Teaching and Making Peace in Every Relationship

Peace Education

Series Editor: Laura L. Finley

Peace education is an important part of peace-building, which helps avoid major conflicts by building a culture of peace through generating peaceful attitudes, dispositions, values, behaviors, action-orientations, and social structures. Books in this series will address how education can contribute to building a culture of peace by teaching: tolerance; diversity affirmation; common understanding; intercultural empathy; reconciliation; renewal; compassion; conflict management skills; and a variety of nonviolent, peace-building skills. The editors welcome studies from a wide variety of disciplines: curriculum theory, educational psychology, history, philosophy, anthropology, and sociology of education, teacher education, comparative and international education, critical theory, cultural studies, language education, feminist studies, religious studies, and environmental education. In our times, peace education efforts can be positive, integrative, restorative, generative, and transformative. In other words, rather than defining peace education in the negative such as education for the elimination of violence, peace education efforts can be understood in the positive as creative, generative efforts that integrate knowledge and action, that integrate differences in ways that both honor diversity and establish common ground. Peace education works on bringing people together. This series on peace education hopes to illuminate the problems, challenges, and rewards associated with using educational means to diminish/eliminate and avoid conflicts. How effective is peace education in bringing about peace? What are its strengths and weaknesses as a strategy to achieve peace? How is peace education carried out in different venues, colleges, schools, and community groups? How is peace taught in different cultures? The editors welcome manuscripts about war and peace and other peace studies themes that exhibit a clear connection to teaching and learning for solutions to promoting harmony and to building a peaceful world.

OTHER TITLES IN THE SERIES

Shiksha Speaks: A White, Non-Jew's Understanding of the Cuban Jewish Diaspora and Its Legacy
Crafting Peace Through Autoethnography: Reflexive Pedagogies for Navigating Difficult Times
Teaching Peace Through Popular Culture

Teaching and Making Peace in Every Relationship

Strategies for Teaching About Dating and Domestic Violence

By

Laura L. Finley

Barry University, USA

emerald PUBLISHING

United Kingdom – North America – Japan
India – Malaysia – China

Emerald Publishing Limited, Floor 5, Northspring, 21-23 Wellington Street,
Leeds LS1 4DL

First edition 2026

Cover photo: iStock and CherriesJD

Reprints and permissions service
Contact: www.copyright.com

British Library Cataloging in Publication Data
A catalog record for this book is available from the British Library

ISBN: 978-1-80686-962-6 (Print hardback)
ISBN: 978-1-80686-964-0 (Print paperback)
ISBN: 978-1-80686-961-9 (PDF)
ISBN: 978-1-80686-963-3 (Epub)

Typeset by TNQ Tech
Cover design by TNQ Tech

I dedicate this book to all of my amazing students. I am blessed every day
to learn from you. Even more, I dedicate this book to the most
spectacular student I know—my daughter Anya Finley.
My best achievement ever is to have raised you to be exactly
who you are—wicked smart, hardworking, funny,
loving, and uniquely you.

CONTENTS

About the Author ix

Preface xi

Acknowledgments xiii

Introduction 1

PART ONE

1 Scope, Extent, and Forms of Abuse 19

2 Understanding Victims 39

3 Understanding Abusers 65

4 Short and Long-Term Effects of Abuse 85

PART TWO

5 Educational Institutions and Legal Requirements Related to Domestic and Dating Violence 103

6 Prevention Curricula and Programs for Schools and Other Institutions 121

7 Using Popular Culture to Address Dating and Domestic Violence 139

8 School-Campus Partnerships 163

Conclusion 177

ABOUT THE AUTHOR

Laura L. Finley, PhD, is Professor of Sociology & Criminology at Barry University in Miami Shores, Florida. She is author, co-author or editor of more than 40 books as well as dozens of peer-reviewed articles and book chapters. As well, Dr Finley is a syndicated columnist with Peace Voice. In addition, Dr Finley is an advocate and activist for peace, justice, gender equality and human rights.

PREFACE

I am fortunate not to have grown up witnessing abuse in my home nor have I ever had to endure an abusive relationship. So, how did I come to write a book like this?

First, I studied sociology and criminology, earning a PhD in Sociology in 2022. In my studies, I learned a great deal about the horrors of abuse, how criminological theory can help explain it, the importance of holistic, feminist approaches to victim advocacy, and the flaws in how the US criminal justice system handles abuse and abusers. At that point, however, my understanding was purely academic, as I did not know anyone (at least that I was aware of) who was or had been a victim nor had I worked in advocacy.

I moved to Florida in 2005 and was assigned to teach a course on Sociology of the Family. A significant portion of the course addressed domestic violence, dating violence, and child abuse. I thought it would be good to have guest speakers in my class from the local agencies serving victims so I contacted Women in Distress, the domestic violence center in Broward County, Florida. They had a person who was a Trainer (she trained staff on various state requirements for advocates as well as presented externally to groups, like mine, that wanted or needed to know more about abuse) and she agreed to present to my class. I thought that she had a really interesting and important job, but I also liked her so we became friends. It turns out she was a police officer previously and wanted to get back into law enforcement, so she notified me several months later that she was leaving her position and recommended that I apply. I did and secured the job while simultaneously teaching.

Both teaching and training about abuse further opened my eyes about the realities of the problem and the limitations in prevention and accountability efforts. I met many victims and their stories broke my heart. I also met many people—from high school students to professionals—who held serious misconceptions about abuse. I was disturbed at how frequently people blamed victims, sometimes subtly and sometimes very overtly. I determined that I would use any platform I had to help correct those misconceptions, not just because they are wrong and hurtful to victims, but they impede the development of effective policies. As an educator and trainer, I have the capacity to reach many people who can further share what they know and, importantly, lobby for social change to better prevent abuse, help victims, and hold abusers accountable. This book follows some of my efforts to teach about dating and domestic violence in various settings.

The book is divided into two parts. In Part One (Chapters 1–4), the focus is on describing the scope and extent of abuse, characteristics of victims, offender characteristics, the barriers to leaving abusers, and the short and long-term effects of abuse. This foundation is an essential part of educating about dating and domestic violence. In Part Two (Chapters 5–8), the emphasis is on educational strategies. This includes formal curricula, lesson ideas using popular culture, programs for medical and legal professionals, bystander intervention approaches, and experiential learning. An example of a campus-community collaboration that involves experiential learning is discussed in Chapter 8. Readers will note that the book includes scholarly research and my personal experience as an educator, advocate, and activist.

It is my hope that this book helps readers better understand abuse and empathize with victims. I also wish that this book allows readers to learn more about abusers so that we can take more effective measures to prevent their abuse, changing their norms, attitudes, and behavior. Finally, I hope that this book helps interested persons educate others about dating and domestic violence, whether that be in the classroom, the workplace, or other settings.

ACKNOWLEDGMENTS

I would like to acknowledge the many amazing and resilient survivors that I know and the fantastic advocates who work with them to promote peace, justice, and healing. I am eternally grateful to my mentors at Western Michigan University who, through my doctoral work, not only imparted knowledge but shared their passion to use what we know sociologically to pursue more effective policy and practice. I am so grateful to be in a position to teach young people and hopefully impact them such that they use their voices for social good.

INTRODUCTION

ABSTRACT

This chapter lays the foundation for the book by framing dating and domestic violence as forms of gender-based violence (GBV). Further, the chapter focuses on international treaties and decisions that see GBV generally and dating and domestic violence specifically as violations of fundamental human rights. Given that a growing body of work emphasizes the responsibilities of states to protect individuals from GBV and to hold abusers accountable, this chapter asserts that failing to enact adequate educational programs, legislation, and policies can be seen as a form of state crime.

Keywords: Gender-based violence; human rights; UDHR; CEDAW; ICCPR; state crime

INTRODUCTION

> Violence against women is perhaps the most shameful human rights violation, and it is perhaps the most pervasive. It knows no boundaries of geography, culture, or wealth. As long as it continues, we cannot claim to be making real progress towards equality, development and peace.

These are the words of former United Nations Secretary General Kofi Annan (in Sveaass & Gaer, 2022, p. 177) in his 1999 address to the Inter-Agency Videoconference for a World Free of Violence against Women. In making these comments, Annan recognized that addressing violence against women is incumbent on ALL States because it is a violation of human rights. In 2006, Annan issued a study on violence against women, prompting the UN General Assembly to discuss the issue. At that time, Annan declared that violence against women was "perhaps the most

Teaching and Making Peace in Every Relationship, pages 1–15

doi:10.1108/978-1-80686-961-920261001

shameful human rights violation" and "perhaps the most pervasive" (Shabazz, 2006). In 2019, the World Health Organization announced that domestic violence was a health epidemic affecting the public globally.

While advancements have been made, there remains much to be done. This chapter provides a review of how violence against women, also called gender-based violence, is a violation of human rights that have been delineated through numerous international treaties, agreements, and acknowledgments. It further discusses how, given that domestic and dating violence are human rights violations, the failure of States to adequately protect victims, prevent abuse, and hold abusers accountable can be considered a crime of the state.

GENDER-BASED VIOLENCE AND HUMAN RIGHTS

Domestic violence is a form of what globally is called violence against women or gender-based violence (GBV). GBV is "violence directed against a woman because she is a woman or which affects a woman disproportionately. It includes physical, mental or sexual harm or suffering, threats of such acts, coercion and other deprivations of liberty" (UN Women, 2024). GBV takes many forms includes feminicide, child marriage, female genital mutilation (FGM), dowry violence, honor killings, sexual assault, sexual harassment, sex trafficking, domestic violence, and more. Femicide is *the killing of women, most often by men, because they are women.* Most often the perpetrator is a family member. While it can be a father or brother, it is typically a husband. According to UN Women, in 2023 approximately 51,100 women and girls worldwide were killed by a family member, approximately 140 each day. The real figures are likely much higher, as many femicides are not investigated as murders (UN Women, 2024). More statistics about the scope of domestic and dating violence specifically is provided in Chapter One.

Domestic violence is abusive behavior by a current or former romantic partner or spouse. In some places, the term also includes abuse by other family members, but the focus in this book is on intimate partner relationships. Dating violence is abusive behavior involving dating partners, typically teens or college-aged individuals. It is important to note (and is addressed in subsequent chapters), that not all countries legally prohibit either domestic or dating violence. This is despite a growing consensus that domestic and dating violence are human rights violations. Gant (n.d.) explained why a human rights focus is necessary.

> The study of domestic violence as a human right violation means that the application of international human rights law can have the effect of reinforcing the state's obligations to respect the individual rights of each and every

> person and thus be held accountable for abuse of those rights by private individuals. Although the state does not actually commit the abuse, its failure to prosecute the abuse and to guarantee legal protection to women victims amounts to complicity in it.

Finley (2010), Libal and Parekh (2009), and Stark (2009) also expressed the need for viewing domestic violence as more than simply an individual act. In particular, a growing body of scholars has emphasized seeing domestic violence as a state crime, owing to the fact that the state has, per international human rights treaties and agreements, a responsibility to prevent, protect, and respond to it.

KEY INTERNATIONAL HUMAN RIGHTS DOCUMENTS, TREATIES, AND DECISIONS

While there are many historical roots of the concept of human rights, the 1948 adoption of the Universal Declaration of Human Rights (UDHR) by the United Nations General Assembly was a significant step in delineating inalienable and universal rights for all people. The UDHR is not binding so there is no way to enforce it, but it does lay out for UN member nations the types of rights they should be ensuring citizens. The UDHR is organized into 30 articles that delineate fundamental human rights. Two of those are most relevant to domestic and dating violence: Article 3: Everyone has the right to life, liberty and security of person; Article 7: All are equal before the law and are entitled without any discrimination to equal protection of the law. All are entitled to equal protection against any discrimination in violation of this Declaration and against any incitement to such discrimination.

Also in 1948, the Ninth International Conference of American States in Bogotá, Colombia adopted the Inter-American Declaration on the Rights and Duties of Man, which established the fundamental human rights for the Americas.

As this book will show, domestic and dating violence are tremendous threats to the life, liberty and security of women globally, as well as in some cases of men. Further, this book will also show that domestic and dating violence legislation and policy, of the lack thereof, is not adequately protecting people.

Subsequent to the UDHR, there have been many international human rights treaties that further carve out the fundamental human rights. One of these is the Convention on the Elimination of Racial Discrimination (ICERD). As the name indicates, the ICERD addresses racial discrimination but one part of that relates to discrimination and how it affects domestic violence victims of color (Finley, 2010).

The International Covenant on Civil and Political Rights (ICCPR), adopted in 1966, includes the same concepts of life, liberty, and security of person and equal protection of the law. Although it makes no specific refence to domestic violence, the United Nations Human Rights Committee has interpreted the ICCPR to include obligations to protect women from GBV. It has done so through the process of general comments, which are findings about a treaty body, based on its assessment of Member States' compliance reports and other research, that that reflect new insights gained about the specific issues included in the treaty (Sveaass & Gaer, 2022). For example, General Comment No. 35, adopted in December 2014, expressed:

> State parties must take both measures to prevent future injury and retrospective measures, such as enforcement of criminal laws, in response to past injury. For example, States parties must respond appropriately to patterns of violence against categories of victims such as intimidation of human rights defenders and journalists, retaliation against witnesses, violence against women, including domestic violence, the hazing of conscripts in the armed forces, violence against children, violence against persons on the basis of their sexual orientation or gender identity, and violence against persons with disabilities. (The Advocates for Human Rights, n.d.).

Adopted in September 2019, General Comment No. 36 explained

> Any deprivation of life based on discrimination in law or in fact is ipso facto arbitrary in nature. Femicide, which constitutes an extreme form of gender-based violence that is directed against girls and women, is a particularly grave form of assault on the right to life. (The Advocates for Human Rights, n.d.).

The UN adopted the International Covenant on Economic, Social, and Cultural Rights (ICESCR) in 1966 and it entered force in 1976. Like the ICCPR, it does not make specific mention about violence against women, but several provisions can be seen as indirectly related. Article 2 expressed the right to non-discrimination and effective remedy while Article 10 declares the protection of family, mothers, children, and young persons.

One of the most important steps in recognizing women's rights as human rights was the 1979 adoption by the UN of the Convention on the Elimination of All Forms of Discrimination Against Women (CEDAW). This was the result of a growing women's rights movement around the globe and was adopted by a vote of 130 to 0 (with 10 abstentions). Compliance with CEDAW is largely overseen by the CEDAW Committee.

CEDAW does not specifically prohibit violence against women, including domestic violence, but it interprets them as a form of prohibited discrimination. Similar to the ICCPR, the CEDAW Committee has pushed forward General Recommendations relevant to the interpretation of CEDAW as it related to violence against women. General Recommendation No. 19, adopted by the committee in 1992, acknowledged that violence against women is discrimination and that, as such, it in interferes with (a) The right to life; (b) The right not to be subject to torture, or to cruel, inhuman, or degrading treatment or punishment; (c) The right to equal protection according to humanitarian norms in time of international or internal armed conflict; (d) The right to liberty and security of person; (e) The right to equal protection under the law; (f) The right to equality in the family; (g) The right to the highest standard attainable of physical and mental health; and (h) The right to just and favorable conditions of work. All of these are rights articulated in CEDAW. It recommends prevention efforts, including media campaigns that address traditional gender role norms that may increase the likelihood of abuse, support services, and accountability mechanisms for perpetrators (Division for the Advancement of Women, n.d.).

In 1984, the UN adopted the Convention Against Torture and Other Cruel, Inhuman or Degrading Treatment or Punishment (UNCAT). It entered into force in 1987. Like the ICCPR and ICESCR, the UNCAT does not specifically address violence against women due to its definition of what constitutes an action by a "public official." Critics have pointed out that failing to include violence against women is a huge omission. One of the first to draw attention to this issue was law scholar Andrew Byrnes in 1992. Byrnes called on members of the body that oversee compliance with UNCAT, the Committee Against Torture (CAT), to "ascertain whether there are particular forms of torture or other ill-treatment which are directed mainly against women" (in Sveaass & Gaer, 2022, p. 179).

Subsequently, the CAT "integrated violence against women in its jurisprudence on torture and ill-treatment by showing that existing provisions could and did incorporate the obligation to protect against and provide redress for torture and ill-treatment directed against women" (Sveaass & Gaer, 2022, p. 177).

Additionally, international decisions helped push forward the idea that violence against women can in some cases constitute torture. The Statute of the International Criminal Tribunal for the former Yugoslavia included rape as a crime against humanity in 1993. Not long after, the International Criminal Tribunal for Rwanda (ICTR) determined that rape was a crime of war, a crime against humanity, and found someone guilty (Jean-Paul Akayesu) of committing rape as crime of genocide. Further, since its inception in 2002, the International Criminal Court (ICC) has included wartime sexual violence as war crimes and crimes against humanity (Sveaass & Gaer, 2022).

In addition, the adoption of two comments, similar to with the ICCPR, further elucidated that violence against women should be included in efforts to adhere to the UNCAT. General Comment 2, adopted in 2007,

> notably points out that States bear international responsibility not only for the acts but also for the omissions of their officials as well as the acts of State agents, private contractors, and others acting in official capacity or on behalf of the State or under its direction or control. It points out that each State party has obligations to prohibit, prevent and redress torture and ill treatment in a wide variety of contexts in which it has control: this can include prisons, hospitals, schools, institutions that care for "children, the aged, the mentally ill or disabled, in military service, and other institutions as well as contexts where the failure of the State to intervene encourages and enhances the danger of privately inflicted harm." (para 15)

Additionally, General Comment 2 acknowledged.

> The contexts at which women are at risk include deprivation of liberty, medical treatment, particularly involving reproductive decisions, and violence by private actors in communities and homes [...]." (para 22)

Further, General Comment 2 addressed States' efforts at prevention and clearly expressed that these must be more than just words.

General Comment 3 focused on the right to redress and violence against women. Adopted in 2012, it addressed Article 14 of UNCAT, which specified the obligation of Member States to "ensure in its legal system that the victim of an act of torture obtains redress and has an enforceable right to fair and adequate compensation, including the means for as full rehabilitation as possible." General Comment 3 specifically noted the obligation in cases of domestic violence "to prevent, to protect, to investigate, to punish perpetrators (all discussed earlier under GC2) and the obligation to provide redress, reparation and/or rehabilitation to victims of such violence" (Sveaass & Gaer, 2022, p. 184).

In GC3, the emphasis in on using gender-sensitive approaches to train officials in the healthcare, immigration, and criminal justice systems. In particular, GC3 recognizes the inherent importance of giving weight to the voices and testimony of women and girls and to avoiding revictimization (Sveaass & Gaer, 2022).

In 1993, the World Conference on Human Rights, held in Vienna, Austria, resulted in many recommendations for strengthening global human rights. Among them was a plan titled the Vienna Declaration and Program of Action. That document acknowledged that "the human rights of women and of the girl-child are an inalienable, integral and indivisible part of universal human rights," that violence against women and girls was a human rights violation, and led to the creation of the post of the High Commissioner for Human Rights and a Special Rapporteur on Violence Against Women (SRVAW), with an appointee designated in 1994. Also in 1993, the UN issued a Declaration on the Elimination of Violence Against Women, affirming the creation of the SRVAW. The Declaration defined VAW to mean

> ...any act of gender-based violence that results in, or is likely to result in, physical, sexual or psychological harm or suffering to women, including threats of such acts, coercion or arbitrary deprivation of liberty, whether occurring in public or private life. DEVAW further outlines the scope of private and public to include violence in the family, violence in the community, and violence perpetrated or condoned by the State, wherever it occurs. (The Special Rapporteur..., 1992, p. 10).

It also called for the universal ratification of the Convention on the Rights of the Child (CRC) by 1995. The CRC will be discussed in greater length later in the chapter.

Since 2006, the SRVAW has reported to the UN Human Rights Council. The establishment of the position "was part of a series of developments that finally accorded explicit recognition to violence against women (VAW) as a human rights concern within the United Nations."

> The creation of this mechanism and the scope of its mandate was a hard-won victory for women's rights movements globally. With the victory came the onerous responsibility upon the SRVAW for covering a vastly neglected and obstacle-ridden legal terrain—that of developing legal doctrines for distinct forms of gender-based violence faced by women, including those that are cognizant of the multilayered violations of women, to examine communications and make recommendations for eliminating violence as well as its root causes.

In 1995, the Beijing Platform for Action brought further attention to women's human rights and is considered the most expansive blueprint for advancing them. It was adopted by 189 Member States and covers 12 areas: poverty; education and training; health; violence; armed conflict; economy; power and decision-making; institutional mechanisms; human rights; media; environment; and the girl child. Specific objectives and actions for governments and other stakeholders fleshed out the roadmap toward gender equality. More than 25 pages of the Platform for Action were devote to violence against women. More specifically, it recognized that certain marginalized groups of women and girls are at greater risk for experiencing violence, that violence and the fear of it inhibits the achievement of equality, and that States have failed to protect victims and hold abusers accountable. It called on governments to ratify or implement international human rights norms and instruments that would address violence against women, including those contained in the Universal Declaration of Human Rights, the International Covenant on Civil and Political Rights, the International Covenant on Economic, Social and Cultural Rights, and the Convention against Torture and Other Cruel, Inhuman or Degrading Treatment or Punishment (UN Women, 2015).

In 2000, Beijing +5 updated it and added actions to accelerate the advancement of women's human rights. It cited achievements and obstacles related to each of the 12 areas. Regarding violence against women, Beijing +5 noted.

> It is widely accepted that violence against women and girls, whether occurring in public or private life, is a human rights issue. It is accepted that violence against women, where perpetrated or condoned by the State or its agents, constitutes a human rights violation. It is also accepted that States have an obligation to exercise due diligence to prevent, investigate and punish acts of violence, whether those acts are perpetrated by the State or by private persons, and provide protection to victims. (UN Women, 2015).

As obstacles, Beijing +5 stated that violence against women was still too often seen as a private matter and was still occurring far too often. Further, it noted the general inadequacy of prevention and educational efforts as well as the lack of comprehensive programs to change the behavior of perpetrators (UN Women, 2015).

A 15-year review by the SRVAW also assessed the advancements made on ending violence against women. It assessed country reports and other data provided by groups that have a role in overseeing women's human rights, including the Commission on the Status of Women (CSW), the General Assembly, the Secretary-General and the Security Council, United Nations agencies, and regional human rights mechanisms such as the Inter-American Commission on Human Rights, the African Commission on Human and People's Rights, and the Council of Europe (Ertürk, 2009).

One achievement it noted was in the broadened understanding of what constitutes a "family" and therefore, who could be considered victims of domestic or dating violence. The report noted that,

> The definition of the family has been expanded by the mandate to encompass intimate-partner and interpersonal relationships, including noncohabitating partners, previous partners and domestic workers. This has allowed inclusion of "wives, live-in partners, former wives or partners, girl-friends (including girl-friends not living in the same house), female relatives (including but not restricted to sisters, daughters, mothers) and female household workers" to be recipients of State protection.

Further, the report noted that there had been growth in understanding that States' obligations go beyond laws and support services. States are obliged to engage in comprehensive prevention efforts (Ertürk, 2009).

As will be discussed in greater detail in subsequent chapters, children are also victims of domestic violence, either directly experiencing abuse or growing up with the negative effects of exposure to parental violence. As such, ensuring that children's human rights are met is also an important when addressing domestic violence. The primary international human rights treaty relevant to children and youth is the Convention on the Rights of the Child (CRC). Article 19 of the CRC guarantees children and youth the right to live free from violence and obliges Member States to protect them. This seemingly covers domestic violence as well.

In 2014, the Council of Europe Convention on Preventing and Combating Violence Against Women and Domestic Violence, known as the Istanbul Convention, specified that European States parties must take action to prevent violence against women, to protect children from it, and to prosecute perpetrators. This includes both experiencing and witnessing domestic violence. Prevention campaigns, per the Istanbul Convention, are to specifically address emphasize the consequences on children (Council of Europe, n.d.). Likewise, the European Court of Human Rights has issued several judgments acknowledging that states can bear responsibility for violence against women if they do not do enough to respond or prevent it, per the European Convention on Human Rights (McQuigg, 2021).

Numerous international courts have made rulings that support the concept of domestic violence as a human rights issue. For example, in 2011, the Inter-American Commission on Human Rights (IACHR) ruled that the United States had violated a victim's rights by failing to enforce a restraining order against her abuser. Jessica Gonzalez had obtained a restraining order against her abusive ex-husband in Castle Rock, Colorado in 1999. Simon Gonzalez kidnapped their three daughters in violation of the order, yet despite multiple efforts to get assistance from the police for more than 10 hours no action was taken. After 10 hours at around 3:30a.m., Simon drove to the police department and opened fire. The police returned fire and the three daughters were all killed. It remains unclear whether Simon killed them or if they died from the police crossfire. Gonzalez (later Lenahan) had sought relief through the United States Supreme Court, which, in 2005, ruled that she had no constitutional right to police protection. "In an opinion written by Justice Scalia, the court maintained that although Colorado law says that the police 'shall' arrest if an order of protection is violated, police always have discretion. In essence, 'shall' does not mean 'shall'" (Lapidus, 2017).

In contrast to the Supreme Court, the IACHR found that the US had violated Jessica and her daughters' human rights because it failed to take adequate steps to protect them from domestic violence (Lapidus, 2017). It declared.

> ...that the United States violated her human rights by failing to adopt reasonable measures to protect her and her daughters from her abusive husband's acts of violence, when the police should have known that they were at risk of being harmed. The Commission recommends that the United States provide redress to Jessica, and in addition implement reforms to federal and state laws and policies that proactively address and prevent gender-based violence, including domestic violence. (University of Miami Law, 2011).

The University of Miami Law (2011) further explained that,

> While state and federal laws exist to provide some protections and remedies for victims of domestic violence, human rights law requires that responsible government entities, including in particular law enforcement agencies, take a more proactive role in preventing and responding to the epidemic of such violence. As the Commission found in Jessica's case, the U.S. has not even sufficiently implemented existing laws aimed at protecting victims of domestic violence. The Commission also identified gaps in U.S. laws aimed at addressing domestic violence and urged the United States to adopt further laws and policies aimed at preventing and eradicating violence, to comply with its human rights obligations.

Jessica's was the first domestic violence case brought by a survivor before an international human rights body. The IACHR was established in 1959 to examine allegations of human rights violations by all 35 member-states of the Organization of American States, including the United States. The IACHR issued a number of recommendations to the United States regarding police response to domestic violence. However, the ACLU and several other groups tested before the court in 2014 about the United States' failure to address the recommendations.

Finally, in December 2015, the Justice Department issued new guidance based on the IACHR's recommendations. Titled "Identifying and Preventing Gender Bias in Law Enforcement Response to Domestic Violence and Sexual Assault," it explained how police departments should respond to domestic violence to comply with civil rights laws and to ensure human rights. Additionally, many cities and counties across the US, based on the IACHR ruling and recommendations by the ACLU and other advocacy groups, enacted ordinances declaring that freedom from domestic violence is a fundamental human right. New York City, Miami, and Seattle are among the cities that address domestic violence as a human rights issue. Further, the IACHR's case has been used to inform other countries. For example, Kenya's high court ruled that the police had violated the human rights of 12 girls when they refused to investigate reported sexual assault and child abuse (Lapidus, 2017).

LIMITATIONS OF A HUMAN RIGHTS APPROACH

While these treaties and international articulations seem to clearly require Member States to take significant action related to domestic violence, one limitation is that not every country is a Member State. 173 States have ratified the ICCPR, meaning that they are obliged to adhere to its provisions (i.e, they are Member States). That is a significant percentage of the 193 UN Member States. Yet, some countries like the United States have issued what is called Reservations, Declarations, and Understandings (RUDs). RUDs are essentially exceptions to the way something is worded in the treaty or convention or exceptions to a particular component of it. In general, these are related to restrictions on freedom of speech and association, the right to continue imposing the death penalty, the acknowledgment that the ICCPR's prohibition on torture and cruel, inhuman, and degrading treatment align with those delineated by the Fifth, Eighth, and/or 14th Amendments, and the treatment of juveniles as adults in the criminal justice system. Those RUDs could potentially limit the activity the United States is willing to take in regard to preventing and responding to domestic violence, in particular as it connects to degrading treatment by abusers.

The United States has never ratified the ICESCR. This is in large part because it is far more progressive on social issues like the right to housing, healthcare, fair pay, and more. The provisions in the ICESCR are much more aligned with those of socialist democracies like those in Western Europe and Scandinavia than they are with the capitalist emphasis on the free market and individual responsibility. As such, the United States is not required to adhere to the specifications of the ICESCR. Like the ICCPR, 173 UN Members have ratified it, making the United States in company with approximately 10 percent of Member States.

Likewise, the United States has not ratified CEDAW. The failure to do so makes the United States an even bigger outlier, as 189/193 (98%) of Member States have ratified it. Iran, Somalia, Sudan, Palau, Tonga, and the United States are those that have not ratified CEDAW, with the United States the only established democracy not to do so. In large part the opposition to CEDAW has been from conservative politicians and religious leaders who fear it will conflict with their views on reproductive rights and gender norms (Lowen, 2020).

The United States and Canada are the only countries in the Americas not to have ratified the Inter-American Convention on the Prevention, Punishment, and Eradication of Violence Against Women, referred also to as the "Convention of Belem do Para." It entered into force in 1995 and begins by affirming that "violence against women constitutes a violation of their human rights and fundamental freedoms, and impairs or nullifies the observance, enjoyment and exercise of such rights and freedoms" (Finley, 2010).

Additionally, the United States has not ratified the CRC. It is the only UN Member not to do so. According to Human Rights Watch (HRW) (2023), the concern is that ratification would require significant legislative and structural changes, as every state falls short of meeting the standards for children's international human rights. "Children in the US can be legally married in 41 states, physically punished by school administrators in

47 states, sentenced to life without parole in 22 states, and work in hazardous agriculture conditions in all 50 states." A year later HRW noted some improvement with seven states scoring higher than a "D" on their scorecard of children's rights. Little progress was made regarding corporal punishment, which is connected with domestic violence.

Simply ratifying international human rights treaties is not enough, however. There are some countries that have ratified the treaties described here but that still need improvement. Yet at least the UN Committee and other oversight bodies can help push those governments that are resistant if they are Member States. Further,

> Within the last decade alone, skeptics may cite such breaches as the genocide of nearly one million Rwandans, the ethnic cleansing of hundreds of thousands of former Yugoslavs, and the displacement of nearly two million Colombians. But continued atrocities do not disprove the case for international human rights law; the fact that it has not triumphed everywhere does not mean that it serves no useful purpose anywhere. (Cassel, 2001, p. 122).

Conrad and Ritter (2019) argued that human rights treaties do work and they are most effective against the more repressive governments. Using data from 25 years and 140 countries, Conrad and Ritter (2019) analyzed how each country would behave when they were party to a treaty and when they were not. Using their model to predict repression, they found that the most repressive countries will repress less when a treaty is in place. So, while treaties do not entirely fix the problems or prevent human rights violations, they are an important improvement. Further, in an interview about the book, Ritter explained,

> Treaties do more than just reduce repression, they also increase protest. They create this expectation that the leader won't repress them if they come out to the streets and so people are demanding more. Treaties make it possible for people to ask for what they need and want—they actually change what people expect from their government. (Vanderbilt University, 2019).

Although not true for all of the international human rights treaties described herein, violations of some of them can result in international accountability for responsible state leaders in the International Criminal Court (ICC). Cassel (2001) asserted that international human rights law helps advance human rights consciousness. This can then help ensure that norms included in human rights treaties filter into constitutions and are thus enshrined as rights of the people in a given country and fostering government compliance that can be overseen by domestic judicial bodies. Additionally, the push of international nongovernmental organizations helps advance human rights in that these entities help hold governments accountable. Further, human rights treaties help forge a common language about human rights issues across the globe and legitimizes rights claims by citizens. "Human rights groups can (and regularly do) say to governments, 'It is not we who say that torture is illegal and must be investigated and punished; it is you who so declare, as parties to the Convention Against Torture'" (Cassell, 2001, p. 127).

DOMESTIC AND DATING VIOLENCE AS CRIMES OF THE STATE

Another way to look at domestic violence is that it is a patriarchal state crime. Rather than simply understood as an individual offense affecting individual victims, some scholars and activists maintain that the state is responsible for not doing enough to protect women from experiencing abuse (Finley, 2010; Rose, 2021). "State crime occurs when the state acts against its own citizens or the citizens of another country during the course of a conflict, or when the state fails to act when it is obligated to do so" (Finley, 2010, p. 10). Another definition offered by Rothe and Kauzlarich (2016) is that state crime is "an act or omission of an action by actors within the state that results in violations of domestic and international law, human rights, or systematic or institutionalized harm of its or another state's population, done in the name of the state regardless whether there is or is not self-motivation or interests at play" (p. 102). Green and Ward (2000) argue that state crime should be defined as "state organisational deviance involving the violation of human rights" (p. 101).

Other criminologists focus more on state-produced harm, noting that because the state controls what is and is not illegal, some things are not technically criminal but should be because they are injurious and because they violate fundamental human rights. Many criminologists have applied a state-produced harm lens, for instance to the inadequate response to Hurricane Katrina (Faust & Kauzlarich, 2008), the handling of domestic violence (Finley, 2017), sexual assault (Collins, 2016), and the use of torture (Collard, 2019; Hamm, 2007).

CONCLUSION

As this chapter has outlined, there is growing consensus among advocates and legal bodies internationally that being free from gender-based violence, including dating and domestic violence, is a fundamental human right. States have an obligation to enact laws, policies, and programs designed to protect people from victimization and to hold abusers accountable. A key part of doing so, however, is ensuring that people are educated about the problems of dating and domestic violence. Without factually correct information about the scope and extent of abuse, people cannot push their legislators and other leaders to enact adequate measures for protection and accountability. As such, this book focuses on educating about abuse.

REFERENCES

Cassel, D. (2001). Does international human rights law make a difference? *Chicago Journal of International Law, 2*(1), 121–135. https://chicagounbound.uchicago.edu/cgi/viewcontent.cgi?article=1122&context=cjil

Collard, M. (2019). *Torture as state crime: A criminological analysis of the transnational institutional torturer.* Routledge.

Collins, V. (2016). *State crime, women, and gender.* Routledge.

Conrad, C., & Ritter, E. (2019). *Contentious compliance: Dissent and repression under international human rights law.* Oxford University Press.

Council of Europe. (n.d.). *Council of Europe Convention on preventing and combating violence against women and domestic violence (Istanbul Convention).* https://www.coe.int/en/web/children/domestic-violence

Division for the Advancement of Women. (n.d.). *CEDAW general recommendation no. 19: Violence against women.* https://www.legal-tools.org/doc/f8d998/pdf/%26ved=2ahUKEwi4r8KY2dX

Ertürk, Y. (2009). *15 years of the United Nations Special Rapporteur on violence against women, its causes and consequences.* https://www.ohchr.org/sites/default/files/15YearReviewofVAWMandate.pdf

Faust, K., & Kauzlarich, D. (2008). Hurricane Katrina victimization as a state crime of omission. *Critical Criminology, 16,* 85–103.

Finley, L. (2010). *Examining domestic violence as a state crime: Nonkilling implications.* Center for Global Nonkilling.

Finley, L. (2017). *Failure to protect: State obligations to victims and state crime.* Crimes of the Powerful Conference, York University. May 25-26.

Gant, A. (n.d.). *Domestic violence against women as a human rights violation.* https://www.corteidh.or.cr/tablas/r26304.pdf

Green, P., & Ward, T. (2000). State crime, human rights, and the limits of criminology. *Race, Class, and State Crime, 27*(1), 101–115.

Hamm, S. (2007). "High crimes and misdemeanors": George W. Bush and the sins of Abu Ghraib. *Crime, Media, Culture: An International Journal, 3*(3), 259–284.

Human Rights Watch. (2023, September 7). *No US state meets child rights standards.* https://www.hrw.org/news/2023/09/07/no-us-state-meets-child-rights-standards

Lapidus, L. (2017, June 9). *Jessica Lenahan lived through a domestic violence nightmare and emerged as a heroic advocate for police reform.* ACLU. https://www.aclu.org/news/womens-rights/jessica-lenahan-lived-through-domestic-violence-nightmare

Libal, K., & Parekh, S. (2009). Reframing violence against women as a human rights violation: Evan Stark's coercive control. *Violence Against Women, 15*(12), 1477–1489.

Lowen, L. (2020, January 3). *Why won't the U.S. ratify the CEDAW human rights treaty?* Thoughtco. https://www.thoughtco.com/why-wont-u-s-ratify-cedaw-3533824

McQuigg, R. (2021). The European Court of Human Rights and domestic violence: Volodina v. Russia. *International Human Rights Law Review, 10*(1), 155–167.

Rose, E. (2021). *Domestic violence as state crime: A feminist framework for challenge and change.* Routledge.

Rothe, D., & Kauzlarich, D. (2016). *Crimes of the powerful: An introduction.* Routledge.

Shabazz, S. (2006, November). *Violence against women a global phenomenon.* New America Media. http://news.newamericamedia.org/news/view_article.html?article_id=8f3648e416500579%20ce78928fb304850a

Stark, E. (2009). Rethinking coercive control. *Violence Against Women, 15*(12), 1509–1525.

Sveaass, N., & Gaer, F. (2022). The Committee Against Torture tackles violence against women: A conceptual and political journey. *Torture, 32*(1–2), 177–192.

The Advocates for Human Rights. (n.d.). *Stop violence against women.* https://www.stopvaw.org/international_covenant_on_civil_and_political_rights_iccpr

University of Miami Law. (2011). *SUMMARY: Jessica lenahan (Gonzales) v. United States.*https://media.law.miami.edu/human-rights-clinic/pdf/2011/gonzales-summary-timeline.pdf

UN Women. (2015). *Beijing declaration and platform for action, Beijing +5 political declaration and outcome.* https://www.unwomen.org/sites/default/files/Headquarters/Attachments/Sections/CSW/PFA_E_Final_WEB.pdf

UN Women. (2024, November 25). *Facts and figures: Ending violence against women.* https://www.unwomen.org/en/articles/facts-and-figures/facts-and-figures-ending-violence-against-women

Vanderbilt University. (2019, June 17). *Human rights treaties benefit the world's most oppressed.* https://news.vanderbilt.edu/2019/06/17/human-rights-treaties-benefit-the-worlds-most-oppressed/

PART ONE

CHAPTER 1

SCOPE, EXTENT, AND FORMS OF ABUSE

ABSTRACT

This chapter provides definitions and statistics about the scope and extent of domestic and dating violence. It also discusses the many types of abuse, including emotional, verbal, physical, sexual, financial, and cyber or technology-facilitated abuse. Additionally, the chapter describes the dynamics of abusive relationships. It also reviews the signs of lethality in abusive relationships and the role of firearms in these cases. Finally, the chapter examines the challenges victims face in trying to leave abusers.

Keywords: Emotional abuse; physical abuse; sexual abuse; financial abuse; technology-facilitated abuse; lethality

DEFINITIONS

As noted in the Introduction, domestic violence "is a pattern of behaviors used by one partner to maintain power and control over another partner in an intimate relationship" (Domestic Violence, 2022). It is sometimes referred to as Intimate Partner Violence (IPV). The World Health Organization (WHO) (2022) this definition:

> Intimate partner violence refers to behavior within an intimate relationship that causes physical, sexual or psychological harm, including acts of physical aggression, sexual coercion, psychological abuse and controlling behaviors.

Teaching and Making Peace in Every Relationship, pages 19–38

doi:10.1108/978-1-80686-961-920261002

> This definition covers violence by both current and former spouses and partners.

Others prefer to use the term domestic abuse, as it helps to enforce the notion that "there are many forms of power and control used by abusers" (Finley, 2016, p. xiii). All 50 states have legal statutes prohibiting domestic violence, although they vary in the specific verbiage. While there is not a uniform set of federal laws, the Violence Against Women Act (VAWA) in 1994 established that it is federal crime to cause an intimate partner or dating partner to cross state lines or leave or enter Indian territory by force.

According to the U.S. Department of Justice Office on Violence Against Women (n.d). refers to dating violence as

> ...violence committed by a person who is or has been in a social relationship of a romantic or intimate nature with the victim and where the existence of such a relationship shall be determined based on a consideration of the following factors: the length of the relationship; the type of relationship; and the frequency of interaction between the persons involved in the relationship." (Domestic Violence, 2022).

Dating violence is sometimes referred to as Teen Dating Violence (TDV) or Adolescent Dating Violence (ADV) so as to differentiate instances of abuse involving youth versus those involving older persons. State laws in the United States draw on these definitions but provide parameters regarding what are domestic violence offenses from a legal setting and what are dating violence offenses legally in those states that have such laws. Similar to domestic violence, every state has some type of legal statute relevant to dating violence, although the specific vary.

Key to all of the above-listed definitions are two factors: The nature of the relationship between the individuals involved and the elements of controlling behaviors. Domestic and dating violence advocates emphasize that the goal of abusers is to obtain and maintain power and control over their victims. They use many tactics to do so. The following section explores those tactics in greater detail.

FORMS OF ABUSE

Abuse takes many forms. The U.S. Department of Justice Office on Violence Against Women (Domestic Violence, 2022) identified the following forms of abuse: Physical abuse, sexual abuse, emotional abuse, economic abuse, psychological abuse, and technological abuse. Physical abuse involves both actions and nonactions. Actions might include hitting, punching, slapping, shoving, biting, strangling, hair pulling and more. Nonactions might involve denial of needed medical care or forced drinking or drug use. Sexual abuse involves coercing or attempting to coerce unwanted sexual contact. Examples include intercourse, oral sex, assault on the genitals, marital rape, and more. Due to the invasive nature of sexual assaults, this form of abuse seems to be the most difficult for victims to report. Undermining someone's sense of self-worth or self-esteem through constant criticism, name calling, harming one's relationship with children or family, and constant criticism are examples of emotional abuse. Economic abuse occurs when a partner controls or restrains the other person's ability to acquire, use, or maintain economic resources. Abusers may use coercion, fraud, or manipulation to control their partner's bank accounts, credit cards, and other assets. Abusers can also ruin their partner's credit or abuse power of attorney privileges. Psychological abuse is the most pervasive form of abuse. It can include but is not limited to intimidation, coercion, threats to the victim, family, friends, or pets, destruction of property, and forced isolation. Technological abuse involves use of phones, computers, cameras, online platforms, and other forms of technology to threaten, control, stalk, harass, exploit, intimidate, or impersonate a partner.

Advocates working with domestic violence victims have long used the "Power and Control Wheel" to help people understand the many forms of abuse, all of which are about the abuser seeking to obtain and maintain power and control over the victim.

This wheel shows that in addition to the above-mentioned forms of abuse, isolation, manipulation of children, minimizing, denying, and blaming, and use of male privilege are considered. Isolation is to an abuser's advantage because it involves separating the victim from people who can offer support and encouragement to get out of the relationship. There are many ways that abusers can isolate victims. I have personally worked with victims who were locked in their homes for periods of time, which is obviously a very extreme means of isolating someone. More often, however, isolation is more subtle. An example might be when an abuser tells his or her victim how much s/he just wants to spend time with them and implores them not to spend time with family or friends. The effect can be that the victim becomes distanced from their supporters. Another way abusers might try to isolate their victims is through complaining about them and trying to get the victim to "turn" on their family and friends.

In cases where children are involved, abusers will often manipulate the children as a tool of control. This can include all of the things listed in that spoke on the wheel, as well as many more. As the children get older, one of the more common things that abusers is do is play them against the other parent, telling them stories and trying to shift the blame. There is also a significant correlation between domestic violence and child abuse. Research shows that children are also being abused in about half of all domestic violence cases where children are present. Obviously, child abuse has tremendous effects on the children, but so too does simply witnessing the domestic violence or growing up knowing that it is occurring in the home. The co-occurrence of child abuse and domestic violence generally results in worse outcomes for children. This has been referred to as a "double whammy" (Herrenkohl et al., 2008; Moylan et al., 2010). The effects of the double whammy are described in Chapter Four.

Abusers almost always engage in minimizing, denying, and blaming. They tell victims that the abuse is their fault—if they just had not done "xyz" or did more of "abc" then the abuse would not be "necessary." Abusers also deny that the abuse happened. This is what is often referred to as "gaslighting." Sweet (2019) described gaslighting as "a type of psychological abuse aimed at making victims seem or feel 'crazy', creating a 'surreal' interpersonal environment" (p. 851). While many consider gaslighting to be a psychological manipulation, Sweet (2019, p. 852) maintains that t must be understood as a sociological phenomenon.

> Specifically, gaslighting is effective when it is rooted in social inequalities, especially gender and sexuality, and executed in power-laden intimate relationships. When perpetrators mobilize gender-based stereotypes, structural inequalities, and institutional vulnerabilities against victims with whom they are in an intimate relationship, gaslighting becomes not only effective, but devastating.

Studies show that gaslighting is very common in domestic and dating violence situations and that it prevents victims from accessing resources.

Although not all abusers are male, which will be discussed in the next chapter, most research shows a decided gender skew when it comes to perpetration. This can be connected to male privilege and patriarchy. Those will be addressed in greater detail in Chapters Two and Three, but in brief, a patriarchal society is one that is male-dominated and male-identified. In such societies, males hold more power and influence. As such, they may feel as though it is normal for them to control and dominate their partners. Research shows that abuse is more common in patriarchal societies. For example, an analysis of data from Grenada, Guyana, Jamaica, Suriname, and Trinidad and Tobago from 2016–2019 found that women ages 15–64 who had been in relationships with men who held patriarchal ideas about men's dominance over women were more likely to have experienced domestic dating violence (UN Women, 2023). Saunders et al. (2022, pp. 1999–2000) explained,

> Violence against women should not be viewed as something that only occurs in the context of one violent partner, one household, or even one community. It contributes to and is a consequence of political, economic, and other inequalities women face daily. Violence against women is fueled mainly by

> perpetrators' negative sociocultural beliefs about women (patriarchal norms) *and* systemic, structural failures to respond based on the same negative beliefs that lead to unequal treatment and status.

Dating violence takes many of the same forms. According to the Centers for Disease Control and Prevention (CDC), these are generally the same as for domestic violence, although some forms, especially cyber-abuse or technology-facilitated abuse (TFA), are more common in abusive teen relationships than they are in abusive domestic relationships (About Teen Dating Violence, 2024). Additionally, teen abusers are more likely to use social status to control their victims. Since social status can be so important to teens, abusers can use that to make their victims feel like they will not be "cool" or "popular" without them. They can use technology as well as traditional verbal and written means to spread rumors that socially isolate a victim.

Using the constant threat that you will commit suicide is also a form of control that is common among both adults and teens. One study from Australia found that 39% of women who had been in abusive relationships had been subject to their abuser's threat to self-harm (Woodley, 2024). Like the Power and Control wheel referenced earlier, there is a Teen Power and Control wheel that illustrates the many ways that teen abusers try to control their victims, including making all the decisions in the relationship. This might be about simple things such what the victim is "allowed" to wear, but even those small things tell victims that they have no agency in the relationship.

SCOPE AND EXTENT OF DOMESTIC AND DATING VIOLENCE

According to the WHO, almost one-third of women ages 15-49 across the globe who have been in a relationship report physical and/or sexual abuse. Estimates of lifetime victimization range from 20% in the western pacific, 22% in the higher-income countries in Europe, 25% in the Americas, 33% in Africa, 31% in the Eastern Mediterranean, and 3% in Southeast Asia (World Health Organization, 2024). One of the first studies to address the scope of abuse globally found rates as high as 71% in Ethiopia, compared to 15% in Japan (Garcia-Moreno et al., 2005). Globally, domestic violence is one of the biggest killers of women. In 2022, around 48,800 women and girls worldwide were killed by their intimate partners or other family members. On average, then more than five women or girls are killed every hour by someone in their own family (UN Women, 2023). Nearly 40% of murders of women globally are perpetrated by current or former intimate partners (World Health Organization, 2024). Gender-based violence, a term that refers to a host of violence perpetrated against women by men, is the most frequently occurring form of violence that women experience globally.

In contrast to the United States, globally, younger women in middle and low-income countries were at greater risk. Specifically, women under the age of 35 were at higher odds of abuse in Sri Lanka, India, rural Bangladesh, Rwanda, and Nigeria. Men over 29 were the most likely to perpetrate abuse in most countries (Ghoshal et al., 2023). Also unlike the United States, the Ghoshal et al. (2023) metaanalysis found that married women were more likely to experience abuse than nonmarried women.

In the United States, as many as one in four women and one in nine men are victims of domestic violence. Stalking and harassment are very common in abusive domestic relationships and are often the precursors of lethal violence. Law enforcement often do not do much to address stalking and harassment, however, instead largely relying on physical violence to make arrests or urge victims to seek help. A review of 430 domestic violence homicides in Florida found that in 80% there had been no prior reports to police about physical violence but there had been threats, coercion, and stalking. Almost 80% of those killed by a current or former partner had been stalked in the year prior (Peace, 2025).

Dating violence is common globally as well. As with domestic violence, it is sometimes difficult to find accurate statistics about victimization because there are many countries in which it is still not prohibited. UN Women (2023) found that globally, 24% of girls ages 15–19 has experienced physical or sexual violence from a dating partner or spouse. Sixteen percent of girls in that age range had experienced the abuse in the previous 12 months. This means that nearly 19 million women will have experienced physical or sexual violence from an intimate partner by the time they are 20 years old (World Health Organization, 2024). The World Health Organization found that rates of dating violence were highest in Oceania (47%) and central subSaharan Africa (40%). The lowest rates were found in central Europe (10%) and central Asia (11%). Research in England and Wales found that in 2024, people ages 16 to 19 were the most likely group to experience abuse in a relationship (Office for National Statistics, 2024). Dating violence is most common in low-income countries and regions and is correlated with limited educational opportunities, weaker property ownership and inheritance rights, and higher rates of child marriage (World Health Organization, 2024).

Studies have repeatedly found that dating violence is one of the most frequently occurring forms of violence experienced by youth in the United States. The CDC reports that one in 12 high school students had experienced physical violence in the year prior (Teen Dating Violence, 2025). Other studies have found that between 10 percent and one-third of teenagers in the United States had experienced physical dating violence while as much as 69% has experienced either physical abuse, psychological abuse, or sexual dating violence (Taylor & Mumford, 2016; Vagi et al., 2015). Ybarra et al. (2016) found that of young people ages 14 to 21, 51% of females and 43% of males reporting experiencing at least one form of dating violence. Males were more.

Psychological dating abuse is the most frequently occurring form, with a lifetime prevalence ranging from 17% to 88% (Abrams, 2023; Piolanti et al., 2023). Stalking and harassment by current or former dating partners occurs frequently as well. One study in which the researchers analyzed the Survey on Teen Relationships and Intimate Violence (STRiV) found that of youth ages 10–18 who had been in relationships, 48% experienced stalking and 43% had been harassed (Rothman et al., 2021).

Stonard (2021) found that as much as 75% of youth in dating relationships had experienced cyber-abuse. A study of university students in Spain found that 35.8% of female and 26.5% of male students had either been a victim or perpetrator of TFA (Villora et al., 2019). A study of 540 college students in the United States found that three quarters had experienced TFA from a current or former partner (Marganski & Melander, 2018). Another study conducted by the Economist Intelligence Unit (2021) focused on 45 countries with the largest online populations. In its sample of 4,500 women, the researchers found that 38% had experienced online TFA and 85% had witnessed it being perpetrated against another woman. A survey of survivors of domestic violence in the UK found that of the sample of 307, 45% had experienced TFA during their relationship and 48% after leaving their partner (Laxton, 2014). A Rogers et al. (2022) reviewed studies conducted between 2020 and 2022 that involved TFA in dating partnerships involving adults ages 18 and older. The 20 studies in the review were conducted in the UK and Ireland, United States, Canada, New Zealand, and Australia. It found that TFA takes many forms. One of these is image-based abuse, often referred to as sexting, which involves the sharing of sexual content such as texts, images, and videos via a new form of technology. Sexting can occur in domestic and dating relationships. An Australian study of 4,122 women found that 63% had experienced some form of image-based abuse by a current or former partner (Office of the e-Safety Commissioner, 2017). Another form of TFA involves constant texting or calling, typically done as a way to identify at all times where the victim is and what he or she is doing. This is a form of coercive control. Restricting access to or ownership of devices, limiting access to or controlling social media platforms, destruction of devices, hacking of accounts, changing passwords, removing friends, deleting messages or context, and using children's accounts and devices were all methods found by Rogers et al., 2022). Surveillance apps are another form of TFA, as well as the use of spyware or other tracking devices. Harassment can also occur over social media and networking platforms. Because it is not dependent on the perpetrator being physically near the victim, TFA can occur with greater frequency (Woodlock, 2017).

Another common form of abuse in teen relationships is reproductive coercion. This refers to

> ...any situation in which one partner is exerting power over the other in a way that impacts their reproductive health, such as forcing someone to engage in sexual activity, refusing to use contraception or interfering with a partner's contraception usage, or restricting a partner from seeing a reproductive health care provider.

After the Supreme Court's ruling in *Dobbs v. Jackson Women's Health Organization* in 2022 that overturned *Roe v. Wade's* right to an abortion, the National Domestic Violence Hotline saw a 98% increase in calls about reproductive coercion (Gerson, 2024).

Research is clear that domestic and dating violence increase during crises. From environmental disasters like the Exxon Valdez oil spill in 1999 and the BP oil spill in 2010 to the COVID-19 pandemic, rates of abuse increase due to personal and financial stress. This is discussed in greater detail in other parts of the book.

DYNAMICS OF ABUSIVE RELATIONSHIPS

It is important to note that each abusive relationship is different. No abuser uses the same tactics in different relationships, and the tactics a specific abuser uses may change over time.

Research is clear that abusive relationships tend to escalate over time. They typically do not involve physical abuse in the early phases of the relationship, as few people would continue a new relationship that involved hitting, punching, slapping, or other physical assaults. Instead, abusive relationships tend to start more subtly, with signs of the abuser needing to obtain and maintain power and control over the victim. Estimates are that about half of abusive relationships become physical, which might indicate that the abuser simply chooses different forms of abuse. It could also indicate that the victim left the relationship before it became physically abusive. Once the relationship becomes physical, however, it tends to continue being physical and the violence usually gets more frequent and more severe. Escalation sometimes happens gradually while in other cases it occurs suddenly. Examples of gradual escalation might include increasingly harmful and degrading insults, more demanding control of who the victim sees or what he or she does, and more alarming threats. This might go from "You make me so mad I could punch a wall," to "I'm going to punch you if you say that again." A sudden escalation may be the first time the abuser hits, pushes, or strangles the victim, or the first time the abuser threatens to harm children or pets. It might also be the first time the abuse occurs in a public space (Kippert, 2020).

In a study of 372 intimate partner homicides in the UK, criminology Dr. Jane Monckton Smith identified an eight-stage pattern that were common to nearly all of the murders. These include:

- A prerelationship history of stalking or abuse by the perpetrator
- The romance developing quickly into a serious relationship
- The relationship becoming dominated by coercive control
- A trigger to threaten the perpetrator's control—for example, the relationship ends or the perpetrator gets into financial difficulty
- Escalation, or an increase in the intensity or frequency of the partner's control tactics, such as by stalking or threatening suicide
- The perpetrator has a change in thinking, choosing to move on either through revenge or by homicide
- Planning—the perpetrator might buy weapons or seek opportunities to get the victim alone
- Homicide—the perpetrator kills his or her partner, and possibly hurts others such as the victim's children (BBC, 2019).

These dynamics can make it hard for people to see what is happening. Lenore Walker (1989) offered the Cycle of Violence theory to explain how the dynamics of abusive relationships play out and to address why it is difficult sometimes for people, victims included, to understand. Walker noted that not all abusive relationships look the same, but that many share similar characteristics. She based her three-stage model on behavioral reinforcement theory. The first phase is *tension-building*. In this phase,

> ...the woman does have some minimum control of the frequency and severity of the abusive incidents. She can slow them down by trying to give the man what he wants or speed them up by refusing to meet his (sometimes unreasonable) demands. Her efforts are more successful at the beginning of this phase than toward its end. (p. 697)

Over time, the couple reaches the *period of inevitability*. Here the abuser realizes his attempts to control the victim are not working and explodes, resulting in an *acute battering incident*. This is often when others get involved, such as when the police are called. Medical attention might also be sought, although that occurs in only about half of such cases. This phase is short but serious and, according to Walker, due to the physiological release of tension it provides, there is next a period of *loving contrition* or at least no tension. As Walker explained, "the battered woman may not perceive this cycle, and she may respond to the love and violence as randomly occurring events in the relationship" (p. 697).

CHALLENGES TO LEAVING ABUSERS

Victims find many barriers to leaving abusers. While each individual's situation is different, fear tends to be at the top of the list of reasons why victims stay with abusers. Fear can include many things: fear that the abuser will retaliate against them or the victim's family, as well as fear of the unknown and fear of how a victim might take care of him or herself and children. People with a history of childhood victimization may find it harder to leave abusers, as their trauma may be deeper and unaddressed. Those who are more financially dependent on abusers face significant barriers and, as was noted earlier, many victims experience financial abuse during the relationship that makes this barrier even more challenging. Victims may also lack self-efficacy, or the belief in their ability to accomplish a given task or achieve a specific outcome. This is likely due to the minimizing, denying, and blaming as well as emotional and verbal abuse that has weakened their belief in themselves. Victims may have internalized the blame and therefore think that, rather than leaving the abuser, the responsibility is on them to change something about their behavior. Cultural factors can play a role as well, as victims from certain religious or ethnic backgrounds may receive different messages from family and friends that can either discourage or encourage leaving abusers. Likewise, those who are immigrants or who are not fluent in English can struggle to understand cultural norms and how or where to seek help (Fernandez, 2015). Mirpour et al. (2021) found that victims were more likely to prolong the relationship when they felt emotionally blackmailed. The following were examples of emotional blackmail that were reported: "He proposed to have sex, and I rejected! so, he broke up for 10 days and sent me sad songs" and "If you refuse sex, I will end the relationship" (p. 130). Victims also reported that financial ransom was a significant reason for why they stayed with abusers. Further, victims typically experience self-blame that prevents them from ending the relationship. Additionally, Mirpoor et al. (2021) found that some victims did not want to leave the relationship due to concerns about social status and familial expectations around divorce.

Walker (1989) focused on the idea of learned helplessness in trying to understand the challenges victims face in leaving abusers.

> Learned helplessness explains the loss of the ability to predict contingent outcomes after exposure to repeated random and variable inescapable aversive stimuli. This model helps one understand the psychological changes in battered women that partially account for their staying in abusive relationships. Learned helplessness can be prevented by psychologically strengthening the potential victim or reversed by empowerment through additional competence training and skill-building activities. (p. 697)

Teens may find it difficult to leave abusers for similar reasons, as well as for those that are more unique to their age group. As noted, the threat that the abuser will commit suicide can be a powerful tool for keeping a victim in the relationship. Even while people want the victimization to end, most do not want someone's suicide to supposedly be their fault. Teens fearing loss of social status if they end a relationship may find it harder to break things off. Further, since teens and young adults often date someone who attends the same school or college as them, it can be tough to be completely free from their abuser who walks the same halls, may attend the same classes, or may even live in the same residence halls as they do.

A lack of resources or inadequate understanding of available resource is another significant barrier. In some countries, there are minimal, if any, resources specific to victims of domestic and dating violence. The scant resources available may be very difficult to access. While the United States began opening domestic violence shelters and crisis lines for victims of domestic violence in the 1970s, much more still needs to be done. Some communities still do not have an easily accessible shelter, and in those that do, demand often exceeds available services. Those in need of immediate and safe shelter may be turned away if the shelter is at capacity. This is discussed in greater detail in Chapter Three.

Cultural barriers may also prevent someone from seeking help at a traditional domestic violence shelter. Victims have reported, for instance, that the typical living arrangements in shelters are communal, with rooms like dorms or college residence halls. This is not something everyone is comfortable with. Certain groups face unique issues in seeking help, which is discussed in Chapter Two.

Different groups of victims may face unique barriers. For example, LGBTQ individuals may face different issues relevant to being "out," to finding appropriate supports, and more. The barriers faced by LGBTQ individuals and other groups are addressed in more detail in Chapter Two.

Many people do not think about it but concerns about pets can also inhibit help-seeking. Research has shown that up to 70% of domestic violence victims have beloved pets. Between 48% and 71% of those victims said that their pets have been threatened or killed. Abusers can manipulate the love for pets in much the same way that they manipulate children, using the pet as a tool for control and for keeping the victim around. At least 20% and as much as 65% of victims say that concerns about their pet delayed their leaving abusers. Although some shelters have capacity to care for pets or have arrangements with local providers, many still are not able to accommodate survivors in need of shelter who have animals with them (Animal Abuse, 2019).

Victims return to abusers for the same reasons that they find it difficult to leave. Yamawaki et al. (2012) found that people are more likely to blame victims who returned to abusers, which is a form of secondary victimization. As a result, these victims are more likely to blame themselves, which impedes their healing. Victims who engage in less healing and help-seeking behavior are thus more likely to return again to their abusers.

Ending the relationship does not necessarily end the abuse, however, as it is not atypical for abusers to continue to harass and harm victims after the relationship has ended. In some cases, ending the relationship escalates the abuse. There are several tools that have been developed to assess risk in an abusive situation. The Empowerment Process Model focuses on managing risk. It is based on the question "Under what circumstances might violence occur, and how might we change them?"

In the worst cases, abusers escalate to murder. Bureau of Justice Statistics data from 2021 found that of 4,970 female victims of murder and nonnegligent manslaughter, 34% were killed by an intimate partner. This is in comparison to the approximately six percent of male victims of murder and nonnegligent manslaughter who were killed by an intimate partner, making the intimate partner homicide rate five times higher for women than for men (Smith, 2022). Other studies have found even higher rates of domestic violence homicides, with nearly half of all female and one-tenth of male homicide victims are killed by intimate partners (Fridel & Fox, 2019; Jack et al., 2015). Approximately 75% of domestic or dating related homicides occur around when the victim has indicated he or she intended to leave the relationship. Homicide is the leading cause of death of women who are pregnant or recently had a baby, and it is most often perpetrated by current or former partners (Miller, 2022).

Experts and advocates have developed a Danger Assessment tool to determine the level of danger a victim has of being killed by a partner. It has been in use for more than 25 years. It was originally developed by Jacqueline Campbell in 1986. The tool involves two components: a calendar to assess the severity and frequency of abuse in the previous year and a 20-item scoring instrument which weighs risk factors for homicide, including the partner's employment status, past death threats, access to firearms, and more. Researchers revised the tool in 2008 to develop a danger assessment specific to women in same-sex abusive relationships. The following are typical questions involved in the Danger Assessment tool or other tools to assess potential lethality: prior victimization; batterer's drug and alcohol problems; batterer's obsessive-possessive behavior and excessive jealousy; batterer's threats to kill the victim or her children; batterer possession of, access to, familiarity with, and degree of fascination with weaponry, especially guns; batterer's use of violence in settings outside the home (e.g. bar fights); stalking behavior; batterer's suicidal ideations, plans, threats, and past attempts; the status of the relationship in terms of whether the parties are separated, separating, estranged, or whether she is in the process of fleeing (Websdale & Dedolph, 2000). Studies using the Danger Assessment tool have found that women who were threatened or assaulted with a gun or weapon were 20 times more likely to be murdered by their abusers than other women (Campbell et al., 2003).

The case of Gladys Ricart highlights how an abusive situation can be on-again, off-again, and can escalate when the victim chooses to move on to another relationship. Her case was also the inspiration for the Brides March and the College Brides Walk, both of which are discussed in subsequent chapters about education and activism.

Gladys, a beautiful woman from the Dominican Republic, had been in a long-term, on-again, off-again seven-year relationship with fellow Dominican, a respected businessman named Agustin Garcia. He was abusive to her and eventually she decided to break up with him for good. Several months late, Gladys met another man, James Preston Jr. They fell in love and made arrangements to marry. On the day she was supposed to wed, September 26, 1999, Gladys was at her home posing for photos and video with loved ones, including her 20-year0ild son and nine bridesmaids, before she was to meet her fiancé at the chapel. As they enjoyed the moment, Garcia arrived at the home and said he had been invited. At around 4 p.m. Garcia walked into her living room wearing a business suit and carrying a briefcase. He pulled out a 0.38 caliber revolver and shot Gladys twice. He fired his gun three more times, hitting Gladys again while her brother wrestled him to the floor. Gladys was rushed to the hospital, where she died from gunshots to her head, spine, and upper arm. Neighbors said that Garcia had stalked Gladys for months after she broke up with him. One said that "nobody liked him" and "the son absolutely hated him" (Associated Press, 1999). Garcia attempted to use a "crime of passion" defense. His attorneys argued that he suffered from a temporary mental illness upon the shock of learning that Gladys intended to marry another man. The judge, particularly disturbed by graphic video of the murder, did not believe Garcia's defense and sentenced him to life in prison in 2002 (Ivers, 2013).

Researchers have also developed strategies to assess the risk to children. Studies have found that while many women believe the children will be at less risk after they have left the abuser, in reality they are often at greater risk than when they lived with the abuser. This is because the risk may be mediated by the mother's efforts to protect her children while they are in the home. Drawing from the victim's reports, the children themselves, past partners, school officials, medical records, child protective service reports, court and police records, and any witnesses, the following 13 factors can identify the risk to children (Campbell et al., 2003):

1. Level of physical danger to the mother. The more frequent and severe physical abuse against the mother increases the risk that children too will endure physical abuse. Similarly, the abusers history of sexually assaulting the victim increases the risk of physical

violence to children. Other questions that can help assess the risk to children include: Has the batterer ever choked the mother? What types of injuries has he caused? Has he ever violated a restraining order? Has he made lethal threats against her or the children? Has he killed or attacked pets? Is he extremely jealous or possessive? Does he have access to weapons? Is he depressed, despondent, or paranoid? Does he stalk her? Is he escalating? What is his criminal record? Does he chronically abuse substances? Has he been violent toward the children, or toward nonfamily members? Does he use pornography?

2. History of physical violence toward the children. This includes the abuser's use of physical disciplinary techniques. Questions to consider include: Does he spank the children? Has he ever left marks? Does he ever grab the children roughly? Has he been involved in fights (including any that appeared mutual) with his older children? Does he minimize or justify physically abusive behaviors he has used in the past?
3. History of sexual abuse or boundary violations involving the children. The following questions can be considered when assessing this: Does the batterer respect his children's right to privacy, and maintain proper privacy himself? Does he expose the children to pornography? Does he pressure the children for unwanted physical affection or engage them in inappropriate sexual conversation? Does he make inappropriate comments about the children's bodies or physical development? Are there indications of secret-keeping?
4. Degree of psychological cruelty to the victim and children. Many victims express that the psychological abuse they endure is more painful than the physical abuse. To assess how psychological cruelty increases the risk to the children, researchers recommend the following questions: What have been his most emotionally hurtful acts toward the mother? What behaviors of his have caused the greatest distress to the children? Has he ever deliberately harmed the children emotionally?
5. Level of coercive or manipulative control in the relationship. The more controlling an abuser is the more he is likely to manipulate the children. Manipulative abusers are also more likely to be authoritarian parents and to physically abuse the children. Relevant questions include: Has he interfered with her social or professional contacts? Is he economically coercive? Does he dictate major decisions, showing contempt or disregard for her opinions? Does he monitor her movements? Is he dictatorial or minutely controlling toward the children?

6. Level of self-centeredness and entitlement. Entitled and self-centered abusers have been found to be more psychologically demanding on children and less focused on their needs. Some research also links higher levels of self-centeredness with the propensity to commit incest. Some questions to consider include: Is the batterer frequently and unreasonably demanding, becoming enraged or retaliatory when he is not catered to? Does he define the victim's attempts to defend herself as abuse of him? Does he have double standards regarding his conduct and that of other family members? Does he appear to view the children as owned objects?
7. History of undermining the mother's parenting and/or using children as weapons. A history of this behavior has been found to continue and often escalate postseparation. Relevant questions include: Has the batterer mistreated the children out of anger at the mother? Has he taught them negative beliefs about her? Has he ever prevented her from caring for a child? Has he every threatened to harm, kidnap, or take custody of the children? Has he used the children to frighten her, such as by driving recklessly with them in the car? Has he threatened to quit his job in order to avoid paying child support? Does he involve the children in activities that he knows the mother does not permit, or undermine her authority in other ways?
8. History of putting children and physical or emotional risk while abusing the mother. This type of violence in front of children increases the risk to children and is associated with more severe physical violence. The following are questions to consider: Has the batterer been violent or mentally cruel during any of the mother's pregnancies? Has he been violent in the presence of the children, assaulted her while a child was in her arms, or pushed a child out of his way to get at her? Has he ever thrown objects in a way that has risked hitting the children? Has he verbally abused or humiliated the mother in the children's presence? Has he neglected the children when angry at her?
9. History of neglectful or seriously uninvolved parenting. Abusers who are uninvolved or neglectful are less likely to consider the children's needs, including their safety. Relevant questions include: Does the batterer have a history of disappearing for hours, days or weeks at a time? Has he ever refused to attend to children's medical needs? Has his lack of attentiveness ever put the children in danger? Has he shown an abrupt interest in the children, perhaps including seeking custody, in response to the dissolution of the parental relationship?

10. Refusal to accept the end of the relationship. This also includes refusal to accept if the mother enters a new relationship. Severe jealous and retribution has been linked to increased dangerousness to the victim and children. Useful questions to consider include: Is the batterer depressed or panicked about the break-up, or insisting that the relationship is not over? Is he stalking her? Did he abruptly demand custody or expanded visitation upon learning that the mother had decided definitively not to go back to him, or when she began a new romantic involvement? Has he ever threatened or assaulted a new partner of hers, or warned her not to let any man other than him be around the children? Has he attempted to frighten the children about the mother's new partner, or to induce guilt in them for developing an attachment to him?
11. Level of risk to abduct the children. This is especially important if previous threats to take the children were made. Indicators of this risk might include efforts to take the children's passports, unexplained travel plans, surprise appearances at schools, or job-seeking in other states.
12. History of substance abuse: Many studies show that a history of substance abuse increases the risk of physical abuse to the mother and children, even including the risk of homicide.
13. Mental health history. While most abusers do not suffer from mental illness, certain mental disorders like antisocial personality disorder, obsessive/compulsive disorder, major depression, and borderline personality disorder may increase the risk of physical violence.

In cases involving teens or dating partners, this risk of homicide during the end of the relationship is often called break-up violence. Seven percent of teen homicide victims were murdered by their current or former dating partner according to a 2019 study (King, 2025). Teens are already at-risk for gun violence, with it being the leading cause of death for children and teens in the United States.

The murder of Lauren Astley in July 2011 highlights the dangers of break-up violence. She went missing on July 3. Just after daybreak her body was found in a marsh. Lauren had been strangled, and her throat was cut. Lauren, a popular, talented, kind, and beautiful girl, had started dating classmate Nathaniel Fujita during high school. He was her first serious boyfriend. Friends described him as generally nice, albeit a little quiet and a good football player. The two dated for three years and while at first it seemed great, friends began to describe the relationship as a "rollercoaster." They began to fight regularly and would break up and get back together, repeatedly.

In the spring of senior year and on her 18th birthday, Lauren broke up with Fujita. He was reportedly very sad about the breakup. Lauren and about 150 classmates were celebrating their graduation when Fujita came over to try to get her to talk to him. She did not want to and told to get away from her, then cried and complained to friends that he would not leave her alone. Fujita punched a pole that was holding up the tent they were partying under, causing a big scene. Fujita was told to leave. It was one month later that Lauren's body was found. Fujita and his mother had been questioned three times after she went missing but both told the same story each time: she had stopped by for five minutes that night but never got out of the car. Upon further investigation, police began to identify that Fujita had exhibited troubling behavior in the weeks leading up to Lauren's murder. He had basically stopped hanging out with friends and was drinking and smoking a lot of pot. His mother took him to a psychologist and asked Lauren if she would reach out. On the night of her murder, which she did. On the night of her murder, video surveillance at the mall where Lauren worked showed on the phone with Fujita around 6:45 p.m. At 7:05 p.m. her phone showed that she had texted Fujita just one word: "here," meaning she had arrived at his home. When investigators went to Fujita's home the morning her body was found, his father was there but Fujita was not. They obtained a search warrant and found blood in the garage as well as additional blood evidence, bungee cords, and a black gym bag that contained a pair of wet, muddy sneakers. In Fujita's bedroom they found in a crawl space about the ceiling a pair of bloody sneakers and bloody, wet clothing. After Fujita was arrested, police learned from friends that Fujita has been possessive and would look through Lauren's phone and things (Smith, 2013). Fujita tried to use an insanity defense but was found guilty of first-degree murder and sentenced to life in prison without parole.

CONCLUSION

As this chapter has shown, domestic and dating violence are among the most frequently occurring forms of violence globally and in the United States. Having a better understanding of the forms of abuse that can occur, the dynamics of abusive relationships, and the challenges of leaving abusers can help inform policy and programs to assist victims. The personal stories of those who have been impacted by abuse can and should be central to any decision on policy as well as in crafting prevention programs, including educational initiatives. Subsequent chapters will address how the information included in this chapter can be used in educational settings at all levels, in traditional classrooms, as well as in nontraditional environments.

REFERENCES

About teen dating violence. (2024, May 16). Centers for Disease Control and Prevention.https://www.cdc.gov/intimate-partner-violence/about/about-teen-dating-violence.html

Abrams, Z. (2023, October 1). *Up to 19% of teens experience dating violence. Psychologists want to break the cycle.* American Psychological Association. https://www.apa.org/monitor/2023/10/disrupting-teen-dating-violence

Animal Abuse. (2019). *DV Awareness.org.* https://www.dvawareness.org/sites/default/files/2019-06/AnimalAbuse-TalkingPointsForm.pdf

Associated Press. (1999, September 28). Bride shot before wedding. *CBS News.* https://www.cbsnews.com/news/bride-shot-before-wedding/

BBC. (2019, August 28). *Domestic abuse: Killers "follow eight-stage pattern," study says.* https://www.bbc.com/news/uk-49481998

Campbell, J., Webster, D., Koziol-McClain, J., Block, C., Campbell, D., Curry, M., Gary, F., McClane, J., Sachs, C., Sharps, P., Ulrich, Y., & Wilt, S. (2003). *Assessing risk factors for intimate partner homicide.* https://www.ojp.gov/pdffiles1/jr000250e.pdf

Domestic Violence. (2022). *U.S. Department of Justice office on violence against women.* https://www.justice.gov/ovw/domestic-violence

Fernandez, M. (2015). *Immigrant mothers in abusive relationships: Decisions and actions* (Doctoral dissertation). University of Miami.

Finley, L. (2016). *Domestic abuse and sexual assault in popular culture.* Praeger.

Fridel, E., & Fox, J. (2019). Gender differences in patterns and trends in U.S. homicide, 1976–2017. *Violence and Gender, 6*(1), 27–36.

Garcia-Moreno, C., Jansen, H., Ellsberg, M., Heise, L., & Watts, C. (2005). *WHO multi-country study on women's health and domestic violence against women: Report on the first results* (pp. 55–89). World Health Organization.

Gerson, J. (2024, February 22). More teens are reporting that a partner has threatened their reproductive health. *The 19th.* https://19thnews.org/2024/02/teens-national-domestic-violence-hotline-reproductive-coercion/

Ghoshal, R., Douard, A. C., Sikder, S., Roy, N., & Saulnier, D. (2023). Risk and protective factors for IPV in low-and-middle-income countries: A systematic review. *Journal of Aggression, Maltreatment & Trauma, 32*(4), 505–522.

Herrenkohl, T., Sousa, C., Tajima, E., Herrenkohl, R., & Moylan, C. (2008). Intersection of child abuse and children's exposure to domestic violence. *Trauma, Violence, & Abuse, 9,* 84–99.

Ivers, D. (2013, May 16). *Court upholds life sentence for NYC man who gunned down ex hours before her wedding.* New Jersey.com. https://www.nj.com/bergen/2013/05/nyc_man_who_gunned_down_ex_hours_before_her_wedding_loses_appeal.html

Jack, S., Petrosky, E., Lyons, B., Bliar, J., Ertle, A., Sheats, K, & Betz, C. (2015). Surveillance for violent deaths — National Violent Death Reporting System, 27 states. *MMWR Surveillance Summaries, 67*(11), 1–32.

King, A. (2025, February 21). Violence in teen relationships is more common than you think. *Time.* https://time.com/7259942/teen-relationship-violence-epidemic-mental-health-misogyny-essay/

Kippert, A. (2020, April 20). Abuse almost always escalates. *Domestic Shelters.* https://www.domesticshelters.org/articles/identifying-abuse/abuse-almost-always-escalates

Laxton, C. (2014). *Virtual world, real fear: Women's aid report into online abuse.* Women's Aid. [Google Scholar]. https://womensaid.org.uk/virtual-world-real-fear/

Marganski, A., & Melander, L. (2018). Intimate partner violence victimization in the cyber and real world: Examining the extent of cyber aggression experiences and its association with in-person dating violence. *Journal of Interpersonal Violence, 33*(7), 1071–1095.

Miller, K. (2022, October 24). Homicide is a leading cause of death for pregnant women, new study finds. Yahoo!Life. https://www.yahoo.com/lifestyle/homicide-leading-cause-death-pregnant-women-224016183.html?guccounter=1&guce_referrer=aHR0cHM6Ly93d3cuZ29vZ2xlLmNvbS8&guce_referrer_sig=AQAAAMHM2u5-CZHEmB–Zy6rsYQBQ3V-G5r8hi5b4X0RMxsTdLcB-s9PHQd6kMu4q2W2bBWkJyS8atoAYCAiviYH877glEhoq79KnYJYY4v16Yhpc_SEjPYAsFbKHbPgidD5Fpt9Gqp6cdNnqseJYC0t90UCN40XlNOaVs-L5hpQRs7-G

Mirpour, Z., Rahmani, M., & Ghorbansharoodi, S. (2021, April). Explaining the concept of re-experiencing abusive relationships. *Journal of Holistic Nursing and Midwifery, 31*(2), 124–134.

Moylan, C., Herrenkohl, Sousa, C., Tajima, E., Herrenkohl, R., & Russo, J. (2010). The effects of child abuse and exposure to domestic violence on adolescent internalizing and externalizing behavior problems. *Journal of Family Violence, 25*(1), 53–63.

Office for National Statistics. (2024, November 27). *Domestic abuse victim characteristics, England and Wales: Year ending March 24.* https://www.ons.gov.uk/peoplepopulationandcommunity/crimeandjustice/articles/domesticabusevictimcharacteristicsenglandandwales/yearendingmarch2024#sex

Office of the e-Safety Commissioner (2017). *Image-based abuse: National survey, summary report.* eSafety.gov. https://www.esafety.gov.au/sites/default/files/2019-07/Image-based-abuse-national-survey-summary-report-2017.pdf

Peace, L. (2025, April 29). 6 ways Florida's public safety system leaves domestic violence victims vulnerable. *Tampa Bay Times.* https://www.tampabay.com/news/crime/2025/04/29/what-to-know-florida-police-domestic-violence/

Piolanti, A., Waller, F., Schmid, I., & Foran, H. (2023). Long-term adverse outcomes associated with teen dating violence: A systemic review. *Pediatrics, 151*(6).

Rogers, M., Fisher, C., Ali, P., Allmark, P., & Fontes, L. (2022). Technology-facilitated abuse in intimate relationships: A scoping review. *Trauma, Violence, & Abuse, 24*(4), 2210–2226. https://pmc.ncbi.nlm.nih.gov/articles/PMC10486147/

Rothman, E., Bahrami, E., Okeke, N., & Mumford, E. (2021). Prevalence and risk markers for dating abuse-related stalking and harassment victimization and perpetration in a nationally representative sample of U.S. adolescents. *Youth & Society, 53*(6), 955–978.

Saunders, D., Jiwatram-Negrón, T., Nanasi, N., & Cardenas, I. (2022). Patriarchy's link to intimate partner violence: Applications to survivors' asylum claims. *Violence Against Women, 29*(11), 1998–2021.

Smith, E. (2022). *Female murder victims and victim-offender relationship, 2021.* Bureau of Justice Statistics. https://bjs.ojp.gov/female-murder-victims-and-victim-offender-relationship-2021

Smith, T. (2013, October 28). Lauren Astley murder draws attention to teen breakup violence. *CBS News.* https://www.cbsnews.com/news/lauren-astley-murder-draws-attention-to-teen-breakup-violence/

Stonard, K. (2021). Technology-assisted abuse in relationships. In J. Devaney, C. Bradbury-Jones, R. J. Macy, C. Overlien, & S. Holt (Eds.), *The Routledge international handbook of domestic violence and abuse* (pp. 356–372). Routledge.

Sweet, P. (2019). The sociology of gaslighting. *American Sociological Review, 84*(5), 851–875.

Taylor, B. G., & Mumford, E. A. (2016). A national descriptive portrait of adolescent relationship abuse: Results from the National Survey on Teen Relationships and Intimate Violence. *Journal of Interpersonal Violence, 31,* 963–988.

Teen dating violence. (2025). Centers for Disease Control and Prevention. https://www.cdc.gov/intimate-partner-violence/about/about-teen-dating-violence.html

UN Women. (2023, November 24). *Facts and figures: Ending violence against women.* https://eca.unwomen.org/en/stories/explainer/2023/12/facts-and-figures-ending-violence-against-women#:%7E:text=Globally%2C%20an%20estimated%20736%20million,women%20aged%2015%20and%20older

Vagi, K., Olsen, E., Basile, K., & Vivolo-Kantor, A. (2015). Teen dating violence (physical and sexual) among US high school students: Findings from the 2013 National Youth Risk Behavior Survey. *JAMA Pediatrics, 169*(5), 474–482.

Villora, B., Yubero, S., & Navarro, R. (2019). Associations between feminine gender norms and cyber dating abuse in female adults. *Behavioral Sciences, 9*(4), 35–47.

Walker, L. (1989). Psychology and violence against women. *American Psychologist, 44*(4), 695–702.

Websdale, N., & Dedolph, B. (2000). *Lethality assessment tools: A critical analysis.* VAWNET. https://vawnet.org/material/lethality-assessment-tools-critical-analysis

Woodley, J. (2024, June 13). *Suicide threats are a weapon of family violence. How can police balance mental health needs with protecting victims?* The Conversation. https://theconversation.com/suicide-threats-are-a-weapon-of-family-violence-how-can-police-balance-mental-health-needs-with-protecting-victims-231594

Woodlock, D. (2017). The abuse of technology in domestic violence and stalking. *Violence Against Women, 23*(5), 584–602.

World Health Organization. (2022). *Intimate partner violence.* https://apps.who.int/violence-info/intimate-partner-violence/

World Health Organization. (2024, March 25). *Violence against women.* https://www.who.int/news-room/fact-sheets/detail/violence-against-women

Yamawaki, N., Ochoa-Shipp, M., Pulsipher, C., Harlos, A., & Swindler, S. (2012). Perceptions of domestic violence. *Journal of Interpersonal Violence, 27*(16), 3195–3212.

Ybarra, M., Espelage, D., Langhinrichsen-Rohling, J., Korchmaros, J., & Boyd, D. (2016). Lifetime prevalence rates and overlap of physical, psychological, and sexual dating abuse perpetration and victimization in a national sample of youth. *Archives of Sexual Behavior, 45*(5), 1083–1099.

CHAPTER 2

UNDERSTANDING VICTIMS

ABSTRACT

Although anyone can be a victim of domestic or dating violence, certain demographic groups are at greater risk. This increased risk is the result of social, economic, and political factors that result in racism, sexism, homophobia, transphobia, and classism. Understanding the risk factors for abuse can help advocates, activists, and educators better tailor policies, programs, and educational initiatives designed to prevent abuse. This chapter reviews the risk factors faced by women of color, immigrants, LGBTQ+ individuals, persons with disabilities, and males. Further, the chapter describes help-seeking behavior by victims from these demographic groups as well as unique barriers to receiving assistance.

Keywords: Women of color; immigrants; socioeconomic status; LGBTQ+; disabilities; male victims

WOMEN OF COLOR

Women of color in general are at greater risk for experiencing abuse. Further, systemic racism and other factors may make them less likely to report abuse, less willing to engage in help-seeking behaviors, and more likely to be revictimized. The Women of Color Network (2022) identified the following barriers to reporting, leaving abusers, and help-seeking: cultural or religious beliefs related to keeping relationships together or involving the help of outsiders; strong racial, cultural, or familial bonds; distrust of law enforcement, criminal justice, and/or social services; lack of culturally and

Teaching and Making Peace in Every Relationship, pages 39–63

doi:10.1108/978-1-80686-961-920261003

linguistically appropriate service providers; fear that their experience will reinforce stereotypes about their racial, ethnic, or cultural group; concerns about legal status in the United States; revictimization due to the intersection of various social identities.

Black women suffer from more frequent and more serious abuse than do White women, in general. More than 40% of Black women suffer physical abuse by a current or former partner in their lifetime. Rates of psychological abuse are higher than for other demographic groups as well (Green, 2017). Black teens also experience dating violence twice as often as their White peers (Black Health Matters, n.d.). Further, African American women are more likely than women of any other racial group to be murdered by an intimate partner. African American women are murdered at younger ages, on average, at age 36, which is five years younger than women in other racial groups, and the perpetrator is almost always an intimate parter (Violence Policy Center, 2024). Despite the increased risk of lethality, Black women are more likely to remain with abusive partners than are other women (Waller et al., 2022).

One difficulty for African American women in seeking help is the stereotype of the "Superwoman." They are applauded and often expected to take care of things on their own, rather than seek help. African American women have long been stereotyped as "Mammys," "Jezebels," and "Sapphires." Such images normalize exploitation and violence against African American women (Waller et al., 2022, pp. 3–4). The Sapphire depiction, which was popular from the 1800s to the mid-1900s, showed Black women as domineering, sassy, and emasculating. Sapphires were loud, angry, and aggressive—a stereotype that persists today in the form of the "angry Black woman." In contrast, Mammy's, a stereotype constructed during slavery and popularized in minstrel shows, emphasized Black women's work as domestics who cared for White families. Mammys were undyingly loyal to slaveholders, serving to legitimize slavery as an institution. This image was often used to promote consumer goods and emphasized the supposed "contentment" Black women had with their position in society. Especially insidious is the portrayal of Black women as sexually promiscuous jezebels, compared to the sexually pure and modest historical depiction of White women (Popular and pervasive stereotypes of African Americans, n.d.; The Jezebel stereotype, 2024)

Additionally, "African American women are often socially perceived as betraying their partner and the entire African American community when they violate their socially prescribed role of protecting their man from the police rather than secretly suffer from victimization" (Waller et al., 2022, p. 2). "Intersectionality illuminates the 'triple jeopardy' sociological barriers of racism, capitalism, and sexism that African American women experience" (Waller et al., 2022, p. 3).

Although African American women do receive help from police, shelters, and professional sources, due to cultural traditions they often receive assistance from their churches or places of worship (Waller et al., 2022). Research has found that African American women tend to delay help-seeking and are more likely to report negative experiences with police and service providers than are other women. They may also not be aware of available supports. For instance, Few (2005) found that only a fifth of Black women in their study had been informed about their local shelter by police, compared to three-fifths of White respondents. Few (2005) found that none of the Black victim respondents felt that police were a viable source of assistance. In another study, a Black victim reported to Monterrosa (2019, p. 12) "I never called the police...We were taught that the police were not our friends...The police are not there to help Black people. For Black people, we don't tell our business. Calling the police was out of the question." Another victim explained that because the was Black, poor, and gay, the police mistreated her. When police responded to her call, they told her they did not like her attitude and they "pulled me, you know, slammed me against the floor, handcuffed me and took me to jail" (Simpson & Helfrich, 2014, p. 245).

Studies show that based on internalized stereotypes, many African American women believe they can handle the abusive situation better than can the police. Research has also shown that bidirectional abuse is more common in African American relations, with some African American women reporting that they intended to exact their own revenge. In addition to distrust of police, African American women report greater distrust of the legal system and are thus less likely to cooperate with legal processes. Additionally, African American women routinely report racist and discriminatory interactions with domestic violence shelter staff. Despite often needing emergency shelter, several studies have found that shelters are the place that African American are least likely to seek help. African American victims in need of medical attention often report delaying treatment due to distrust of the system and previous racist interactions. Similarly, African American women report being minimized and even dismissed within the mental healthcare system and, consequently, often do not seek such help or discontinue it before they should. Instead, African American victims are more likely to turn to self-care such as prayer or meditation (Waller et al., 2022). Although religious institutions can indeed be helpful, they may not always be equipped to provide the necessary assistance to victims of domestic violence. Bent-Goodley and Fowler (2006) found that members of faith-based groups and clergy often used Bible quote to encourage victims to stay with their abusers.

Hispanic or Latina women also suffer from domestic violence, although at similar rates as White women. Just over one-third (34.4%) of Latina women will experience domestic violence during their lifetime while one in 12 (8.6%) reported it in the previous 12 months. Rates tend to be lower among immigrant Latinas than US-born Latinas. Rates are higher among Latina women living near the Mexico border, 37.5%. Approximately 10% of pregnant Latina women reported physical abuse and 19% reported emotional abuse. This is slightly less than for all pregnant women. A study of Latina college students found that 31% had experienced dating violence since they enrolled (Esperanza United, 2021).

Latina and Hispanic women are significantly less likely to tell others about the abuse. This is in part due to the cultural emphasis on familismo, which refers to a strong family unit in which the father is the breadwinner and the mother is responsible for the wellbeing and cohesiveness of the family. Additionally, Latina and Hispanic women often put their children before themselves and thus may think keeping the family together is more important than getting free from abuse. Religion is another factor, as many Latina and Hispanic women are raised in religious traditions that emphasize the sanctity of marriage (Esperanza United, 2021).

Like Black women, Latina and Hispanic women are less likely to seek help than are their White peers. Rather than formal supports, Latina and Hispanic women are more likely to seek help from family, friends, and neighbors. This is especially true for undocumented immigrants. They are also less likely to seek mental health assistance. Further, a study of Latina's who did seek shelter found that they were less likely to know what an order of protection was, thereby making that an unlikely source of assistance. The language barrier can also be an issue. Financial insecurity as well as lower levels of education is also associated with decreased help-seeking among Latina and Hispanic women (Esperanza United, 2021).

Native American. Alaskan Native and Pacific Islander women are at significantly greater risk for experiencing domestic violence, sexual assault, and stalking. Approximately 39% of Native American, Alaskan Native, and Pacific Islander women report being abused in their lifetime. Although it is older data now, the U.S. Department of Justice stated in 2004 that the rate of abuse among Native American, Alaskan Native, and Pacific Islander women is 50% higher than for other demographic groups (Futures Without Violence, n.d.). Another study found that 46% of Native American women had experienced lifetime physical violence, rape, or stalking (Breiding et al., 2014).

One explanation for the increased risk of abuse among native peoples is the imposition of cultural values by American colonists and the federal mistreatment of them through genocidal policies. Many Native American youths were removed from their homes and sent to Boarding Schools, where the intent was to promote cultural assimilation and sever the ties to their culture and community. Youth sent to the Boarding Schools were often subject to physical and sexual abuse as well, and some died or were murdered. "The legacy of harm resulting from Boarding Schools is apparent in the continued disruption of physical, mental, and spiritual health, and traditional family systems/parenting passed from one generation to the next...This contextualization is important for understanding and interpreting the role of family systems in NA communities today and how they impact experiences of intimate partner violence" (Jock et al., 2022, p. 3). One survivor explained the link this way: "Because it becomes intergenerational. It starts from one generation and moves into the next and the next, and there's nothing wrong with it because that's a way of life. [As] a child, if you're exposed to it, then that becomes a way of life so when they 're grown up, there's nothing wrong with that" (Jock et al., 2022).

Furthermore, the loss of jurisdictional power held by tribal nations has reduced their sovereignty and deeply affected how crime is addressed on reservation lands. During the 18th and 19th centuries, not only did the federal government renege on all of the treaties it negotiated with Native peoples, decisions like that in *Oliphant v. Suquamish* (1978) essentially dismantled tribes' ability to prosecute in tribal courts nonIndians who commit crimes on reservation land. "This created the perfect storm to create a legal gap for nonNative people to murder, brutalize, and assault NA women without legal repercussions and further complicated by U.S. attorneys' offices declining to prosecute sexual assault cases and underfunding of tribal law enforcement": (Deer, 2017). Finally, the 2013 Violence Against Women Act (VAWA) Reauthorization allowed some federally recognized tribes to criminally prosecute nonNative perpetrators of domestic violence (Hart & Lowther, 2008; Reed, 2018; Whitebear, 2019). More than 90% of cases involve nonNative perpetrators (Logan, 2016). As of 2021, 26 of the 574 federally recognized tribes are implementing VAWA Special Domestic Violence Criminal Jurisdiction. One victim noted how the jurisdictional issues increase the likelihood of abuse: "...those who come to the reservation and target Native women specifically. They feel there's some kind of protection. The state police aren't gonna be there. The sheriff's department's not gonna be there. I think there's a belief they can get away with stuff on the reservation. They actually target Native women and come to reservations." Native American victims are critical of the lack of systemic supports. "I left my abuser and I had a PFA (protection from abuse) on him and he got served, and when he got served, he said, 'It was just a piece of paper.' He said other things on top of that, but he did make it very clear that he didn't care about the paper and he did violate it many times. He made contact with me either indirect or directly... and I reported so many things and nothing was done about it. Nothing, and that's really upsetting." Another victim expressed how the support varies depending on exactly where someone is located when the incidents happen. "If this person were to appear at my house, I could pick up the phone, call tribal police, and hope that they get there. When I'm off the reservation, I got nothing. I got nobody to call. I got no protection. I'm extremely vulnerable every time I leave. Yeah. That makes me uneasy" (Jock et al., 2022).

Native people also face several unique barriers to leaving and staying free from abusers. These include culturally specific forms of abuse, such as: historical and intergenerational trauma stemming from colonization and oppression; jurisdictional issues on Native lands that limit criminal justice response and make it more difficult to hold abusers accountable, especially nonNative perpetrators; poverty; lack of infrastructure for tribal police, courts, and victim's services; limited availability and enforcement of protection orders; lack of confidentiality in small, isolated Native communities; accessibility of medical services; and lengthy investigations when Federal Bureau of Investigations (FBI) is involved due to jurisdictional issues (Identify Abuse, n.d.). Many Native American victims fear that they will receive a racist response from healthcare and other providers. "Additionally, silence is a trauma response that must be recognized and understood by providers. This is because AI women's voices have been silenced over hundreds of years through colonial power imbalances and they may feel that it is not safe to speak out about the violence that they experience" (Deer, 2017). While there are many benefits of living in tight-knit communities like most Native Americans do, a drawback is that "everybody knows everybody." One victim reported, "What is both a risk factor and a resiliency factor is the extended family network aspect. Something that could be scarier, but also could be something that protects you. Knowing that you have a bunch of relatives you could go stay with." Families may also fiercely support abusers. As one victim put it, "…if he has a support system that's backing him…she's very unsafe, because they have ears and eyes all over the reservation of where she's going to be. I think that's a huge risk factor, too…" Cultural beliefs that emphasize the family "no matter what" may mean that loved ones support victims but it might mean that victims are encouraged to keep the family unit together despite the abuse. Many Native survivors emphasize keeping the family together so that their children have a father figure and out of fear that the children will be taken by legal systems. Fear that family or community may ostracize victims prevents them from reporting abuse and seeking help, with many victims concerned that they did not want the abuse to reflect poorly on their family. As one victim expressed, "Well in the Native way too, family and community is everything. When you have the breakdown in trust of a family member, it's you against your family. Your family doesn't come to support you. You're the odd man out because you're disrupting this community and that's hard for anybody to be singled out like that." Another victim commented on the issue: "Well, in a small community such as ours, families tend to side with families, and so we have large families…[the abuser's] uncle might be the chief of police, so that person is gonna have more leeway than somebody else, if you get what I'm saying…" (Jock et al., 2022).

Another issue lies in the cultural belief to try to get the abuser help, rather than simply leave him.

> See [the] Westernized way…is they have to leave their perpetrator and that's the fix. Well, that doesn't work so…well in [a] Native community. Part of it is trying to get the perpetrator help… If I talk about healing him from that place that his father learned from residential school, and that it's not their fault, and I remove the blame of the colonization, and the…historical trauma, I move that blame away from that person, then we can really start making progress, but we also have to heal our community.

Victims and advocates recognize the need for interventions that focus on extended families and cultural practices that also encourage "intergenerational healing."

> Intergenerational healing is about empowering individuals to remember where we came from, a strengths-based perspective of how culturally rich our people are. That is not anything money can buy, but the intergenerational healing is about rejuvenating our cultural practices, our ceremonies, our self-esteem, our sense of self-care. Really to truly embrace life as a blessing versus it's hard when somebody's always talking about the trauma…What are we going to do with that? You're here. You have the ability to address these issues and not pass them to your children. That's called intergenerational healing. If your children see you fighting, then they're more likely higher risk to repeat the behaviors and the relational detachment that they learn growing up…We've already endured the trauma, and who is going to either end that cycle, or continue to feed it? (Jock et al., 2022)

Other countries have similar issues with disproportionate violence against indigenous peoples, especially women. Australia, New Zealand, and Canada, all countries that like the United States are settler colonialist (meaning colonists took over the land, imposed different systems, and never left) have similar rates and issues. In Australia, Aboriginal women and women from the Torres Straits are significantly more likely—32 times—to be hospitalized for injuries due to violence than nonindigenous women. This is most often due to abuse by partners (Longbottom et al., 2024).

IMMIGRANT VICTIMS

Immigrant Latina women face unique challenges with domestic violence. They may come from countries that hold deeply patriarchal beliefs, making the likelihood of abuse greater. Family and religious factors discourage women from ending relationships with abusers. Cultural views on marriage were found to effect Latina victim's perceptions of abusive behavior and impede help-seeking. Latina women's predominately Catholic beliefs also hinder help-seeking. Women report that faith leaders often side with abusers. One victim explained that her Catholic priest interpreted abuse: "as an unchangeable circumstance designed by god as a challenge to be met with dignity in order to enter heaven after death" (Vidales, 2010, p. 537).

Fatalism, the belief that problems are predetermined and due to fate or destiny, is prominent among Latinos and Latinas, which also may contribute to the high rates of abuse and the inclination for help-seeking. Victims in Mexico reported that cultural beliefs about men's entitlement to women contributed to physically abusive behavior (Vidales, 2010). One woman reported, "In Mexico it is normal to have fights . . . is like there is still machismo in Mexico . . . like everything is part of marriage . . . I thought it (domestic violence) was part of marriage" (Reina et al., 2014, p. 602). Machismos is the norm for men, where as "marianismo" emphasizes that women must maintain relationships and the peace. A quote from a Latina woman highlights the point: "If your husband says something that you do not like, your obligation is to shut up and put up with it, because he is your husband, I mean you already got married, you are there and you put up with it" (Silva-Martínez, 2016, p. 531). Women may also be afraid to leave abusers in cultures that emphasize the importance of virginity, as they may fear that they won't find another partner. "Sometimes I felt that I wasn't worth anything, because of what people in Mexico said to me. That if you aren't a virgin anymore, you are worthless… if I didn't have him [her abuser in the US], nobody else was going to love me" (Parson et al., 2016, p. 24). All of these beliefs may be brought with them to the United States when they immigrate (Ogbonnaya et al., 2015).

When they move to the United States, immigrant women are typically isolated from family so do not have that source of support. Those without proper documentation are concerned about contacting police out of fear they will be deported, which is very legitimate. This is especially true at times when antiimmigrant sentiment is high (Esperanza United, 2021) and there are frequent raids by immigration and customs enforcement, as is the case at the time of this writing in May 2025. Even though shelters are typically not government-run and staff do not usually have to ask about immigration status, many victims are not aware of that and are thus hesitate to seek this kind of help as well (Florian, 2022). Connie Chung Joe, chief executive officer of Asian Americans Advancing Justice Southern California, explained,

> When you send enforcement agents into courthouses and you take such broad immigration actions, you're actually making it less safe for survivors because of this chilling effect. Now victims are more scared about getting detained or separated from their children and family, and that becomes scarier than [not] being able to protect themselves against their abusers. (McShane, 2025)

Abusers will also use the threat of deportation as a tool of control. Research has shown that many undocumented immigrant victims had relocated to their husband's host country. One woman explained, "My visa expired but (they) were not ready to apply for indefinite leave for me. His mother always used to say, 'Deport her!'" (Anitha, 2008, p. 194). Another undocumented immigrant victim whose son was a citizen, said, "Every time I wanted to leave, he would tell me 'If you say something I will go to immigration and accuse you. If you talk with the police, I will tell them that you are illegal and you won't ever see the boy again'" (Silva-Martinez, 2016, p. 537). Abusers may lie to victims, telling them that they had submitted immigration paperwork as a spouse but not doing so. I worked with an immigrant victim from Guyana who found out after she left her abuser that she was actually undocumented and he had been lying about her paperwork. Further, as Hulley et al. (2023) noted, "perpetrators can weaponize any asymmetries between the couple, using his language proficiency, residency and knowledge of local laws and customs in order to further threaten, abuse and control his victim" (p. 1008). In cases like these in the United States, there is a provision in the VAWA that allows people to self-petition for legal residency status if they were in a bonified marriage and can provide evidence of the abuse. Many victims are unaware of this, however.

Another tactic abusers use is to limit their victim's opportunity to learn the local language. This hinders help-seeking in a variety of ways. One Mexican immigrant victim explained, "When the police came, they could tell I couldn't speak English, so they started to talk to my husband. I could understand enough of their conversation in English to make out some of what they were saying. My husband told them it was his home and that he wasn't sure if he'd let me stay here. Soon the police were asking him to please let me stay. I was crying and really frustrated because the police didn't take the time to understand what I wanted to say…After a while the police and my husband began talking about football and laughing. It was like they were part of a male club or something" (Vidales, 2010, p. 536). In another example, an immigrant victim reported that her husband attacked her one night. She grabbed a nearby object and scraped him in self-defense. But when the police came, her abuser explained in English what had happened and could not communicate with her. She was arrested and the police left her abus werith their children (Parson et al., 2016).

Even when they do seek help, immigrant women have a harder time receiving it. One study found that minority ethnic women made 17 contacts with formal services before receiving help, compared to 11 contacts by non-minority ethnic women (Hulley et al., 2023). A Latina immigrant in the United States explained, "When you don't know where they are [services], when you don't know where to turn, when you don't know the language, when you don't know the people, you realize that you are blind and you need to stay where you are" (Silva-Martinez, 2016, p. 532).

Other groups have cultural norms that might make abuse more acceptable and help-seeking less likely. Research with South Asian victims has found that culturally, domestic violence is a private, family issue that is considered to be normal. Male dominance and female subordinance are common beliefs in China and can contribute to abuse. One Chinese woman reported her husband saying, "The woman whom I marry should be as docile as a sheep, and should never talk back" (Rai & Choi, 2018). Further, sex is considered the marital right of the husband in much of South Asia so sexual abuse in a relationship is not recognized as a problem (Hulley et al., 2023). Another woman from India noted, "As the cultural Indian girl, I'm not allowed to leave him, because I can change the man by changing my tactics. It will be a disgrace to the family. The children will have a black spot on their name, and no one will marry them when they grow older" (Sabri et al., 2019, p. 247). Another woman noted the cultural emphasis on honor and how leaving an abusive husband would be perceived as a dishonor to her family. 'My father said, "if you divorce, you are dead to me, do not come back home" (Tonsing & Barn, 2017, p. 633). Marrying cousins is also common in South Asian culture and thus leaving an abuser is uniquely disruptive to the family 'I am married to my first cousin so tolerated it because women get divorce then many families get affected ... it will disrupt family...' (Tonsing, 2016, p. 22). In addition, women also fear that if they discuss abuse or attempt to leave abusers, they will jeopardize the marriage prospects of their sisters. In some cases, the in-laws are also abusive. While some South Asian victims have reported that their religion helped them understand and get free from abuse, other report that abusers also use religion as a form of abuse. For example, an Indian victim described how religion meant that women were unable to refuse their husband sex. If they refuse, the man has the right to leave the woman (Sabri et al., 2019).

African women also report widespread cultural acceptance of abuse (Ogunsiji et al., 2012; Ting & Panchanadeswaran, 2009). For example, one woman explained, "In my country, it is okay for men to discipline their wives. I told myself this was not abuse, this was 'normal discipline'. Other wives I know said the same thing? 'oh yes, my husband hits me too; that's normal', so that is how we believed, and how we all survived" (Ting, 2010, p. 353). Another African woman commented on how family members often interfere in marital relationships in ways that inhibit help-seeking. "My mother-in-law, she tell me she will tell the police I am the troublemaker, that I am the crazy one" (Ting & Panchanadeswaran, 2009, p. 825). In predominately Muslim cultures, women have often reported that their mosques and religious leaders were helpful, although that is not always the case. One Muslim victim reported that her Imam pressured her to stay with her abusive husband.

> He told me that the woman who is patient with her husband's bad deeds will go to paradise. They said to me million times until I said to them, I don't want to go to paradise this much quick. If I stay with him, I will die soon; someone should help me. They just kept telling me I have to be patient. (Ghafournia, 2017, p. 157)

Single women in many African cultures are viewed negatively, as are single parents. Women leaving abusers fear that they will be ostracized (Ogunsiji et al., 2012; Ting & Panchanadeswaran, 2009). As with many places, African women may lack financial independence, causing them to remain in abusive relationships. One victim explained, "He wouldn't let me go back to school. He wouldn't let me go to work. He wouldn't let me do anything. Just stay at home being a mom" (Tam et al., 2016, p. 533). After being paid a bride price, African women are traditionally sees as their husband's property and are this financially obligated to remain with him (Ting & Panchanadeswaran, 2009).

SOCIOECONOMIC STATUS

Many studies link domestic violence and lower socioeconomic status. For instance, Bonomi et al. (2014) studied domestic violence incidents reported to police involving urban couples and found that abuse rates were highest in the poorest neighborhoods. Poverty interacts with other identities; for example, poor women of color are at greater risk for experiencing abuse than are poor White women. This is true in the United States as well as globally (Gillum, 2019). As was noted earlier, finances are a significant reason why victims remain with or return to abusers. As well, victims may not be able to seek certain kinds of help, such as therapy, due to financial reasons.

It is important to remember, however, that middle and upper-class women also experience abuse (Weitzman, 2001), but less is known about their experiences. Women with more financial resources may seek certain kinds of help, such as from friends or private therapists, rather than from police or domestic violence shelters. Nonetheless,

> Many survivors who live in upscale neighborhoods will not likely report abuse, feeling shame or embarrassment in sharing what's really going on at home. Many of the services they'd utilize from professionals to help respond to or escape from abuse (such as doctors, dentists, attorneys, etc.) are probably neighbors, belong to the same country club, and likely socialize together. Even though seeking services to escape abuse may seem more accessible to those in upper-middle-class areas, this shame to disclose is often a barrier. (Peterson, 2024)

LGBTQ+ VICTIMS

Research shows that LGBTQ+ individuals as well as those who identify as nonbinary are as likely if not more likely to experience dating and domestic violence in their lifetimes. The CDC's 2010 National Intimate Partner and Sexual Violence Survey found that lesbian and bisexual women were more likely to experience abuse than were straight women, with 61% of bisexual women and 44% of lesbian women reporting lifetime abuse compared to 35% of straight women. Rates of abuse were also higher for bisexual men than for straight men, with 37.3% of bisexual men reporting lifetime abuse. Rates of abuse among gay men were slighting lower than for straight men, 26% to 29%. Some of the highest rates are among trans and nonbinary individuals, according to the 2015 United States Transgender Survey. It found that 54% of trans and nonbinary individuals had experienced abuse during their lifetimes.

The abuse LGBTQ+ individuals experience often begins with they are young. Almost one-fifth of Lesbian, Gay, Bisexual and Transgender high school-aged students report having been forced to have sex with a dating partner, for example. This is much higher than the six percent of straight youth reporting that experience. The rate of trans youth reporting being forced to have sex with a dating partner is even higher, at 24%, compared to the 15% reported by their cisgender peers. Rates of physical violence and other types of sexual violence by dating partners are also higher, with 13% of LGB high school-aged youth reporting physical violence and 16% reporting sexual violence. This compares to seven percent of straight youth who reported physical and sexual violence by a dating partner. Rates of physical and sexual violence by dating partners are still higher among trans youth compared to cisgender youth, with reported rates of physical violence 26% for trans youth and 15% for cisgender youth and 23% of trans youth and 16% of cisgender youth reporting sexual violence.

One reason that rates of abuse are higher among LGBTQ+ individuals is due to societal marginalization and discrimination. Abusers can capitalize on social, economic, and political vulnerabilities. In this case, abusers can weaponize existing homophobic and transphobic feelings and systems to perpetuate control.

LGBTQ+ victims may find it difficult to tell others about the abuse or to seek help due to homophobia and transphobia. Further, because many LGBTQ+ individuals are not "out" or have only told a few people about their gender identity or sexual orientation, abusers use the threat of "outing" them to family, friends, and coworkers as a tool of control. Abusers can capitalize on the fact that many victims are already marginalized or isolated from loved ones to further isolate them. Abusers also gaslight LGBTQ+ victims into believing that domestic and dating violence only happens in traditional heterosexual relationships. Bisexual individuals are often stereotyped as being hypersexual, which might affect the likelihood that they will be believed, or at least their belief that others will take them seriously. Abusers can also exploit this stereotype to pressure bisexual individuals into unwanted sexual activity. Transgender women, especially Black transgender women, are at heightened risk for enduring domestic and dating violence. Poverty, racism, transphobia, and inadequate supports are all factors that increase the risk, especially among younger adults, many of whom are with older partners (Human Rights Campaign, 2022).

Globally, the challenges are even more stark for LGBTQ+ individuals who are in abusive relationships. The Human Dignity Trust noted that 65 jurisdictions criminalize private, consensual, same-sex activity. Twelve countries even allow for the imposition of the death penalty for private, consensual, same-sex activity. It would be nearly impossible for someone living in one of these countries to receive any sort of formal support, and even informal supports may be quite limited. Further, as was noted in the Introduction, while there are many international human rights treaties, agreements, and case precedents related to domestic violence and the state's responsibility, few specifically include LGBTQ+ individuals. The wording of some country's domestic violence legislation still emphasizes that only females can be victims (Serra, 2013).

PREGNANT WOMEN

Pregnant women are especially at risk for experiencing domestic or dating violence. Most often, the abuse predates the pregnancy but escalates during it. 50–70% of pregnant women who endure abuse experienced abuse before they were pregnant. Up to 20% of pregnant women endure abuse, making it more common that preeclampsia and gestational diabetes (both conditions that are routinely screened for during pregnancy). The risk for experiencing physical abuse is two to four times greater when the pregnancy is unintended. This means the risk is generally greater for pregnant teens than for pregnant adults (National Coalition Against Domestic Violence, 2016). More than 45% of homicides of pregnant women or women within one year of pregnancy were related to domestic violence (CDC, 2024).

Pregnant women may delay help-seeking for various reasons. They may want to keep the relationship together, believing that the abuser will change due to the addition to the family. Unfortunately, that does not typically happen. Pregnant women may also feel mentally, physically, and financially overwhelmed and thus not want to reach out to shelters, police, or other support services.

The effects of abuse during pregnancy, for the mother and the baby, are discussed in detail in Chapter Four.

MALE VICTIMS

Approximately one-third of men in the United States have experienced some form of domestic or dating violence in their lifetime. Other studies have found that between 3.4% and 20.3% of men globally have experienced physical domestic violence. Interestingly, most of the men who endured abuse have also perpetrated it. The most likely predictor of a male being abused by a partner is growing up in an abusive home, with 10.6% to 40% reporting that they had endured abuse or maltreatment as children (Kolbe & Büttner, 2020). More than half (56%) endured the abuse by their partner before age 25, with many experiencing the abuse before age 18 (CDC, n.d.) Like Black women, Black men also experience domestic violence at higher rates than White men. 40.01% of Black men have experienced physical violence, sexual violence, or stalking from their intimate partner (Black Health Matters, n.d.).

While some research shows that male victims can more easily leave abusers, perhaps due to the fact that they tend to be more in control of finances and thus have more resources to get out, they also face unique barriers. One is in simply recognizing the abuse and naming it what it is. Some males do not believe that women can abuse men, so when they are experiencing any of the forms of power and control described in the previous chapter, they may chalk it up to their wife or girlfriend being "crazy" or a "bitch." Thus, rather than seeking support, they may try to deal with it or move on but never really address what is truly happening. Still others feel stigma or shame that they may be experiencing abuse at the hands of a female. This can tie into gender role norms that many men adhere to which tell them that they are to be strong, not emotional, take charge, solve problems, and not be submissive. These qualities are what sociologist R. Connell referred to as "hegemonic masculinity."

Some assert that growing up in a patriarchy prepares boys for violence when they are young, as they are often encouraged to play rough, contact sports, "to exhibit fearlessness in the face of physical confrontations, and to accept the harm and injury associated with violence as 'natural'" (Anderson & Umberson, 2011, p. 363). While this might make them more prone to be abusers, it can also prohibit them from acknowledging when they are abused and inhibit help-seeking behavior. These cultural norms that depict men as tough, hard, and strong mean that men who are victimized may be less likely to be believed (Levell & Hester, 2023). Tillapaugh (2022) found that "hegemonic masculinity ultimately serves as a secondary form of violence among men who survived sexual violence in college." The author claimed that, "(1) the inevitability of masculinity as violence; (2) masculinity as violence and its impact on coping; (3) the shame, fear, and frustration of masculinity as violence; and (4) systemic administrative (masculine) violence in higher education" (Tillapaugh, 2022, p. 1).

Another issue for male victims of dating and domestic violence is the scarcity of resources to help. When in the 1970s under the second wave of the feminist movement, or what is often called the Women's Liberation Movement, activists began paying more attention to domestic violence and the need for legislation and resources, the emphasis was solidly on helping female victims. Research and understanding of male victims and their unique needs is still developing. Many shelters and resources still have names or titles that use the word "woman" as well. Even though some may be able to assist men, a name like the "Violence Against Women Act" does not necessarily make it obvious that men can benefit from its provisions.

VICTIMS WITH DISABILITIES

Persons with disabilities or with limited capacity such as some elderly individuals also at greater risk of experiencing abuse. This includes people with cognitive or learning disabilities, mental illness, and physical disabilities. Women with disabilities are at 40% greater risk for experiencing violence in general, with the perpetrator most frequently being a current or former partner. The risk is especially acute for severe physical abuse. Disabled victims of violence are often dependent on their abusive primary caretakers and run the risk of losing their caretaker if they report abuse. Many fear being institutionalized or losing their basic decision-making rights if they are viewed as unable to take care of themselves (NCADV, 2017).

Services may not be easily accessible to persons with disabilities. For instance, some people with transportation or mobility issues may find it difficult to access domestic violence shelters or supports. Some people with cognitive or emotional disabilities may have limited ability to act independently and thereby cannot or do not seek help. As with many other victims, persons with disabilities may not be aware of services. This could be in part because they are not promoted in ways that are accessible, for instance, in large print, Braille, or via audiotape. The NCADV (2017) noted that only 35% of shelters offered disability awareness training to their staff. Just 16% had a specific employee devoted to delivering services to victims with disabilities. The VAWA provides support for victims with disabilities. The original version in 1994 did not, but the 2000 reauthorizations expanded funding for education and technical assistance to service providers so they could better serve victims with disabilities. The 2005 reauthorization provided additional coverage for victims. The Americans with Disabilities Act of 1990 requires that domestic violence shelters be accessible. This is defined as admitting people with disabilities into the shelter, providing reasonable accommodations, and eliminating structural barriers to access (NCADV, 2017).

DATING VIOLENCE VICTIMS

Teen victims experience abuse somewhat differently than do adults. For one, bidirectional abuse is more common. When the abuse becomes physical or sexual, it is more often perpetrated by males against females, especially the more severe forms. Further, due to their lack of experience in romantic relationships, youth may mistake the abuse for interest or see the "drama" of the relationship as normal or even desirable. Although adults do this as well, youth who are being victimized often try to change themselves to please their partner, believing that doing so will stop the abuse.

Youth most often rely on informal sources of support, largely friends and parents. Many cite mistrust, shame, and embarrassment as inhibitors of more formal help. Some research also shows that racial and ethnic factors such as negative conceptions of father figures, familism, adherence to traditional gender role norms, and distrust of authorities also inhibit help-seeking by youth. Many youth are simply unaware of resources to assist them.

In the United States, women ages 18 to 24 are at greatest risk for experiencing abuse. This makes college students particularly vulnerable. Research has shown that 10% to 50% of college students experience some type of dating or domestic violence. These rates vary tremendously by campus, however. Larger schools typically having higher rates (Kaukinen, 2014). An estimated 20% to 37% of college dating relationships involve physical assault (Shorey et al., 2008). College students face some unique challenges in seeking help. Many are new to campus and do not know where to report abuse or what services are available. Some students live in the same residence halls as their abusers, making it even more difficult to stay safely away. Even having the same classes as your abuser can make it challenging for victims to want to speak up. Like teens, college students may fear stigma or loss of relationships if they tell anyone about the abuse.

Globally, research has shown that youth in abusive relationships may respond in slightly different. A study in Ghana, for instance, found that teen victims of dating violence were more prone to isolate themselves, to dabble in illicit drugs, and/or to seek spiritual guidance (Pastor-Bravo et al., 2023).

HELP-SEEKING GLOBALLY

One factor that makes help-seeking difficult globally is that some countries do not have legislation prohibiting domestic and/or dating violence. UN Women's database shows that 145 countries have some type of relevant legislation. Several countries in Africa and the Middle East do not legally prohibit domestic or dating violence. As of 2023, Afghanistan, Cameroon, the Democratic Republic of Congo, Oman, Qatar, Somalia, Sudan, South Sudan, Equatorial The West Bank and Gaza, Yemen, Guinea, Eritrea, Estonia, Guinea, Haiti, Iran, Iraq. Libya, Mauritania, Myanmar, Niger, Syrian Arabic Republic, and Tanzania all lack specific legislation relevant to dating and domestic violence (World Bank Group, 2025). This means victims cannot utilize the justice system for support. Similarly, those countries also tend to offer minimal social service support. Amnesty International noted that Russia's war against Ukraine, the COVID-19 pandemic, and adherence to traditional gender roles had led to rising levels of domestic violence in Eastern Europe and Central Asia and a shortage of appropriate support services. Amnesty's Eastern Europe and Central Asia researcher Natalia Nozadze commented,

> Governments across Eastern Europe and Central Asia are increasingly promoting 'traditional values' and equating the protection of gender equality and women's rights with a loss of cultural and traditional identity, as part of efforts to secure broader support for their antihuman rights agenda. As a result, patriarchal attitudes, misogyny and homophobia have not only become more entrenched, but have flourished.

In 2017, the Russian parliament decriminalized some forms of domestic violence, as did Kazakhstan (Amnesty International, 2022). The following story illustrates the problems with this approach:

> After her husband had dragged her into the woods behind their home and threatened her ith a knife, the mother of two called the police. It was not the first time she had reported abuse, but, under Russian law, her abuser could not be arrested unless the abuse was so violent that she would be hospitalized. Three months later, the police received a call saying that Gracheva's hands had been cut off with an ax. Only then was her husband arrested. (Rollins, 2022)

The law in Russia says that if the abuse leads "only" to bruises or minor injuries, the offender will face no punishment. If the victim sustains severe injuries requiring hospitalization, the abuser can face criminal punishment of a fine of 5,000 rubles ($88) for a first offense. After the law was passed, the number of domestic violence incidents reported to police dropped in half, and one of the few shelters in the country, the Anna Center, reported a 7,000 increase in calls (Rollins, 2022).

Belarus had considered a law prohibiting domestic violence in 2018 but decided that President Alyaksandr Lukashenka opposed it because it supposedly violated "Belarusian, Slavic traditions. He added that a "good belting could sometimes be useful" in relationships. Azerbaijan requires that victims go through mandatory mediation with their abusers so as to promote the "resumption of family affairs." The Council of Europe has established the requirement of one available shelter space per 10,000 people, a standard that none of the countries in this region have met. Russia has only 14 state-run domestic violence shelters for its population of 146 million. Before the war, Ukraine had just 33 shelters across the nation for 42 million people, many of which are now used to house persons displaced by the war rather than victims (Amnesty International, 2022).

As noted in Chapter One, the COVID-19 pandemic both increased rates of domestic and dating violence and further limited the availability of help services. Lockdown orders meant more time in a home with an abuser, who might also be financially and emotionally stressed. China saw a threefold increase in domestic violence cases, while several states in the United States reported 21–35% increases. Spain saw a 47% increase in calls to domestic violence helplines in April 2020 compared to the same time period the previous year. It also reported a 700% increase in women seeking support service electronically, either via social media or email. India also saw a 47% increase in reported domestic violence (Kunasagran et al., 2023).

While the first shelters were started in the 1970s in England and the United States. Most shelters in the United States are based on the Domestic Abuse Intervention Project, more commonly known as the Duluth Model due to where it was developed. This emphasizes victim safety and offender accountability based on the feminist understanding that abuse is the result of power and control. Paymar and Barnes (2017) explained how an understanding of history influenced the development of the model.

> When Europeans came to this continent, they brought religion, laws, and economic systems that institutionalized the status of women as the property of men through marriage. From the church to the state, there was not only acceptance of male supremacy, but also an expectation that husbands would maintain the family order by controlling their wives. Various indiscretions committed by wives were offenses to be punished by husbands. This system of male dominance (like any social structure where one group oppresses another) was perpetuated by: a) a belief in the primacy of men over women; b) institutional rules requiring the submission of women to men; c) the objectification of women which made violence acceptable; and d) the right of men to use violence to punish with impunity.

With victims, the Duluth Model helps develop understanding of the many ways that abusers obtain and maintain power and control. The wheels included earlier in the chapter are one way of helping victims see the tactics their abusers are using. There are some concerns about this model being biased that are discussed in the following chapter.

There was a rapid increase in the number of domestic violence shelters after the 1995 Beijing Declaration and Platform for Action, Article 125(a), which calls on states to "provide well-funded shelters and alleviation assistance for girls and women facing violence, as well as medicine, mental, or other counseling services, and free or cheap legal support, where needed, as well as supportive services." Nonetheless, there remains a shortage of this kind of help (Sharifi et al., 2024).

Nor is the shelter model the only or even necessarily the best option. Most are operated as nonprofit or nongovernmental organizations (NGOs), rather than run by the state. Some activists have asserted that this absolves the state from providing the necessary support. Others have criticized what they refer to as the nonprofit industrial complex (NPIC). It is estimated that there are some 10 million nonprofits and NGOs worldwide and nearly two million in the United States alone. Finley and Esposito (2021) noted that, "In the last decade, however, critics have begun to point out that nonprofits are burdened by some of the same problems as are other institutions; namely, hyperbureaucracy, competition for scarce resources, and kowtowing to the very states and governments they once critiqued." Some scholars and activists have referred to this as the NPIC. The Nonprofit-industrial complex (NPIC) is "a set of symbiotic relationships that link political and financial technologies of state and owning class control with surveillance over public political ideology, including and especially emergent progressive and leftist social movements" (Smith, 2007, p. 8). This has established essentially a "shadow state" that does the work the government should do but has outsourced to the private sector. As Sharifi et al., 2024 Allard (2009) noted, "we effectively have privatized a substantial portion of the contemporary safety net" (p. 31).

Many social service providers, including domestic violence shelters, are bureaucratic, formal, hierarchical, and elitist (Rodriguez, 2007). As Baines (2010) suggests, the acceptance of neoliberal ideology and practice and the bureaucratization of service provision has "...supplanted discourses of collective care, economic equality, and social solidarity" (p. 14). As such, Brainard and Siplon (2004), explained that "the soul of the nonprofit sector seems to be up for grabs" (p. 436) while Bush (1992) described keeping the "nonprofit spirit in a profit world" (p. 391) as the biggest challenge facing nonprofits today.

Nonprofit and NGOs serving victims nearly always struggle to secure adequate funding and resources. This created a competitive environment whereby service providers are fighting for the same pot of money and often not collaborating as they should. As Baines (2010) explained, "scarce funding generates competition among agencies, compelling some to undercut themselves and others in order to continue to provide much-needed programs and retain highly skilled staff" (p. 14). Finley and Esposito (2021) explained,

> Given that neoliberal and conservative funding sources typically require "evidence" of business-like effectiveness and support only "best practices," funding increasingly supports short-term projects that can be easily measured and do not advocate more radical and necessary social changes. At domestic violence shelters, this tends to mean simply tallying the number of people served or showing a change in scores from pre to post tests. Such measures do little to assess whether a victim will remain safe or whether social norms are changing.

Further, research is clear that while the shelter movement was founded on feminist principles, many of these organizations largely shun feminist objectives. Bumiller (2008), Ferarro (1996), Pleck (1987) and others have described how domestic violence advocates are advised to avoid including feminist-based approaches and programs in their requests for funding, as conservative grantors and foundations refuse to fund such work. Finley and Esposito (2021) explained,

> The result is that programs receive grants largely to serve individuals, but not to change social norms that would reduce domestic violence as a structural phenomenon. Furthermore, the now typical neoliberal funding formulas rarely cover all the costs of overhead or operations for the increasingly bloated bureaucratic structures. As a result, organizations must constantly be seeking other sources of funding. Rather than devote their resources to the provision of services or to organizing the community, domestic violence shelters increasingly employ, and pay significant salaries to, "development" officers and grant writers. Competition does not help build movements for social change, nor does it meet the needs of diverse communities.

CONCLUSION

As this chapter has explained, demographic factors affect the frequency of abuse, victim's help-seeking behavior, and the types of support that they receive. So, what can we do with this information? The following is a short list that is developed further in the second half of the book.

- Consider cultural factors when crafting prevention programs, laws, policies, and other resources for support.
- Rethink the reliance on traditional shelters as the preferred method of assistance.
- Address systemic racism and interlocking oppressions that result in some groups experiencing greater victimization and lesser help.

- Develop educational programs in schools, workplaces, and communities—as well as in local, state, and federal political realms.
- Utilize existing international human rights laws to leverage global cooperation to address gender-based violence.
- Improve international human rights law to better include males, LGBTQ+ victims, and other marginalized groups.

REFERENCES

Allard, S. (2009). *Out of reach: Place, property and the new American welfare state.* Yale University Press.

Amnesty International. (2022, December 14). *Eastern Europe and Central Asia: Lack of protection against domestic violence exacerbated by crises and "traditional values"—New report.* https://www.amnesty.org/en/latest/news/2022/12/eastern-europe-and-central-asia-lack-of-protection-against-domestic-violence-exacerbated-by-crises-and-traditional-values-new-report/

Anderson, K., & Umberson, D. (2011). Gendering violence: Masculinity and power in men's accounts of domestic violence. *Gender & Society, 15*(3), 358–380.

Anitha, S. (2008). No recourse, no support: State policy and practice toward South Asian women facing domestic violence in the UK. *British Journal of Social Work, 40*(2), 462–479.

Baines, D. (2010). Neoliberal restructuring, activism/participation, and social unionism in the nonprofit social services. *Nonprofit and Voluntary Sector Quarterly, 39*(1), 10–28.

Bent-Goodley, T., & Fowler, G. (2006). Spiritual and religious abuse: Expanding what is known about domestic violence. *Affilia, 21*(3), 282–295.

Black Health Matters. (n.d.). *Domestic violence in the Black community—By the numbers.* https://blackhealthmatters.com/domestic-violence-and-african-americans-by-the-numbers/

Bonomi, A., Trabert, B., Anderson, M., Kernic, M., & Holt, V. (2014). Intimate partner violence and neighborhood income: A longitudinal analysis. *Violence Against Women, 20*(1), 42–58.

Brainard, L., & Siplon, P. (2004). Toward nonprofit organization reform in the voluntary spirit: Lessons from the internet. *Nonprofit and Voluntary Sector Quarterly, 33,* 435–457.

Breiding, M., Smith, S., Basile, K., Walters, M., Chen, J., & Merrick, M. (2014). Prevalence and characteristics of sexual violence, stalking, and intimate partner violence victimization—National intimate partner and sexual violence survey, 2011. *MMWR Surveillance, 63*(8), 1–18.

Bumiller, K. (2008). *In an abusive state: How neoliberalism appropriated the feminist movement against sexual violence.* Duke University Press.

Bush, R. (1992). Survival of the nonprofit spirit in a for-profit world. *Nonprofit and Voluntary Sector Quarterly, 21,* 391–410.

CDC. (n.d.). *Intimate partner violence, sexual violence, and stalking among.* https://www.cdc.gov/intimate-partner-violence/about/intimate-partner-violence-sexual-violence-and-stalking-among-men.html

CDC. (2024, December 5). *Violence and pregnancy.* https://www.cdc.gov/intimate-partner-violence/about/violence-and-pregnancy.html

Deer, S. (2017). Bystander no more: Improving the federal response to sexual violence in Indian Country. *Utah Law Review, 2017*(4). https://dc.law.utah.edu/ulr/vol2017/iss4/7

Esperanza United. (2021). *Latinas and intimate partner violence: Evidence-based facts.* https://esperanzaunited.org/wp-content/uploads/2021/11/3.11.73-Factsheet_GeneralIPV2021.pdf

Ferarro, K. (1996, fall). The dance of dependency: A genealogy of domestic violence discourse. *Hypatia, 11*(4), 77–92.

Few, A. L. (2005). The voices of Black and White rural battered women in domestic violence shelters. *Family Relations, 54*(4), 488–500.

Finley, L., & Esposito, L. (2021). Neoliberalism and the non-profit industrial complex: The limits of a market approach to service delivery. *Peace Studies Journal, 5*(3), 4–26.

Florian, J. (2022). The effects of IPV on immigrant Latinas. *Family Therapy Magazine, 21*(4). https://ftm.aamft.org/effects-of-ipv-on-immigrant-latinas/

Futures Without Violence. (n.d.). *Safety and health for indigenous women: Working at the intersection of health and intimate partner violence.* https://futureswithoutviolence.org/wp-content/uploads/2025/10/Safety-Health-for-Indigenous-Women.pdf

Ghafournia, N. (2017). Muslim women and domestic violence: Developing a framework for social work policy. *Journal of Religion and Spirituality in Social Work, 36*(1–2), 146–160.

Gillum, T. (2019). The intersection of intimate partner violence and poverty in Black communities. *Aggression and Violent Behavior, 46*, 37–44.

Green, S. (2017, July 13). *Violence against Black women—Many types, far-reaching effects.* Institute for Women's Policy Research. https://bookstore.emerald.com/shiksa-speaks-hb-9781837084944.html

Hart, R. A., & Lowther, M. (2008). Honoring sovereignty: Aiding tribal efforts to protect Native American women from domestic violence. *California Law Review, 96*(1), 185–234.

Hulley, J., Bailey, L., Kirkman, G., Gibbs, G., Gomersall, T., Latif, A., & Jones, A. (2023). Intimate partner violence and barriers to help-seeking among Black, Asian, minority ethnic and immigrant women: A qualitative metasynthesis of global research. *Trauma, Violence, & Abuse, 24*(2), 1001–1015.

Human Rights Campaign. (2022). *Understanding intimate partner violence in the LGBTQ+ community.* https://www.hrc.org/resources/understanding-intimate-partner-violence-in-the-lgbtq-community

Identify Abuse (n.d.). *Strong hearts helpline.* https://strongheartshelpline.org/abuse

Jock, B., Dana-Sacco, G., Arscott, A., Bagwell-Gray, M., Loerzel, E., Brockie, T., Packard, G., O'Keefe, V., McKinley, C., & Campbell, J. (2022). We've already endured the trauma, who is either going to end that cycle or continue to feed it?: The influence of family and legal systems on Native American women's intimate partner violence experiences. *Journal of Interpersonal Violence, 37*(21–22), 1–23.

Kaukinen, C. (2014). Dating violence among college students: The risk and protective factors. *Trauma, Violence, & Abuse, 15*(4), 283–296.

Kolbe, V., & Büttner, A. (2020). Domestic violence against men: Prevalence and risk factors. *Deutsches Artzeblatt International, 117*(31–32), 534–541.

Kunasagran, P., et al. (2023). The global landscape of domestic violence against women during the COVID-19 pandemic: A narrative review. *Korean Journal of Family Medicine, 18*(1), 3–11.

Levell, J., & Hester, M. (2023). Masculinity and domestic violence: Hegemonic masculinity. In T. Schackleford (Ed.), *Encyclopedia of domestic violence* (pp. 1–23). Springer.

Logan, M. (2016). Human trafficking among native Americans: How jurisdictional and statutory complexities present barriers to combating modern-day slavery. *American Indian Law Review, 40*(2), 293–324.

Longbottom, M., McGlade, H., & Cripps, K. (2024, May 10). Indigenous women are most affected by domestic violence but have struggled to be heard. It's time we listened. *The Conversation.* https://theconversation.com/indigenous-women-are-most-affected-by-domestic-violence-but-have-struggled-to-be-heard-its-time-we-listened-229720

McShane, J. (2025, June 12). LA's ICE raids are impacting domestic violence shelters. *Mother Jones.* https://www.motherjones.com/politics/2025/06/la-ice-raids-domestic-violence-shelters/

Monterrosa, A. E. (2019). How race and gender stereotypes influence help-seeking for intimate partner violence. *Journal of Interpersonal Violence, 36*(17–18), 1–22.

National Coalition Against Domestic Violence. (2016). *Domestic violence and pregnancy fact sheet.* https://vawnet.org/sites/default/files/assets/files/2016-09/DVPregnancy.pdf

NCADV. (2017). *Domestic violence and disabilities.* https://www.niwrc.org/sites/default/files/images/resource/fact_sheet_pdfs.pdf

Ogbonnaya, I. N., Finno-Velasquez, M., & Kohl, P. L. (2015, January). Domestic violence and immigration status among Latina mothers in the child welfare system. Findings from the National Survey of Child and Adolescent Well-being II (NSCAW II). *Child Abuse & Neglect, 39,* 197–206.

Ogunsiji, O., Wilkes, L., Jackson, D., & Peters, K. (2012). Suffering and smiling: West African immigrant women's experience of intimate partner violence. *Journal of Clinical Nursing, 21*(11–12), 1659–1665.

Parson, N., Escobar, R., Merced, M., & Trautwein, A. (2016). Health at the intersections of precarious documentation status and gender-based partner violence. *Violence Against Women, 22*(1), 17–40.

Pastor-Bravo, M., Vargas, E., & Medina-Maldonado, V. (2023). Strategies to prevent and cope with adolescent dating violence: A qualitative study. *International Journal of Environmental Research and Public Health, 20*(3), 2355–2370.

Paymar, M., & Barnes, G. (2017). *Countering confusion about the Duluth Model.* Battered Women's Justice Project. https://www.biscmi.org/wp-content/uploads/2015/04/PaymarBarnesArticleDecember06.pdf

Peterson, C. (2024, March 4). Not to people like us. *Domestic Shelters.* https://www.domesticshelters.org/articles/domestic-violence-op-ed-column/not-to-people-like-us

Pleck, E. (1987). *Domestic tyranny.* Oxford University Press.

Popular and pervasive stereotypes of African Americans. (n.d.). *National Museum of African American History & Culture.* https://nmaahc.si.edu/explore/stories/popular-and-pervasive-stereotypes-african-americans#:%7E:text=The%20Sapphire%20caricature%2C%20from%20the,direct%20violation%20of%20social%20norms

Rai, A., & Choi, Y. (2018). Socio-cultural risk factors impacting domestic violence among South Asian immigrant women: A scoping review. *Aggression and Violent Behavior, 38,* 76–85.

Reed, C. (2018). Are we there yet: An analysis of violence against Native American women and the implementation of special criminal domestic violence jurisdiction. *Journal of Race, Gender, and Poverty, 2018*(10), 1–18.

Reina, A. S., Lohman, B. J., & Maldonado, M. M. (2014). He said they'd deport me. *Journal of Interpersonal Violence, 29*(4), 593–615.

Rodriguez, D. (2007). The political logic of the non-profit industrial complex. In INCITE! Women of Color Against Violence (Ed.), *The revolution will not be funded: Beyond the non-profit industrial complex* (pp. 21–40). South End.

Rollins, K. (2022, August 3). Putin's other war: Domestic violence, traditional values, and masculinity in modern Russia. *Harvard International Review.* https://hir.harvard.edu/putins-other-war/

Sabri, B., Rai, A., & Rameshkumar, A. (2019). Violence against women in India: An analysis of correlates of domestic violence and barriers and facilitators of access to resources for support. *Journal of Evidence- Based Social, Work, 19*(6), 700–729.

Serra, N. (2013). Queering international human rights: LGBT access to domestic violence remedies. *Journal of Gender, Social Policy, & the Law, 21*(3), 583–607.

Sharifi, F., Talasaz, Z., & Larki, M. (2024). The establishment of shelters as a new paradigm towards struggling with violence against women: A literature review. *Journal of Family and Reproductive Health, 18*(1), 9–19.

Shorey, R., Cornelius, T., & Bell, K. (2008). A critical review of theoretical frameworks for dating violence: Comparing the dating and marital fields. *Aggression and Violent Behavior, 13*(3), 185–194.

Silva-Martínez, E. (2016). "El silencio": Conceptualizations of Latina immigrant survivors of intimate partner violence in the midwest of the United States. *Violence Against Women, 22*(5), 523–544.

Simpson, E. K., & Helfrich, C. A. (2014). Oppression and barriers to service for Black, lesbian survivors of intimate partner violence. *Journal of Gay & Lesbian Social Services, 26*(4), 441–465.

Smith, A. (2007). Introduction: The revolution will not be funded. In INCITE! Women of Color Against Violence (Ed.), *The revolution will not be funded: Beyond the non-profit industrial complex* (pp. 1–20). South End.

Tam, D. M. Y., Tutty, L. M., Zhuang, Z. H., & Paz, E. (2016). Racial minority women and criminal justice responses to domestic violence. *Journal of Family Violence, 31*(4), 527–538.

The Jezebel stereotype. (2024). *Jim Crow Museum.* https://jimcrowmuseum.ferris.edu/jezebel/index.htm

Tillapaugh, D. (2022). Masculinity as violence: College men sexual violence survivors and the impact of hegemonic masculinity. *International Journal of Qualitative Studies in Education, 0*(0), 1–16.

Ting, L. (2010). Out of Africa: Coping strategies of African immigrant women survivors of intimate partner violence. *Health Care for Women International, 31*(4), 345–364.

Ting, L., & Panchanadeswaran, S. (2009). Barriers to help-seeking among immigrant African women survivors of partner abuse: Listening to women's own voices. *Journal of Aggression, Maltreatment & Trauma, 18*(8), 817–838.

Tonsing, J. C. (2016). Complexity of domestic violence in a South Asian context in Hong Kong: Cultural and structural impact. *Social Work Education, 35*(1), 18–30.

Tonsing, J., & Barn, R. (2017). Intimate partner violence in South Asian communities: Exploring the notion of "shame" to promote understandings of migrant women's experiences. *International Social Work, 60*(3), 628–639.

Vidales, G. T. (2010). Arrested justice: The multifaceted plight of immigrant Latinas who faced domestic violence. *Journal of Family Violence, 25*(6), 533–544.

Violence Policy Center. (2024, October 3). *Black women murdered by men are almost always killed by someone they know, most commonly with a gun.* https://vpc.org/press/black-women-murdered-by-men-are-almost-always-killed-by-someone-they-know-most-commonly-with-a-gun/

Waller, B., Harris, J., & Quinn, C. (2022). Caught in the crossroad: An intersectional examination of African American women intimate partner violence survivors' help seeking. *Trauma, Violence, & Abuse, 23*(4), 1235–1248.

Weitzman, S. (2001). *Not to people like us: Hidden abuse in upscale marriages.* Basic.

Whitebear, L. (2019). VAWA reauthorization of 2013 and the continued legacy of violence against Indigenous women: Critical outsider jurisprudence perspective. *University of Miami Race and Social Justice Law Review, 2019*(9), 75–90.

Women of Color Network. (2022). *Domestic violence fact sheet.* https://womenofcolornetwork.org/publications/index.php

World Bank Group. (2025). *There is legislation specifically addressing domestic violence.* https://liveprod.worldbank.org/en/indicator/sg-leg-dvaw

CHAPTER 3

UNDERSTANDING ABUSERS

ABSTRACT

The emphasis in Chapter 3 is on understanding abusers. It provides risk and protective factors for perpetration, details about offender's characteristics, including female offenders, and offers information on best practices to change abusers' behaviors.

Keywords: Perpetrators; batterers; batterers intervention programs; risk and protective factors; female abusers

RISK FACTORS FOR PERPETRATION

There are numerous risk factors for perpetrating abuse. These are at the individual, relationship, community, and societal levels. Individual risk factors focus solely on the person. Relationship risk factors have to do with family and friends. Community risk factors are related to neighborhood violence and disadvantage, while societal level risk factors focus on broader economic, political, and cultural structures and institutions.

- Low self-esteem.
- Low education or income.
- Young age.
- Aggressive or delinquent behavior as a youth.
- Heavy alcohol and drug use.

Teaching and Making Peace in Every Relationship, pages 65–83

doi:10.1108/978-1-80686-961-920261004

- Depression and suicide attempts.
- Anger and hostility.
- Lack of nonviolent social problem-solving skills.
- Antisocial personality traits and conduct problems.
- Poor behavioral control and impulsiveness.
- Traits associated with borderline personality disorder.
- History of being physically abusive.
- Having few friends and being isolated from other people.
- Economic stress (e.g., unemployment).
- Emotional dependence and insecurity.
- Desire for power and control in relationships.
- Hostility toward women.
- Attitudes accepting or justifying violence and aggression.
- History of physical or emotional abuse in childhood.
- Unintended pregnancy.

Relationship risk factors include:

- Relationship conflicts including jealousy, possessiveness, tension, divorce, or separations.
- Dominance and control of the relationship by one partner over the other.
- Families experiencing economic stress.
- Unhealthy family relationships and interactions.
- Association with antisocial and aggressive peers.
- Parents with less than a high school education.
- Witnessing violence between parents as a child.
- History of experiencing poor parenting as a child.
- History of experiencing physical discipline as a child.

Community risk factors include:

- Communities with high rates of poverty and limited educational and economic opportunities.
- Communities with high unemployment rates.
- Communities with high rates of violence and crime.
- Communities where neighbors don't know or look out for each other and there is low community involvement among residents.
- Communities with easy access to drugs and alcohol.
- Weak community sanctions against intimate partner violence (e.g., unwillingness of neighbors to intervene in situations where they witness violence).

Societal risk factors include:

- Cultural norms that support aggression toward others.
- Income inequality.
- Weak health, educational, economic, and social policies or laws.

Some of these risk factors are more significant than others. One of the strongest predictors is childhood exposure to domestic violence. Experiencing or witnessing childhood can increase the risk of someone becoming a perpetrator as much as three times. Mother-to-father violence is the strongest predictor of dating violence perpetration (Temple et al., 2014). Given that childhood exposure and experience with abuse is such a strong predictor of later violence, many screening tools have been developed to help assess the degree to which young people experience adverse experiences so that assistance can be coordinated and the cycle broken. One of these is the Adverse Child Experiences scales, which were developed by researchers and practitioners with the Centers for Disease Control and Kaiser Permanente in 1995. Practitioners can use the scales developed to assess childhood exposure to the following: Child Maltreatment, including sexual abuse, physical abuse, and verbal abuse; as well as Child's Environment, which includes domestic violence, parental separation, mental illness, alcohol abuse, drug abuse, and parental incarceration. A child who experiences four or more of these is at much greater risk for engaging in future risky behavior, including perpetrating domestic violence (Morton et al., 2022). Another way to look at adverse childhood experiences and their impact on later risky behavior, including domestic and dating violence perpetration, is to focus on "ghosts," or adversity, versus "angels," meaning benevolence, in the nursery (as children grow up) (Narayan et al., 2020).

Harsh parental discipline is another of the more significant factors that increase the risk of later perpetration of violence. In particular, being physically punished, such as being spanked, paddled, pushed, shoved, hit, or slapped, is associated with increased perpetration of violence when the child gets older. Even though as of 2024, 67 countries have banned physical punishment (both at home and in schools), it persists as a relatively common disciplinary tactic in the United States. Further, many of the international human rights treaties discussed in the Introduction require that signatory countries prohibit physical punishment. Abusive parents are more likely to use physical punishment as well (Affi et al., 2017).

How people communicate can be a red flag for abuse. The following are common phrases used by abusers, according to survivors (Kippert, 2022).

- "You can go but I don't want you to go."
- "Couples don't have secrets—I need to be able to read your texts or emails whenever I want to."

- "You'd be much more pretty if…."
- "I bring the money into this house, so I decide."
- "I'll give you money to spend. You don't need to worry about a bank account."
- "How much did you spend? I need to see all your receipts."
- "Where were you today?"
- "I tried calling … why didn't you answer?" [This is after 15 missed calls in a few hours.]
- "Why did you make me do that?"
- "You don't love me as much as I love you."
- "No one will ever understand you like I do."
- "If you loved me, you'd do this."
- "You're always creating drama/making a big deal out of nothing/starting a fight/trying to get the last word in."
- "If you leave me, no one else will want you."
- "You're not smart/successful/strong enough to survive without me."
- "You need to go on a diet."
- "Why don't you look as hot as you did when we first met?"
- "You're such a slut/you dress like a whore."
- "This is why no one likes you."

Related to gender norms, Sileo et al. (2022) described "masculine discrepancy stress," or the intrapsychic stress that men feel when they feel that they have failed to meet internalized masculine ideals. This feeling was associated with higher levels of domestic violence perpetration. In particular,

> We find that discrepancy stress is directly associated with higher levels of anger, lower levels self-esteem, a sense of powerlessness, and a greater odds of perpetrating any physical IPV and severe physical IPV resulting in injuries, but not sexual IPV perpetration in our sample of men. (Sileo et al., 2022, p. 1)

As was noted in Chapter One, pet abuse is also a significant predictor of domestic violence perpetration. Additionally, children who witness animal cruelty are at greater risk of perpetrating violence later in life (Animal Abuse, 2019). The connection is commonly called "the Link." One study in 2017 found that 89% of women who had pets during an abusive relationship reported that they were threatened, harmed or killed by the abuser. Love for a beloved pet is also a major barrier to leaving abusers, as was noted in Chapter One. Historically, domestic violence shelters generally did not allow pets, so victims would delay leaving abusers out of fear for their animals (Animal Legal Defense Fund, n.d.). There have been some improvements, however. Today all 50 states have felony animal cruelty laws, which can allow individuals to be held accountable hopefully before they abuse their partners. Nearly two thirds of states allow pets to be included in domestic violence protective orders, which allows victims and their animals a level of protection. Starting in 2016 the Federal Bureau of Investigations (FBI) began tracking crimes against animals in the national incident based reporting system, which can show where perpetrators are located, including those who might hurt humans as well (ASPCA, n.d.). As of this writing (June 2025), the White House budget request to Congress would eliminate a program known as the Pet and Women Safety Act, which is funded by the Agriculture Department and administered by the Department of Justice, and provides domestic violence shelters with money to support survivors' pets (McShane, 2025).

Although substance abuse is not causal, it is highly correlated with domestic violence (Armstrong et al., 2019). For example, a study involving 216 female victims of abuse who recorded daily surveys of their experiences for 90 days found that abuse was more likely on the days when the abuser used any substance, but in particular, alcohol (Schick et al., 2025).

Advocates are typically cautious about connecting mental illness to domestic violence. People with mental illnesses are far more likely to be victims of violence than they are perpetrators. As Kippert (2022) explained "An abuser who lives with any mental illness simply has two issues—mental illness and propensity to abuse their partner." Yet, abusers do tend to share some psychological traits. These include hostility toward women, adherence to traditional gender roles, sexual objectification of women, intense jealousy, a controlling nature, inability to admit fault and take blame, advancing the relationship very quickly, and hypersensitivity about minor inconveniences or perceived slights.

However, there have been some studies that have found a link between perpetration of domestic violence and certain mental illnesses. Some mental disorders that have been linked to increased propensity to perpetrate domestic violence include Narcissistic Personality Disorder, Borderline Personality Disorder, Psychopathology, and Antisocial Personality Disorder or Sociopathology (Kippert, 2022).

Persons with Narcissistic Personality Disorder typically lack empathy and are constantly seeking attention and validation, often through arrogant or grandiose behavior. They may belittle others in order to feel superior and monopolize conversations. Such individuals are more prone to psychological forms of abuse (Kippert, 2022).

Borderline Personality Disorder can result in difficulty self-regulating emotions and behaviors, intense fear of change, instability, or abandonment, frequent mood swings, impulsivity, and inappropriate anger. This form of mental disorder is also more linked to psychological abuse than other forms (Kippert, 2022).

Psychopaths are unable to feel guilt, shame, or remorse, as are those with Antisocial Personality Disorder. The latter also has a difficult time understanding right from wrong (Kippert, 2022).

Although far more research needs to be done to understand the risk factors for female perpetrators, many studies have found that women abuse men as a response to some form of abuse they are receiving. Past unresolved trauma, such as child abuse, sexual abuse, or previous domestic abuse, is another risk factor for female perpetration (Larance, 2024).

Military members and veterans are also at greater risk for perpetration of domestic violence. Rates of abuse perpetration are higher among veterans than those in active service and by male military members than female members (Kwan et al., 2020). There are many possible reasons why military populations may be overrepresented as abusers.

> Military training may encourage the use violence as a mode of conflict resolution. It is possible that factors associated with military service could result in increased risk of IPV. These could include experiences on deployment, particularly combat exposure, which is known to be associated with violence and offending in general. The general demands of military life can cause military personnel to be separated from their family and support system which may impact on rates of IPV. (Kwan et al., 2020)

Head injuries can also cause someone to become violent. Military members are more likely than most of the general public to sustain head injuries, so this too could be a factor.

It is also important to note that police officers perpetrate abuse at higher rates than do those not working in law enforcement. A systematic review of research published before 2015 found that between 4.8% and 40% of police officers self-reported perpetrating domestic violence. The large discrepancy is likely due to varying methodologies, sample sizes, and the nature of self-reporting. The overrepresentation of police officers as abusers may be due to the traditional hypermasculine subculture of policing. Included in that subculture is what is known as the "Blue Wall of Silence," meaning that officers do not "tell" on their colleagues even when they are engaged in some type of wrongdoing (Mennicke & Ropes, 2016). Since often allegations of abuse, if they are even brought forward at all, are dealt with internally, police officers may not be held accountable for their perpetration. Research has shown that police are perpetrators at higher rates than are civilians in other countries as well, including England, Australia, and Wales (Reeves, 2025).

Unemployment is also a risk factor for domestic violence perpetration. Economic stress has long been associated with increased abuse. Statistics about various crises that were highlighted in Chapter One, including the COVID-19 pandemic, highlight this point. Unemployed or underemployed abusers, especially males, may feel as though they have "failed as men" and take it out on their partners. Additionally, more time at home due to unemployment can exacerbate abusive behavior.

PROTECTIVE FACTORS FOR PERPETRATION

The following protective factors are also at the individual, relationship, community, and societal levels. These are based on data in the United States compiled from the CDC and Yakubovich et al. (2018).

Individual risk factors include:

- Being older
- Being married (not dating, divorced or polyamorous)

Relationship protective factors include:

- Strong social support networks and stable, positive relationships with others.

Community protective factors include:

- Neighborhood collective efficacy, meaning residents feel connected to each other and are involved in the community.
- Coordination of resources and services among community agencies.
- Communities with access to safe, stable housing.
- Communities with access to medical care and mental health services.

Societal protective factors include:

- Less patriarchal beliefs, institutions, and systems.

RISK FACTORS FOR DATING VIOLENCE PERPETRATION

While there are many similar risk factors for dating violence perpetration, there are some that are unique to youth. In a review of 20 previous studies, Vagi et al. (2013) identified 53 risk factors for perpetration. These include: mental health issues such as depression and anxiety; aggressive thoughts/cognitions, for instance, the belief that violence is the way to solve problems; youth violence like bullying and fighting; marijuana and/or alcohol use; poor relationship and quality with family and friends, including abuse in the home; and use of aggressive media. Some studies have found a link between having peers who are abusers and perpetration, while others have not found that to be a significant factor (Foshee et al., 2011). A metaanalysis by Park and Kim (2018), however, found that the biggest predictor of dating violence perpetration was having deviant peers.

There are certain groups who are also at greater risk of becoming perpetrators. This includes athletes, although not everyone who participates in sports is at higher risk. Rather, sports that involve physical contact and encourage aggression, such as football, basketball, wrestling, hockey, and boxing are those in which athletes are overrepresented as abusers (Benedict, 1998; McCauley et al., 2014; McMahon, 2010; Merten, 2008). Research has also found that boys who participate in these kinds of sports are more likely to hold negative attitudes about gender equality and to hold social status that might make them feel as though they can behave in whatever way this wish without consequence (McCauley et al., 2014). Additionally, as noted previously about the military, research has begun to focus on how brain injuries might contribute to abusers' violent behavior. Many boys and men involved in the sports listed above sustain head injuries, sometimes several times (Costello & Greenwald, 2022). College athletes in these sports are also overrepresented as abusers (Cantor et al., 2021).

While they report higher rates of victimization, Lesbian, Gay, and Bisexual (LGB) youth also report higher rates of perpetration. A third of LGB youth reported perpetrating physical dating violence, 37% perpetrated psychological abuse, 18% perpetrated cyber dating abuse, and four percent reported perpetrating sexual coercion. Transgender youth reported the highest rates of perpetration (Dank et al., 2014).

For youth, heavy drinking and marijuana use are risk factors for perpetrating dating violence (Walton, 2010). Another study found similar results but also noted that tobacco use was a risk factor, for both boys and girls as perpetrators (Rothman, 2011).

GLOBAL RISK AND PROTECTIVE FACTORS

Domestic violence is more common in middle and low-income countries, some five times higher than in high-income countries. One reason may be the propensity to emphasize traditional gender roles. If men are unable to succeed as breadwinners due to individual, institutional, or structural factors, they may compensate by taking it out on their partners. In cultures that believe men are to have control over women, the perpetrators can easily reject responsibility for abusive behavior, instead transferring it to women (Ghoshal et al., 2022).

When looking at the most frequent and severe offenders, they are most likely to deflect responsibility and to endorse gender role norms, cultural, and religious beliefs that are misogynistic and patriarchal and thus conducive to perpetration. The most common justification men use for abuse is that their partners disrespect their authority as men (Cunha et al., 2022). Men who suspect infidelity, whether their suspicions are reasonable or not, are more likely to perpetrate abuse.

> Women are considered as property to be possessed, or a conduit to material property in many patriarchal cultures. Male ownership of the woman translates to her expected emotional and physical loyalty to the partner. If she is suspected of intimacy with another male, her partner's insecurities are triggered, leading to violence against her. (Ghoshal et al., 2022, p. 513).

Men who have secondary or higher education are less likely to perpetrate abuse. Like in the United States, data shows that globally substance use and especially abuse increases the likelihood of perpetration (Ghoshal et al., 2022).

Men are more likely to abuse women in countries or areas that are engaged in violent or political conflict. The number and severity of conflicts around the globe has increased since the mid-2000s. The effects of these go beyond the loss of life and injury. Conflicts disrupt infrastructure, trap countries in poverty, reduce investment, and affect education and mental health. Women and girls suffer from gender-based violence at higher rates in conflict zones. Rape, sexual trafficking and other forms of gender-based violence disproportionately affect women and girls, but domestic violence is the most frequently occurring forms of violence in conflict areas. Conflict increases domestic violence in a number of ways. For one, people surrounded by violence can come to see violent behavior as normal. Financial stress that often accompanies conflict due to loss or jobs or reduced hours/pay can exacerbate abuse. Social supports are also diminished in conflict zones (Ringdal, 2024).

Men who come from countries where they have experience with political violence are more likely to perpetrate abuse as immigrants. This might include witnessing the death of many people in a single incident, witness rape, torture, or murder of a family member, or being detained, captured, or kidnapped.

In contrast to the above-listed risk factors, countries in which intimate relationships are more gender equal—in regard to beliefs, financial contributions, household activities, parenting, and intimacy—are less likely to see domestic violence (Ghoshal et al., 2022).

PREVENTING DOMESTIC AND DATING VIOLENCE: WORK WITH ACTUAL AND WOULD-BE ABUSERS

Obviously, preventing domestic and dating violence is the optimal goal. There are three levels of prevention: Primary prevention, secondary prevention, and tertiary prevention. Primary prevention is aimed at the general population and is intended to change values, beliefs, and behaviors such that abuse does not occur. Secondary prevention involves responses immediately after an incident. This includes efforts to address the abuser's behavior as well as to get the victim assistance so as to avoid future incidents. Tertiary prevention seeks to mitigate the long-term consequences of abuse for victims and to more seriously address the root causes of the offender's behavior. Many prevention programs exist and are discussed in subsequent chapters.

An important element of eliminating domestic and dating violence is holding abusers accountable. Before the 1970s women's rights movement and the antidomestic violence movement, law enforcement, when alerted about an incident, would often minimize it and do little, if anything, to help the victim or to hold the abuser accountable. As new laws specifically about domestic violence were enacted in the 1970s and beyond, police had to take the issue more seriously. Officers received training on handling domestic violence cases, which can be very challenging. Police may arrive and find both parties upset or even bearing injuries. Victims may be scared and unwilling to cooperate. There may be no witnesses to the incident so it can seem like a "he said, she said" situation. Abusers may lash out at officers or in extreme cases, kill them. While there have been improvements in the police response, there remain many challenges with relying on the criminal justice system to protect victims and hold abusers accountable.

One controversial effort to make things easier for the police and to purportedly help both victims and offenders is mandatory arrest policies. These began to be introduced in the early 1980s and were bolstered by the release of a 1984 study that scientifically assessed whether arrest was the best response in domestic violence cases. With funding from the National Institute of Justice, the Minneapolis Police Department, and the Police Foundation, Lawrence W. Sherman and Richard A. Berk (1984) compared whether arrest, advice or informal mediation, or a required eight-hour separation was the best at reducing re-offending. They found that arrest was the most effective response in that it resulted in the lowest rates of domestic violence repeat offending. Yet subsequent research found mixed results and no study completely replicated Sherman and Berk's findings, drawing concern from critics. Critics point out that Sherman and Berk used police data and victim self-report, both of which can be skewed. Police data was based on a six-month follow up, so offenses that happened after that would not have been included Victims were less likely to report reoffending but that does not necessarily mean that it did not happen. Maybe the consequences of the abuser's arrest were too hard on the victim to want to rely on the criminal justice system again. Perhaps it is certain types of perpetrators who will not re-offend compared to others that will. For instance, several studies found that employed men who were arrested for domestic violence were less likely to re-offend but not men who were unemployed (Berk, 1992).

Hoppe et al. (2020) conducted a metaanalysis of 11 studies assessing the effectiveness of mandatory arrest. They concluded that there was no statistically significant effect on re-offending when mandatory arrest policies were employed. As with many criminal justice responses, critics also point to mandatory arrest as contributing to the increased use of jail and prison as a sanction. There is also concern that the ways that officers use mandatory arrest can sometimes include arrest of victims who were acting in self-defense. Despite the lack of research consensus, mandatory arrest remains common. In 2023, there were 24 states that provisions for mandatory arrest in domestic violence cases. At least 35 states specify that police must determine and arrest the primary aggressor. This is true in my home state of Florida. Police must arrest that individual and take them to jail. Additionally, Florida has a "no drop" policy which means once the perpetrator is arrested, the victim can not drop the charges. Only the prosecutor can dismiss the case. While some assert that this helps in cases where victims are scared to push forward with prosecutions due to intimidation or] fear of retaliation, others contend that this is disempowering to victims.

Victims may also seek to stop abuse by obtaining a protection order. These are also called restraining orders, family violence orders, domestic violence protection orders, among other names. Protection orders mandate that the abuser stay a specific distance away from the victim for a set period of time. They typically also require that the abuser make no contact with the victim by phone, text, email, etc. Abusers who violate a protection order can be arrested and prosecuted.

While the idea of the protection order is to legally inform the abuser that his or her behavior is not acceptable and that there will be consequences for continued abuse, there are some limitations of them as well. For one, some abusers may take the protection order seriously and at least for that time, refrain from violence. Others may not, and in some cases, the protection order is seen as a threat to their power and control and the abuser escalates the abuse.

What is the best way to change the beliefs and values of offenders? One of the main programs for doing so is called Batterer's Intervention Programs (BIPs). These programs emerged in the late 1970s, alongside the development of shelters for victims. The proliferation of BIPs expanded dramatically in the 1980s, and today there are more than 2,500 (Jeltsen, 2024). Often abusers who take plea deals or are convicted of domestic violence offenses are required to attend BIPs. This includes a host of celebrities. Mel Gibson, Christian Slater, and Chris Brown are just a few who have been mandated to complete a BIP. These are psychoeducational treatment efforts that are generally intended as an alternative to incarceration. In many cases, the offense ends up being considered a misdemeanor so the offender would not be incarcerated any way. Even if incarcerated is an actual option, it is not always considered the best one, as it can have a negative impact financially and socially on the victims and their children. Some victims do not want their abusers to be incarcerated so they will remain in the relationship instead of seeking legal help. Further, jail sentences for domestic violence offenses tend to be short and there is no real evidence that they rehabilitate the offender. Therefore, extended treatment arose as a more promising option.

Many of the BIPs were developed from the Duluth Model, which was mentioned briefly in the previous chapter. Developed by Pence and Paymar (1993), the Duluth Model emphasizes a coordinated community response, a pro-feminist understanding that the victim's needs should come first, and a focus on the need for power and control as the reason for abuser's behavior. Further, the model

> ...proposes that the principal cause of domestic violence is a social and cultural, patriarchal ideology that historically has allowed men to control women through power and violence. Violence perpetrated on women and children originates from their relative positions of weakness and vulnerability socially, politically, economically, and culturally. As such, the model does not assume that domestic violence is caused by mental or behavioral health problems, substance use, anger, stress, or dysfunctional relationships. (National Institute of Justice, 2024)

There are seven core components of the Duluth Model: (1) Written policies that centralize victim safety and offender accountability (2) Practices that link intervening practitioners and agencies together (3) An entity that tracks and monitors cases and assesses data (4) An interagency process that brings practitioners together to dialog and resolve problems (5) A central role in the process for victim advocates, shelters, and battered women (6) A shared philosophy about domestic violence 7. A system that shifts responsibility for victim safety from the victim to the system (Paymar & Barnes, 2017).

The Duluth Model emphasizes the many ways that abusers maintain power and control, using the Power and Control Wheel included in Chapter One. The program then seeks

> ...to convince men to use nonviolent strategies outlined in the "Equality Wheel." The eight items making up this wheel are 1) negotiation and fairness, 2) economic partnership, 3) shared responsibility, 4) responsible parenting, 5) honesty and accountability, 6) trust and support, 7) respect, and 8) nonthreatening behavior. These items are considered to be the foundations of a strong and egalitarian relationship. (National Institute of Justice, 2024)

Typically, the Duluth Model is not a therapeutic one, although some BIPs that focus more on the offender's mental health and utilize psychotherapeutic strategies. Despite these origins, there are many differences between BIPs. State standards direct the specific parameters of BIPs. In California the Probation Department is in charge, whereas in Massachusetts, it's the Department of Public Health.

Many BIPs are male-only group efforts. Price and Rosenbaum (2009, p. 760) noted that

> The group approach is popular not only because it is more cost-effective but also because it provides an opportunity for men to mentor each other, share experiences, and challenge maladaptive attitudes and beliefs in a social context similar to the one from which the behavior is thought to have originated.

The length of BIPs also varies dramatically, with some up to 52 weeks in length. Price and Rosenbaum (2009) surveyed men who had gone to BIPs and found the average length was 31 weeks and the average session lasted 96 minutes. Some BIPs include components related to alcohol and substance abuse, given the strong connection between the two. Additionally, some BIPs address anger management. This is controversial because advocates assert that power and control, not anger, is the root cause of the behavior. The credentials of the person leading the program also vary tremendously.

Although it remains somewhat controversial, another issue that must be considered is when abuse is bidirectional. The Duluth Model focuses on unidirectional domestic violence, but research shows that bidirectional abuse occurs, with some studies finding it to be more frequent than unidirectional abuse (Straus, 2008).

Another concern is that typical BIPs often pay little attention to the trauma the abuser may have endured in past, perhaps due to the fear of diminishing the offender's responsibility for their actions (Sotiroff et al., 2024). Yet trauma has been found to be a risk factor for domestic violence perpetration, both among males and females. Further, critics contend that addressing abusers in group settings may actually make them worse, as they are exposed to others with similar beliefs (Keilhotlz & Spencer, 2022).

Another issue with BIPs is cultural appropriateness. Beyond language barriers, the unique cultural background of offenders is often not considered in the delivery of BIPs. As such, the program may be inadequate to address the root causes of abuse that can vary due to racial, socioeconomic, country of origin, immigrant status and more. More is needed to "take into account the contextual and narrative knowledge of the ethnocultural nuances in their BIP design and strategy with elicited input from program users themselves" (Emezue et al., 2021). Further, research shows that only approximately 10 percent of BIPs target female offenders. BIPs as they have been traditionally run may not meet the needs of LGBTQ+ offenders, either (Sotiroff et al., 2024).

Critics of the Duluth Model also argue that it contributes to overreliance on the criminal justice system in that it emphasizes batterer accountability. Further, as noted, BIPs typically work in conjunction with courts in getting participants.

Cheng et al. (2019) conducted a metaanalysis of studies about the effectiveness of BIPs. It included 14 studies conducted between 1986 and 2016. The emphasis was on domestic violence recidivism reported by the criminal justice system, perpetration reported by the victim, and general recidivism reported by the criminal justice system. They found that the criminal justice system reported less recidivism, in general and specific to domestic violence, but the survivors did not. Persons who completed BIPs were three times less likely to be reported as recidivating a domestic offense by the criminal justice system and 2.5 times less likely to be reported recidivating in general. One criticism of these studies, however, is that they often include people who started but did not complete the program. Between 15 and 58% of participants do not complete the full BIP. Probation officers and others involved with administering BIP routinely fail to inform the courts about dropouts (Jeltsen, 2024).

Jeltsen (2024) observed a BIP program, which started much like an Alcoholics Anonymous meeting. Participants introduced themselves and the name of the person they abused, then were asked to describe their relationships. Absent a talented and detailed leader, abusive men can be vague, provide misinformation, or fail to take ownership—exactly what the program is intended to do. One of the men, Jeremy, minimized that he had engaged in "just" dragging his girlfriend down the stairs and blamed the problems on their mutual insecurities.

The inconsistent findings related to the success of BIP have prompted recommendations for new models that might be more individualized to the needs of the offenders. Offenders are not monolithic; there are many subgroups of offenders who might need different interventions in order to change their behavior. Among these are those with varying levels of risk (i.e., low, medium, high); personality variations; comorbid conditions such as mental health concerns and substance abuse; ethnic or cultural background; LGBTQ+ individuals; and persons from different socioeconomic backgrounds. There are some programs that are focused specifically on subgroups. An analysis of Connecticut program for serious offenders found that participants had a significantly lower one-year arrest rate but not a statistically significant lower arrest rate for new family violence arrests. Again, completion was an issue, with 65% of participants completing the program (Cox & Rivolta, 2021).

Another model for working with abusers is Cognitive Behavioral Therapy (CBT). CBT emphasizes that battering is a learned behavior and that nonviolence can also be learned. It focuses on teaching perpetrators to identify their thought processes and beliefs that contribute to their violent action. Most also help consider their emotions and attitudes toward women. Provided by trained professionals, CBT usually includes six phases: (1) assessment, (2) reconceptualization, (3) skills acquisition, (4) skills consolidation and application, (5) generalization and maintenance, and (6) follow-up treatment. Activities that might be included during these phases are motivational self-talk and affirmations, relaxation techniques, coping strategies for negative thoughts, anger management, social skills role playing, and more. While CBT is typically used with men, its components can be used with female offenders. Studies have generally not found CBT to reduce domestic violence recidivism (National Institute of Justice, 2024).

Couples Therapy is controversial when it comes to domestic violence. Advocates have long argued that any efforts that involve the victim and the offender together are inappropriate because they will be dominated by the abuser in the same way that he controls the relationship. Further, there is concern that engaging the couple together could put the victim at greater risk. Several studies, however, have not found an increased risk when couples therapy was the intervention (e.g., O'Leary et al., 1999). Stith et al. (2011, p. 10) maintained that "violence can end, relationships can be improved, and women and men both can be empowered through the careful application of conjoint couples' treatment." Karakurt et al. (2016) conducted a metaanalysis of research about the effectiveness of couples therapy and found that can reduce or even eliminate domestic violence. It is definitely not the right fit for all couples, however, nor for all therapists. The decision on whether couples therapy is the right approach should be based on a number of factors, including the type and severity of the violence, the commitment of the couple to the relationship, whether substance abuse is involved, mental health issues, access to firearms, and the overall commitment to ending the violence (Keilhotlz & Spencer, 2022).

Another controversial approach with domestic violence cases is restorative justice (RJ).

> RJ views crime not as a depersonalized breaking of the law but as a wrong against another person as well as the community. It attends to the broken relationships between three parties: the perpetrator (the person who has caused harm), the victim (the person who had been harmed), and the community. (Barocas et al., 2020, p. 320)

RJ programs can operate as part of the criminal justice system or separate from it. In RJ circles, as they are often called, offenders must begin by accepting responsibility and acknowledging the harm they did. They must also accept that the harm of a domestic violence offense goes beyond just the immediate victim in that crime of any sort affects the community as well. RJ allows victims to feel empowered in ways that the criminal justice system often does not. It also allows the group to consider what actions the offender could take to repair the harm and how he or she could improve so as not to re-offend. Often, offenders who successfully complete whatever the group comes up with avoid a criminal record, which helps reduce the concern about overuse of the criminal justice system. RJ has been used around the world in domestic violence cases, including in New Zealand, Greece, South Africa, Australia, and more.

Some advocates and activists oppose using RJ in domestic violence cases. They cite concerns about the victim's safety, decriminalization of domestic violence, failing to communicate antiviolence norms to the public, and undermining the feminist principles of the antidomestic violence movement. Yet others note that the feminist antiviolence movement and RJ share many common beliefs.

> Both argue that existing remedies provided by the law fail both victims and perpetrators, that the justice system neglects the needs of victims, and both seek to create victim-centered justice. They both criticize the perpetrator orientation of the system, stress the need for perpetrator accountability, and are concerned with the impact of crime on communities. Both movements seek social justice in the broadest sense, and both are increasingly aligned with the global human rights movement. (Barocas et al., 2020, p. 324)

Sotiroff et al. (2024) conducted a study of the degree to which state standards for domestic violence intervention programs had been updated to address female offenders, treatment of people in LGBTQ+ relationships, bidirectional violence, and the trauma background of the offender. Their review included 47 states, as Mississippi, South Dakota, and Pennsylvania either did not have state laws, standards or guidelines or did not provide them. Of the 47, 30 had guidelines that apply to all offenders, not just males, while 17 states had guidelines that only apply to male offenders. Fourteen of the 47 states included LGBTQ+ individuals specifically. Twenty-two states explicitly prohibited messages about bidirectional violence or mutual violence. Twenty states require that programs should evaluate offenders past trauma. More updated standards could help address the concerns noted above and consequently make BIPs more effective.

CONCLUSION

This chapter has reviewed offender risk and protective factors as well as common interventions with abusers. All of those interventions have limitations, as was noted, and most are reactive rather than preventative. Further, most do little if nothing to address the most prominent risk factors. Outside of these formal responses, however, are a host of informal social controls that can potentially be useful in preventing abuse or curtailing it once it has started. For instance, family, peers, teachers, and faith leaders can play a role in shaping the values and beliefs people hold that contribute to violent actions. As well, they can use their influence to help the abuser she the harm in his or her actions and learn to change.

REFERENCES

Affi, T., et al (2017). The relationships between harsh physical punishment and child maltreatment in childhood and intimate partner violence in adulthood. *BMC Public Health, 17,* 493–503.

Animal Abuse. (2019). *DVAwareness.org.* https://www.dvawareness.org/sites/default/files/2019-06/AnimalAbuse-TalkingPointsForm.pdf

Animal Legal Defense Fund. (n.d.). *The link between cruelty to animals and violence toward humans.* https://aldf.org/article/the-link-between-cruelty-to-animals-and-violence-toward-humans-2/

Armstrong, E. M., Glover Reed, B., & Bennett, L. W. (2019). How and how much: Combined services for domestic violence and substance abuse. *Violence Against Women, 25*(12), 1450–1470.

ASPCA. (n.d.). *Pet-friendly housing and survivors of domestic violence.* https://www.aspca.org/improving-laws-animals/public-policy/housing/pet-friendly-housing-and-survivors-domestic-violence

Barocas, B., Avieli, H., & Shimzu, R. (2020). Restorative justice approaches to intimate partner violence: A review of interventions. *Partner Abuse, 11*(3), 318–349.

Benedict, J. (1998). *Athletes and acquaintance rape.* Sage.

Cantor, N., Joppa, M., & Angelone, D. (2021). An examination of dating violence among college student-athletes. *Journal of Interpersonal Violence, 36.*

Cheng, S., et al (2019). Compared to what? A meta-analysis of batterer intervention studies using nontreated controls or comparisons. *Trauma, Violence, & Abuse,* 1–16.

Costello, K., & Greenwald, B. (2022). Update on domestic violence and traumatic brain injury: A narrative review. *Brain Science, 12*(1), 122.

Cox, S., & Rivolta, P. (2021). Evaluative outcomes of Connecticut's batterer intervention for high-risk offenders. *Journal of Aggression, Maltreatment & Trauma, 21*(7), 931–949.

Cunha, O., et al (2022). Intimate partner violence: Perceptions and attributions of male perpetrators. *Journal of Forensic Psychology Research and Practice, 24*(3), 338–358.

Dank, M., et al (2014). Dating violence experiences of lesbian, gay, bisexual, and transgender youth. *Journal of Youth and Adolescence, 43*(5), 846–857.

Emezue, C., Williams, O., & Bloom, T. (2021). Culturally-differentiated batterer intervention programs for immigrant male batterers (IMB): An integrative review. *Journal of Aggression, Maltreatment & Trauma, 30*(7), 907–930.

Foshee, V., Reyes, H., Ennet, S., Suchindran, C., Mathias, J., Karriker-Jaffe, K., Bauman, A., & Benefield, T. (2011). Risk and protective factors distinguishing profiles of adolescent peer and dating violence perpetration. *Journal of Adolescent Health, 48*(4), 344–350.

Ghoshal, R., et al (2022). Risk and protective factors for IPV in low-and-middle-income countries: A systematic review. *Journal of Aggression, Maltreatment & Trauma, 32*(4), 505–522.

Hoppe, S., et al (2020). Mandatory arrest for domestic violence and repeat offending: A meta-analysis. *Aggression and Violent Behavior, 53.*

Jeltsen, M. (2024, April 18). What I learned inside a Batterer Intervention Program. *The Cut.* https://www.thecut.com/article/batterer-intervention-programs-domestic-violence.html

Karakurt, G., Whiting, K., Can Esch, C., Bolen, S., & Calabrese, J. (2016). Couples therapy for intimate partner violence: A systematic review and meta-analysis. *Journal of Marital Family Therapy, 42*(4), 567–583.

Keilhotlz, B., & Spencer, C. (2022). Couples therapy and intimate partner violence: Considerations, assessment, and treatment modalities. *Practice Innovations, 7*(2), 124–137.

Kippert, A. (2022, June 6). Profile of an abuser. *Domestic Shelters.* https://www.domesticshelters.org/articles/identifying-abuse/profile-of-an-abuser

Kwan, J., et al (2020). Prevalence of intimate partner violence perpetration among military populations: A systematic review and meta-analysis. *Aggression and Violent Behavior, 53.*

Larance, L. (2024). *Broken: Women's stories of intimate and institutional harm and repair.* University of California Press.

McCauley, H., et al (2014). Differences in adolescent relationship abuse perpetration and gender-inequitable attitudes by sport among male high school athletes. *Journal of Adolescent Health, 54,* 742–744.

McMahon, S. (2010). Rape myth beliefs and bystander attitudes among incoming college students. *Journal of American College Health, 59,* 3–11.

McShane, J. (2025, June 5). Republicans want to ban pets from domestic violence shelters. *Mother Jones.* https://www.motherjones.com/politics/2025/06/domestic-violence-pets-shelters-abuse/

Mennicke, A., & Ropes, K. (2016). Estimating the rate of domestic violence perpetrated by law enforcement officers: A review of methods and estimates. *Aggression and Violent Behavior, 31,* 157–164.

Merten, M. (2008). Acceptability of dating violence among young adolescents: The role of sport participation, competitive attitudes, and selected dynamics of relationship violence. *Adolescence, 43,* 31–56.

Morton, S., Curran, M., & O'Gorman, M. (2022). Adverse childhood experiences, domestic violence and substance misuse: An action research study on routine enquiry and practice responses. *Frontiers in Psychology, 13,* 1–12.

Narayan, A., et al (2020). Developmental origins of ghosts and angels in the nursery: Adverse and benevolent childhood experiences. *Journal of Advanced Research, 1,* 121–134.

National Institute of Justice. (2024, July 17). *Practice profile: Interventions for persons who committed intimate partner violence: Duluth Model.* https://crimesolutions.ojp.gov/ratedpractices/interventions-persons-who-committed-intimate-partner-violence-duluth-model

O'leary, K., Heyman, R., & Neidig, P. (1999). Treatment of wife abuse: A comparison of gender-specific and conjoint approaches. *Behavior Therapy, 30,* 475–505.

Park, S., & Kim, S. (2018). The power of family and community factors in predicting dating violence: A meta-analysis. *Aggression and Violent Behavior, 40,* 19–28.

Paymar, M., & Barnes, G. (2017). *Countering confusion about the Duluth Model.* https://www.theduluthmodel.org/wp-content/uploads/2017/03/CounteringConfusion.pdf

Pence, E., & Paymar, M. (1993). *Education groups for men who batter: The Duluth model.* Springer Publishing.

Price, B., & Rosenbaum, A. (2009). Batterer intervention programs: A report from the field. *Violence & Victims, 24*(6), 757–770.

Reeves, E. (2025). "The fact that he was a police officer was probably my number one challenge": Victim-survivor experiences of officer-involved domestic violence in Australia. *Violence Against Women.* Online. https://doi.org/10.1177/10778012251319761

Ringdal, C. (2024, September). Conflict and domestic turmoil: A review of intimate partner violence in conflict settings. *Development Learning Lab.* https://www.cmi.no/publications/file/9373-conflict-and-domestic-turmoil-a-review-of-intimate-partner-violence-in-conflict-settings.pdf

Rothman, E., et al (2011). Drinking style and dating violence in a sample of urban, alcohol-using youth. *Journal of Studies on Alcohol and Drugs, 72,* 555–566.

Schick, M., et al (2025). Patterns of substance-involved intimate partner violence perpetration: Findings from a daily diary study. *Addictive Behaviors, 166.*

Sherman, L., & Berk, R. (1984). *The Minneapolis domestic violence experiment.* Policing Institute. https://www.policinginstitute.org/wp-content/uploads/2015/07/Sherman-et-al.-1984-The-Minneapolis-Domestic-Violence-Experiment.pdf

Sileo, K., et al (2022). Mechanisms linking masculine discrepancy stress and the perpetration of intimate partner violence among men in the United States. *American Journal of Men's Health, 16*(4).

Sotiroff, A., et al (2024). Stuck behind the times: How current controversies related to domestic violence intervention programs are addressed in U.S. state-specific documents. *Journal of Aggression, Maltreatment & Trauma,* 1–21.

Stith, S., Rosen, H., McCollum, E., & Thomsen, C. (2004). Treating intimate partner violence within intact couple relationships: Outcomes of multi-couple versus individual couple therapy. *Journal of Marital and Family Therapy, 30*(3), 305–318.

Straus, M. (2008). Dominance and symmetry in partner violence by male and female university students in 32 nations. *Children and Youth Services Review, 30*(3), 252–275.

Temple, et al (2014). Importance of gender and attitudes about violence in the relationship between exposure to interparental violence and the perpetration of teen dating violence. *Child Abuse & Neglect, 13*(37), 343–352. https://pmc.ncbi.nlm.nih.gov/articles/PMC3670104/#:%7E:text=From%20the%20total%20sample%2C%2028.8,TDV%20and%2073.9%25%20psychological%20TDV

Vagi, K., Rothman, E., Latzman, N., Tharp, A., Hall, D.& Breiding, M. (2013). Beyond correlates: A review of risk and protective factors for adolescent dating violence perpetration. *Journal of Youth and Adolescence, 42,* 633–649.

Walton, M., et al (2010). Effects of a brief intervention for reducing violence and alcohol misuse among adolescents: A randomized controlled trial. *JAMA, 304,* 527–535.

Yakubovich, A., et al (2018). Risk and protective factors for intimate partner violence against women: Systemic review and meta-analyses of prospective longitudinal studies. *American Journal of Public Health, 108*(7), 1–11.

CHAPTER 4

SHORT AND LONG-TERM EFFECTS OF ABUSE

ABSTRACT

This chapter addresses the short and long-term effects of abuse. It includes physical effects, psychological effects, financial effects, and more. Further, the chapter addresses how education is affected by abuse at both the K-12 level and in higher education.

Keywords: Physical effects; mental health effects; effects on children; workplace domestic violence; housing and domestic violence; education and domestic violence; criminal justice and domestic violence

PHYSICAL EFFECTS OF DATING AND DOMESTIC VIOLENCE

The physical effects of dating and domestic violence are vast, ranging from minor injuries to serious, even life-threatening wounds. Some physical effects can also last a lifetime. Minor injuries might include bruises, cuts, bite marks, and cigarette burns. More serious are concussions, broken bones, knife wounds, and migraines. Long-term effects might include disfigurement, loss of hearing and vision, arthritis, hypertension, heart disease, anxiety and depression, and sexually transmitted infections, including human papillomavirus and HIV (Alejo, 2014).

Teaching and Making Peace in Every Relationship, pages 85–99

doi:10.1108/978-1-80686-961-920261005

Female victims of domestic violence are at greater risk for experiencing cervical cancer. Coker et al. (2009) found that 3.5% of victims of domestic violence reported having cervical cancer at some point, compared to 1.3% of the women who had not been victimized. This is likely because victims of domestic violence are more likely to have contracted human papillomavirus, smoked cigarettes, and used illegal drugs, all of which increase the risk of cervical cancer. The risk of cervical cancer was highest among victims who smoked (4.6%).

More than 10 million women in the United States have had a partner try to get them pregnant against their will, either by sabotaging birth control or refusing to allow the victim to prevent pregnancy or refusing to wear a condom. More than two million women have become pregnant as a result of being raped by their intimate partner and 1.8 million women have contracted a sexually transmitted infection due to being raped by their intimate partner. These actions by abusers are often referred to as reproductive coercion. Reproductive coercion is also associated with second-trimester abortions and repeat abortions as well as an increased risk of miscarriage (Planned Parenthood, 2012).

Experiencing violence during pregnancy not only affects the mother but the growing baby as well. The baby may be born prematurely, have low birth weight, there may be obstetric complications, suffer from birth defects, and there may be issues of attachment between the mother and child (World Health Organization, 2011).

As was noted in earlier chapters, the effects of experiencing dating violence can persist into adulthood. An older study found that teen victims were three times more likely than their peers who had not been victimized to experience an abusive dating relationship in college (Smith et al., 2003). Experiencing teen dating violence also increases the likelihood that victims will engage in other risky behaviors, including alcohol use and smoking marijuana as well as a host of mental health outcomes.

One effort that some states have made is requiring medical professionals to have regular training about domestic and dating violence. The idea behind this is that the victim may not have told anyone else but the physician, nurse, or medical professional might identify signs of abuse if he or she is properly trained. If abuse is disclosed, the medical professional can be the first line of support in getting the victim and/or children needed assistance. Learn more about this type of education in Chapter Six.

MENTAL HEALTH EFFECTS OF DATING AND DOMESTIC VIOLENCE

Research has shown, and many victims have expressed, that the emotional damage from abusive relationships are more damaging, especially in the long-term (Hill et al., 2009; McCaw et al., 2007). Common mental health effects of abuse are depression, anxiety, personality disorder, posttraumatic stress disorder, disordered eating, sleeping disorder, social dysfunction, alcohol or substance abuse, and suicidal (Alejo, 2014; McCaw et al., 2007). Victims also report feeling lonely and guilty. The guilt is at leaving their abusers as well as to family who wanted them to keep the relationship together. This feeling of guilt, in term, may result in the victim staying in the relationship longer.

Moreover, those who suffer emotionally or who develop psychological disorders are more likely to be re-victimized. In turn, re-victimization increases the likelihood of other mental health issues and/or exacerbating existing ones (Howard et al., 2010; McCaw et al., 2007). Research has shown that mental health outcomes are similar for women who were victims in the past 12 months as for women who were victimized before that (Alejo, 2014).

Victims report significant consequences of technology-facilitated abuse (TFA) as well. Emotional or mental health consequences range from diagnoses of mental health conditions, especially depression and anxiety, doubting one's sanity after having been gaslighted, and suicidal ideation. Socially, victims of TFA reported reduced contact with significant others and social isolation. In addition to emotional or mental health effects, victims often report that TFA affected them financially. These include a lack of or limited access to finances and online banking, loss of employment, difficulties securing employment, debt, the cost of purchasing new devices, and fees paid to remove images from social media and web-based platforms (Rogers et al., 2023). As Rogers et al. (2023) explained,

> One of the most striking consequences of TFA, marking its distinctiveness from other abuse, is its pervasiveness and reach. Almost all people carry a mobile phone, regularly access the internet and social media. As such, mobile phones can be used to abuse both for coercive control and maleficence on an almost continual basis.

Youth victims of dating violence are at risk for experiencing a host of mental health effects, many of which are the same as for victims of domestic violence. Among these are mental depression, anxiety, low self-esteem, suicidal thoughts, and disordered eating. The risk of suicidal thoughts continues years after the abuse, as does the increased risk of substance abuse problems.

ECONOMIC AND WORK-RELATED EFFECTS OF DATING AND DOMESTIC VIOLENCE

There are numerous workplace effects of domestic and dating violence. Female victims have more disrupted work history, having often had to change jobs more often and be employed in low-paying, part-time or irregular work. Victims also reported negative effects on their workplace in terms of feeling tired or not well, unwanted contact (in-person or otherwise), and how to support victims.

The Institute for Women's Policy Research (2017) reviewed literature about the economic costs of domestic violence, sexual assault, and stalking in the United States. It noted that victims often have work-related consequences of the abuse. Some 64% of victims reported that the abuse affected their ability to work. Another study found that 60% of victims surveyed by the Maine Department of Labor had to quit their jobs or were terminated as a result of the abuse. Victims whose work was affected by the abuse experience what has been called a "wage penalty" of 88 cents per hour. Abusers can also destroy their victim's credit and get them into debt, which then affects their access to safe housing, their ability to pay other household builds, and their opportunity to provide financially for their children. In all, the Institute for Women's Policy Research (2017) found that, in 2017 dollars, the total cost of domestic violence was $9.3 billion.

Just getting to work can be sabotaged by abusers. Some physically restrain their victims or make it so that they do not have access to transportation. Victims of domestic violence tend to take more time off, sometimes to deal with injuries or other facets of the abuse, which contributes to job loss for an estimated 5% to 27% of victims. Studies have found that between 36 and 75% of victims report their abuser harassing them at work, for example with constant phone calls, which negatively affects their performance. In one study, more than half of participants who had experienced domestic violence reported that the abuse continued at or near their workplace, with the most frequent form being phone calls, threats to show up there, and emotional abuse like telling the victim she is worthless or her colleagues do not care about her. Importantly, most of the research on workplace effects has been conducted with female victims. The little research with male victims finds that experiencing abuse has less effect on their work. Domestic violence is also one of the leading causes of workplace homicide for females. One study that reviewed workplace homicides of women from 2003 to 2008 found that one-third were related to domestic violence (Tiesman et al., 2015). In April 2025, Indiana Guzman's estranged husband Reynoldo Sandoval showed up at her workplace, Del Toro Insurance in Miami, Florida. He shot Guzman before turning the gun on himself. The couple were separated and Guzman obtained a restraining order against Sandoval. He had previously worked at Del Toro and despite the restraining order still had access to the building. Guzman had requested a transfer to another site but that did not happen. Her sister, Maria Guzman, has questioned why Sandoval was not banned from the premises (Pastrana, 2025).

Abusers will also harass and threaten co-workers. As well, studies show that coworkers feel stressed about the situation. In the most extreme cases, abusers have physically assaulted or even killed coworkers (Wathen et al., 2016). Workplaces are encouraged to train employees about abuse, to establish protocol for instances in when an abuser may make.

EFFECTS OF DOMESTIC VIOLENCE ON HOUSING

Abuse may impact the ability of victims to have safe housing for themselves and their children. This is especially true for females, owing to the gender wage gap and financial dependence many have on their abusers. Affordable housing is difficult to come by in many major cities, let alone if your ability to work regularly for decent wages has been manipulated by your abuser. According to the American Bar Association, 38% of domestic violence victims have experienced homelessness at some point in their life. Domestic violence is also one of the leading causes of homelessness for children, with one quarter of homeless children having been exposed to abuse in the home. Yet resources are scarce, and victims have to wait, on average, 6 to 10 months to secure housing. The Violence Against Women Act, discussed in previous chapters, prohibits discrimination against domestic violence victims seeking housing through federal programs like Section 8 Housing Choice Vouchers, Project-based Section 8, and Low-Income Housing Tax Credit programs (American Bar Association, 2025).

Some cities have adopted a Domestic Violence Housing First initiative. This is part of a broader approach to get unhoused people into safe homes before addressing any of their other needs. With victims, it entails finding safe and affordable places for victims and their children to live before addressing other things like work-related needs, trauma-informed therapy, and more.

EFFECTS ON BATTERERS AND OTHERS

Children are often considered to be the silent victims of domestic violence. Experiencing abuse in the home is considered to be an adverse child experience (ACES). Children who are exposed to abuse in the home are more likely to exhibit aggressive behavior, have low self-esteem, have poor social skills, and struggle academically. According to the US Department of Health and Human Services Office on Women's Health, in the short-term children living in homes where there is abuse often feel anxious and fearful, making them always on guard. That will manifest differently depending on their age and other variables. Preschool children often regress, such as wetting the bed after they previously had mastered potty training, sucking their thumbs, whining or crying. They may also have difficulty sleeping or speaking. Children in elementary school often feel guilty and blame themselves for the abuse, which in turn hurts their self-esteem. Many do not participate in extracurricular activities, have few friends, tend to get into trouble (especially boys), and may not do well academically. Teens who grow up abusive homes are more likely to act out, such as skipping school, fighting, having unprotected sex, or using drugs and alcohol. Again, the outward display of these effects is more common among boys, whereas girls are more likely to internalize the abuse. Disordered eating, self-mutilation, and depression are common effects for teen girls.

The effects of experiencing ACES like domestic violence can persist into adulthood, as research shows that adults who were exposed to ACES are more likely to suffer from health problems including diabetes and heart disease as well as mental health problems such as poor self-esteem, depression, and anxiety. They are at greater risk for heart attacks. Further, experiencing ACES results in greater anger and hostility as an adult (Monnat & Chandler, 2015).

The International Association of Chiefs of Police and the Childhood Violence Trauma Center also identified that youth who were exposed to abuse in the home are at greater risk for involvement with the juvenile and criminal justice systems, perpetrating community violence, and even early death. All of these risks are increased when first responders like police fail to identify youth who have experienced trauma and when there is a lack of adequate social supports to help those youth.

CRIMINAL JUSTICE EFFECTS

Although it would seem logical that the abusers might land behind bars, with some frequency it is the victims who do, or who as well. Abusers may force or coerce their victims into assisting them in the commission of crime. In other cases, victims were punished because they failed to protect their children from abusers. Researchers from Stanford Criminal Justice System found one woman who was in prison because her abusive expartner killed one of her children while she was at work, after he discovered supplies she had packed to leave him. California law says that she can be punished because she put their child in a dangerous situation. The Marshall Project found nearly 100 cases in which victims—mostly women—were punished for their abuser's actions under obscure laws like "failure to protect" and "accomplice liability." The specifics vary, but every state has some version of accomplice liability. Several women in that study said that they were punished for actions they took while trying to leave their abusers. One woman explained, "I fled from my house with four of my children. I was hit in the back of my car by my exhusband which caused me to crash." When one of their children died as a result of the crash, she was convicted of vehicular manslaughter and sentenced to prison. Sixteen of the women were incarcerated for incidents related to driving under the influence while they were drinking or using drugs to cope with the abuse.

In some cases, victims will kill their abusers. Researchers from Stanford Criminal Justice System found that a significant number of women who had been convicted of manslaughter or murder had been in abusive relationships and had retaliated against their abusers. They surveyed 649 women and almost three-quarters had been abused in the year prior to their offense. One stabbed an exboyfriend who had stalked her for months, while another killed her partner who had raped and beaten her. She contacted police and they did nothing to help her.

Some states have made improvements in the legal realm. New York allows the victim's history of abuse to be considered in sentencing. Oklahoma now allows survivors to serve shorter sentences in certain cases. April Wilkens, who served 26 years for killing her fiancé, was the first person to seek resentencing under the new law. Wilkens' abuser had handcuffed and raped her but she was not previously able to use that evidence to apply for early release. Illinois has done something similar, with legislation since 2016 that allowed for abuse to be considered during sentencing if it was directly connected to the case (Weiss, 2025).

Marissa Alexander's situation offers and interesting and sad case involving a victim who did not use violence against her abuser but was convicted and incarcerated regardless. Alexander was arrested, prosecuted, and incarcerated for firing a warning shot in the home she had shared with her estranged husband, Rico Gray.

On July 31, 2010, then-29-year-old Alexander, a mother of three, returned to the home she had shared with Gray to get some belongings when she believed he would not be home. He showed up unexpectedly with his two sons from a previous relationship in tow. She tried to be cordial, showing him some photos of their newborn on her phone. But things turned sour when she went to the bathroom and Rico saw some text messages on her phone. He began yelling at her and threatening to kill her. This was not surprising, given that he had abused Alexander and had been arrested three times for domestic violence. She responded by trying to leave, but when she got to her truck she could not do so because the garage door was broken. Fearing for her life, she grabbed a gun that she lawfully owned from the glove compartment, went back inside the home, and fired a warning shot into the kitchen wall. Gray fled and called 911, reporting that Alexander had fired at him and his sons. At the time, Alexander had just given birth to the couple's daughter nine days prior. Regardless of the circumstances and her explanation, she was arrested and charged with three counts of aggravated assault (Amber, 2020).

Gray undermined the case against Alexander four months after, when he gave a deposition to a state prosecutor admitting that he had physically abused Alexander and three of his other "baby mamas." He also acknowledged that women had to walk on eggshells around him and that they never knew when he might explode and hit or push them. Importantly, he also stated that his initial report about Alexander pointing her gun at him and his children had been a lie. When a few days before her trial Alexander went to Gray's home to get him to sign some paperwork so that their daughter could be on her health insurance, he again attacked her, and she ended up in the hospital with wounds on her arms from blocking his punches. Gray again lied, saying that Alexander had injured his eye. She was arrested, her bond was revoked, and she was returned to jail (Amber, 2020).

Gray continued to lie, however, when during Alexander's trial several months later he recanted that statement. This time he said he had "begged for his life." The judge refused to allow Alexander to use a "Stand Your Ground" defense, which generated significant controversy. After deliberating less than 15 minutes, the jury found Alexander guilty despite Gray's lies and her own lack of criminal record. Due to Florida's mandatory minimum law related to discharging weapons, she was sentenced in May 2012 to 20 years, even though she hurt no one. Florida Congresswoman Corrine Brown commented,

> The Florida criminal justice system has sent two clear messages today. One is that if women who are victims of domestic violence try to protect themselves, the Stand Your Ground law will not apply to them...the second is that if you are Black, the system will treat you differently. (Amber, 2020)

Alexander's conviction and lengthy sentenced outraged people around the country and generated protests and petitions to "Free Marissa." After several month, her conviction was overturned because a judge ruled that the jury had been given inadequate instructions. She then struck a deal, pleading guilty to three felony charges of aggravated assault. Her sentence was three years in prison but she was allowed to return home on January 27, 2015 due to the fact that she had already spent more than 1,000 days behind bars. Alexander has become a vocal national advocate for victims of abuse and criminal justice reform (Amber, 2020).

In some cases, battered women who have killed or have attempted to kill their abusers are able to use a legal defense similar to self-defense. The defense, often called battered women's self-defense, asserts that the act was legally justified because it was necessary to protect themselves or someone else, typically children. In some cases, the response by the victim may not appear to be her only option but an understanding of the dynamics of abuse and how it escalates, as well as its psychological impact on victims (battered woman syndrome) has informed the concept of battered women's self-defense. Prior to the advancement of this legal defense, battered women who killed or attempted to kill were typically told to please guilty or, in rare cases, plead not guilty due to some form of insanity.

Battered woman syndrome emphasizes the dynamics of abusive relationships, the cycle of violence discussed in Chapter One, and what Walker (1992) referred to as learned helplessness. Walker (1992) and colleagues identified five childhood factors that were most associated with learned helplessness. Additionally, they identified seven factors from the adult abusive situation that were significant predictors of learned helplessness. The five childhood learned helplessness factors include (1) witnessing or experiencing violence in the home; (2) sexual molestation or abuse in childhood or adolescence; (3) major hardships, such as early parent loss through death or divorce, frequent moves, alcoholism in one or both parents, sibling problems, and poverty; (4) being raises with strict and stereotypical gender role expectations; and (5) chronic or serious illness in childhood.

The seven factors that predicted the development of learned helplessness from an abusive adult relationship include: (1) escalation of violence in the relationship following the cycle of violence; (2) sexual abuse in the relationship; (3) numerous exhibitions of power and control, such as the batterers' intrusiveness, overpossessiveness, isolation, and jealousy; (4) threats to kill the victim and/or others; (5) routine psychological torture, such as putdowns, humiliation, mind control, waking her during the middle of the night or not letting her sleep, and more; (6) abusers use of violence against other people, pets, and objects; and (7) abuse of alcohol and drugs.

To successfully use battered women's self-defense, defense attorneys must involve expert witnesses who can testify about victim and abuser behaviors. Walker (1992, p. 323) explained,

> The psychologist is asked to evaluate first if the woman was a battered woman; second, if the abuse caused the development of Battered Woman Syndrome (which is a subcategory of the Post Traumatic Stress Disorder explained further below), and third, if so, how that impacted on the woman's state of mind at the time of the action for which she is charged.

Since the defense was first popularized in the 1970s and 1980s, it has been broadened to include battered children who kill their abusive parents, battered men who kill their partners (both male and female), battered women who kill their female partners, rape victims who kill their attackers, and battered roommates.

The Battered Woman's Self-Defense is a significant departure from the normal criteria used to prove someone acted in self-defense. Most states require in their legal definitions of self-defense a "reasonable person" standard. That is, whether a reasonable person would have perceived the danger they defended themselves against. In the case of battered women, expert testimony helps judges and juries assess how a reasonable victim of abuse would perceive the danger, given general patterns and dynamics of abuse as well as her specific history and the context of the situation.

Another typical component of self-defense is imminent danger. This is typically considered to a danger that is on the brink of or about to happen. Walker (1992, p. 324) explained how imminent danger is perceived in cases of domestic violence,

> ...frequently the women are hypervigilant to cues of impending danger and accurately perceive the seriousness of the situation before another person who had not been repeatedly abused might recognize the danger. They may make a preemptive strike before the abuser has actually inflicted much physical damage, anticipating his next moves from what they know from previous experience. Or, they might wait until the man has stopped for a while, knowing that he will begin his assault again.

Walker (1992) went on to note that many victims know that their abusers are dangerous even when they are sleeping and that most abusers stalk and harass their victims when they try to leave, as Mickey did to Francine. In some, "Imminent danger takes on new meanings in domestic violence situations" (Walker, 1992, p. 325).

A third component of self-defense is use of a reasonable amount of force to repel the danger. As Walker (1992) notes, the context of repeated and escalating abuse makes this somewhat different in domestic violence cases than in other cases involving self-defense.

One of the earliest cases to focus on Battered Woman Syndrome and how it might affect a woman who killed her abuser involved that of Francine Hughes. Her story was told in a book (1980) and 1984 film titled "The Burning Bed." For 13 years her husband (and later exhusband) James "Mickey" Hughes had routinely beat Francine, often in front of their children. Growing up, Francine witnessed her father abusing her mother. Francine dropped out of high school to marry Mickey, and the pair lived in the small town of Dansville, Michigan. They had four children and then divorced in April 1971, but Mickey moved back in after a serious car accident. The abuse continued and even escalated as Mickey recovered, with him beating Francine, destroying furniture, and even killing his daughter's cat. He constantly threatened to kill Francine, making it impossible for her to kick him out or leave him out of fear for her own life and that of her children.

Upon returning home from a secretarial course she was taking on the afternoon of March 9, 1977, Francine found Mickey drunk and irate. He berated her and yelled at her to quit attending classes and refused to allow her to make food for the kids. He hit her and Francine called the police, but they did nothing, saying that they had not witnessed Mickey assault her. As she again attempted to make food Mickey swept it onto the floor then grabbed Francine by her arm and forced her to clean up the mess. After she finished that he dumped the contents of the trash can onto the floor and made her clean that up as well. He forced her to agree to quit school and then burned her textbooks. Taking it even farther, Mickey forced Francine to make him dinner then raped her. Francine waited until Mickey fell into a drunken sleeping stupor, told the three kids who were home to wait in the car, and burned the house down with Mickey in it. She then drove to the police station and confessed. She was tried for the crime and found not guilty by reason of insanity.

Francine remarried and her new husband encouraged her to pursue her dream of becoming a nurse. In 1984, she told People magazine,

> I learned that if I fought back, it only made him more angry. I thought, well, maybe I could kill myself. But then I thought, if I kill myself, who is going to take care of the kids? Nobody could love them like me. I would conjure up schemes about how I would sneak off to the airport with the kids and leave. But I would picture us sitting on a park bench with nowhere to go. Then I would get scared thinking about what he would do if he found me. (Album, 2017)

Francine died in 2017 at age 69.

Some states have revised their definitions of self-defense to better address situations involving victims of domestic violence. Court cases have also affirmed that the self-defense statutes apply in these cases (Kinports, 2004).

There have been several criticisms of battered women's self-defense. These include that the theory implies pathology or mental disorder rather than reasonableness; that it creates a new "battered woman syndrome" defense; that it suggests a model for all battering relationships that does not fit some women; and that the learned helplessness portion of the theory is inconsistent with a woman's use of self-defense (Kinports, 2004). Even domestic violence advocates have sometimes been critical of battered woman syndrome in that they are concerned that it emphasizes that something is "wrong" with victims, especially owing to the word "syndrome." Others feel that it creates a new category of defense for women that is in effect "special treatment." Still others have criticized Walker's work on the cycle of violence, noting that not all abusive relationships that model. Finally, some find it difficult to juxtapose the idea of passive victims who have learned helplessness with the idea of killing a spouse (Kinports, 2004).

EDUCATIONAL EFFECTS OF DATING AND DOMESTIC VIOLENCE

Many children exposed to abuse in the home manifest signs that educators could possibly identify. This typically involves unexpected or frequent tardiness, truancy, significant changes in submission and quality of schoolwork, misbehavior, difficulty getting along with others, engage in fewer social interactions or activities, exhibit inappropriate sexual behavior, or signs of withdrawing/depression (Lloyd, 2018). Because victims of domestic violence are at risk for experiencing unstable housing or homelessness, children's school stability is also affected. In other cases, however, children exposed to abuse throw themselves into their school work as a means of escape (Lloyd, 2018).

Victims of teen dating violence also struggle with being late for school or having multiple absences. Many struggle academically, even if they did not before the abuse. Teen dating violence victims also tend to hold more negative views of school (Ackard & Neumark-Sztainer, 2002; Banyard & Cross, 2008; Coker et al., 2000; National Center for Injury Prevention and Control, 2022). Experiencing dating violence also increases the likelihood that a victim wll drop of out school. Diette et al. (2017) found that victims are 25% more likely to drop of out school, either due to physical or mental health effects or out of fear of their abuser (Diette et al., 2017).

Klencakova et al. (2021) conducted a metaanalysis of 10 articles the addressed the educational effects of abuse. Low attendance and attachment were among the most common school-related effects, especially among female sexual and racial minorities. One of the studies they reviewed, Dank et al. (2014), found that LGBTQ victims had a rate of failing grades (D/F) 10 times higher than did heterosexual victims. Women who had endured psychological abuse expressed the belief that they would never "be anything" and that they were "only good for stripping" (Wiklund et al., 2010).

In one study, Foshee et al. (2011) found no long-term educational impact of having experienced dating violence. However, even the authors acknowledged that their study did not address all aspects of education, and that questions like "how important was it" to graduate from high school may have resulted in respondents answering generally and not specifically how that related to their victimization.

Some have asserted that victims will go in the opposite direction, treating education as an escape and a safe place (Sterne & Poole, 2009). While this is possible the research seems to indicate that abuse is disruptive to the acquisition of education.

At the college level, victims of abuse are more likely to miss class, show reduced engagement in class, have lower GPAs, or drop out entirely (Klencakova et al., 2021). Women who had experienced sexual violence and coercion in abusive relationships were less likely to attend college than other women in that age group who had not been victimized. If they did attend, they typically experienced a decline in their grades that was not found to be statistically significant among male victims (Martz et al., 2016). Cyber abuse has similar effects, as Dank et al. (2014) found that it affected attendance and grades. Yet, as Klencakova et al. (2021) noted, "Particularly for young females, education is a powerful protective factor against re-victimisation and economic dependence which often forces women to remain trapped in abusive relationships" (p. 1172).

CONCLUSION

As this chapter has shown, the effects of abuse go way beyond the obvious physical and mental injuries and stressors. Abuse can impact someone's ability to work, to have safe housing, to go to school, even to stay out of prison. Furthermore, abuse affects children in myriad ways. These are fundamental human rights, as outlined in the Introduction. When States do nothing or not enough to protect victims from the effects of abuse on their human rights, they can be considered to be in violation of many of the human rights treaties described in the Introduction. As such, States should consider numerous ways to prevent and respond to abuse. These should be multifaceted and should cover education as well as other institutions. Efforts to do so are the focus of the second part of this book, starting with Chapter Five.

REFERENCES

Ackard, D., & Neumark-Sztainer, D. (2002). Date violence and date rape among adolescents: Associations with disordered eating behaviors and psychological health. *Child Abuse & Neglect, 26*, 455–473.

Album, M. (2017, April 1). *40 years after burning bed, domestic violence issue still smolders.* Detroit Free Press. https://eu.freep.com/story/sports/columnists/mitch-albom/2017/04/01/mitch-albom-domestic-violence/99886102/

Alejo, K. (2014). Long-term physical and mental health effects of domestic violence. *Themis: Research Journal of Justice Studies and Forensic Science, 2*, 81–98. https://scholarworks.sjsu.edu/cgi/viewcontent.cgi?article=1016&context=themis#:%7E:text=Some%20of%20the%20mental%20health,Howard%2C%20Trevillion%2C%20&%20Agnew%2D

Amber, J. (2020, October 27). In her own words: Marissa Alexander tells her story. *Essence.* https://www.essence.com/news/marissa-alexander-exclusive/

American Bar Association. (2025). *Five facts about domestic & sexual violence and homelessness.* https://www.americanbar.org/groups/domestic_violence/Initiatives/five-for-five/five-facts-homelessness/

Banyard, V., & Cross, C. (2008). Consequences of teen dating violence: Understanding intervening variables in ecological context. *Violence Against Women, 14*(9), 998–1013.

Coker, A., Derrick, C., Lumpkin, J., Oldendick, R., & Potter, R. (2000). Severe dating violence and quality of life among South Carolina high school students. *American Journal of Preventive Medicine, 19*, 220–227.

Coker, A., Hopenhayn, C., DeSimone, C. P., Bush, H. M., & Crofford, L. (2009). Violence against women raises risk of cervical cancer. *Journal of Women's Health, 18*(8), 1179–1185.

Dank, M., Lachman, P., Zweig, J. M., & Yahner, J. (2014). Dating violence experiences of lesbian, gay, bisexual, and transgender youth. *Journal of Youth and Adolescence, 43*(5), 846–857.

Diette, T., Goldsmith, A. H., Hamilton, D., & Darity, Jr, W. A. (2017). Child abuse, sexual assault, community violence and high school graduation. *Review of Behavioral Economics, 4*(3), 215–240.

Foshee, V., Reyes, H., Ennet, S., Suchindran, C., Mathias, J., Karriker-Jaffe, K., Bauman, A., & Benefield, T. (2011). Risk and protective factors distinguishing profiles of adolescent peer and dating violence perpetration. *Journal of Adolescent Health, 48*(4), 344–350.

Hill, T., Schroeder, R. D., Bradley, C., Kaplan, L. M., & Angel, R. J. (2009). The long-term health consequences of relationship violence in adulthood: An examination of low-income women from Boston, Chicago, and San Antonio. *American Journal of Public Health, 99*(9), 1645–1650.

Howard, L., Trevillion, K., & Agnew-Davies, R. (2010). Domestic violence and mental health. *International Review of Psychiatry, 22*(5), 525–534.

Institute for Women's Policy Research. (2017). *The economic cost of intimate partner violence, sexual assault, and stalking.* https://iwpr.org/wp-content/uploads/2020/10/B367_Economic-Impacts-of-IPV-08.14.17.pdf

Kinports, K. (2004). So much activity, so little change: A reply to the critics of battered women's self-defense. *St. Louis University Public Law Review, 23,* 155–192. https://insight.dickinsonlaw.psu.edu/cgi/viewcontent.cgi?referer=&httpsredir=1&article=1175&context=fac_works

Klencakova, L., Pentaraki, M., & McManus, C. (2021). The impact of intimate partner violence on young women's educational well-being: A systematic review of literature. *Trauma, Violence, & Abuse, 24*(2), 1172–1187.

Lloyd, M. (2018). Domestic violence and education: Examining the impact of domestic violence on children, young children, and young people and the role of schools. *Frontiers in Psychology, 9,* 1–11.

Martz, D., Jameson, J., & Page, A. (2016). Psychological health and academic success in rural Appalachian adolescents exposed to physical and sexual interpersonal violence. *American Journal of Orthopsychiatry, 86*(5), 594–601.

McCaw, B., Golding, J. M., Farley, M., & Minkoff, J. R. (2007). Domestic violence and abuse, health status, and social functioning. *Women & Health, 45*(2), 1–23.

Monnat, S., & Chandler, R. (2015). Long-term physical health consequences of adverse childhood experiences. *The Sociological Quarterly, 56,* 723.

National Center for Injury Prevention and Control. (2022, February 28). *Fast facts: Preventing dating violence.* https://www.cdc.gov/violenceprevention/intimatepartnerviolence/teendatingviolence/fastfact.html

Pastrana, L. (2025, April 15). Murder-suicide at Miami Del Toro Insurance office highlights domestic violence struggles. *CBS News.* https://www.cbsnews.com/miami/news/murder-suicide-at-miami-del-toro-insurance-office-highlights-domestic-violence-struggles/

Planned Parenthood. (2012, August). *Intimate partner violence and reproductive coercion.* https://www.plannedparenthood.org/files/3613/9611/7697/IPV_and_Reproductive_Coercion_Fact_Sheet_2012_FINAL.pdf

Rogers, M., Fisher, C., Ali, P., Allmark, P., & Fontes, L. (2023). Technology-facilitated abuse in intimate relationships: A scoping review. *Trauma, Violence, & Abuse, 24*(4), 2210–2226.

Smith, P., White, J., & Holland, L. (2003). A longitudinal perspective on dating violence among adolescent and college-age women. *American Journal of Public Health, 93*, 1104–1109.

Sterne, A., & Poole, L. (2009). *Domestic violence and children: A handbook for schools and early year settings*, Routledge.

Tiesman, H., Gurka, K. K., Konda, S., Coben, J. H., & Amandus, H. E. (2015). Workplace homicides amongst U.S. women: The role of intimate partner violence. *Annals of Epidemiology, 22*(4), 277–284.

U.S. Department of Health and Human Services Office on Women's Health. (2021). *Effects of domestic violence on children.* https://www.womenshealth.gov/relationships-and-safety/domestic-violence/effects-domestic-violence-children

Walker, L. (1992). Battered women syndrome and self-defense. *Notre Dame Journal of Law, Ethics, and Public Policy, 6*(2), 321–334.

Wathen, C., MacGregor, J., & MacQuarrie, B. (2016). The impact of domestic violence in the workplace. *Journal of Occupational and Environmental Medicine, 57*(7), 65–71. https://pmc.ncbi.nlm.nih.gov/articles/PMC4676385/#:%7E:text=11%20Domestic%20violence%20can%20also,or%20harm%20from%20the%20perpetrator

Weiss, D. (2025, September 8). Domestic abuse survivor who was inspiration for reduced sentencing law loses bid for release. *ABA Journal.* https://www.abajournal.com/news/article/domestic-abuse-survivor-who-served-as-inspiration-for-new-reduced-sentencing-law-loses-bid-for-release

Wiklund, M., Malmgren-Olsson, E., Bengs, C., & Öhman, A. (2010). "He messed me up": Swedish adolescent girls' experiences of gender-related partner violence and its consequences over time. *Violence Against Women, 16*(2), 207–232.

World Health Organization. (2011). *Intimate partner violence during pregnancy.* https://iris.who.int/bitstream/handle/10665/70764/WHO_RHR_11.35_eng.pdf;jsessionid=F32F8CBE3341293DED9449281712D620?sequence=1

PART TWO

CHAPTER 5

EDUCATIONAL INSTITUTIONS AND LEGAL REQUIREMENTS RELATED TO DOMESTIC AND DATING VIOLENCE

ABSTRACT

Chapter 5 discusses the responsibilities that schools, colleges, and universities have in regard to responding to allegations of abuse as well as to preventing it. Regarding the latter, the chapter discusses legislation that requires dating violence education. While the focus is on the United States, the chapter briefly addresses international efforts that align with the human rights agreements outlined in the Introduction. Additionally, the chapter discussed educational requirements for others institutions, including law, social work, and healthcare.

Keywords: Title IX; tort liability suites; Jeanne Clery Act; healthcare professionals; criminal justice system

INTRODUCTION

Given that dating violence often occurs in or around schools or universities, it is essential that systems have in place policies and practices related to prevention and response. Teenagers and young adults often date someone who attends the same school or university that they do, which makes it likely

Teaching and Making Peace in Every Relationship, pages 103–119

doi:10.1108/978-1-80686-961-920261006

that educators, staff, and administrators will see abusive relationships manifest on school grounds. Since we know that abusers can target more than just their victims, dating violence incidents on school or campus grounds are a threat to everyone's safety. In fact, there are actually several ways that schools and universities can be held legally liable for incidents of dating violence that occur at school or school-sponsored events.

One of these is Title IX, 42 US.C. §1983. Title IX, as it is typically called, requires that schools and universities keep students, faculty, and staff, safe from hostile and discriminatory environments. A claimant could assert that a school, district, college, or university deprived him or her of this right (National Women's Law Center, 2017).

Another area of legal recourse is a tort liability suit claiming that the school, district, college, or university was negligent in that it failed to provide adequate protection (National Women's Law Center, 2017).

The following is an example of case involving a Title IX claim against a school related to dating violence. In 2017, the National Women's Law Center filed a suit on behalf of "Jane Doe" as well as other survivors or dating violence. It asserted that Pennridge School District in Perkasie, Pennsylvania, along with Superintendent Jacqueline Rattigan and Principal Gina DeBona, had failed to ensure Doe and other students' safety from abuse, in violation of Title IX. According to the suit, the district was aware that Doe had endured verbal and physical abuse, cyber-abuse, and stalking from her boyfriend. Further, the district was aware that the abuse had escalated when Doe broke up with her boyfriend, at which point he enlisted his friends to harass her as well. For two years she endured their verbal harassment. Her boyfriend also physically assaulted her on school grounds. When Doe informed the school about the abuse they repeatedly told her there was nothing they could do.

Doe begin exhibiting some of the same effects of abuse that were discussed in Chapter Four. She began avoiding school so that she did not have to see her exboyfriend. Her grades dropped from all As and Bs to mostly Cs and Ds. The district informed Doe during her junior year that they could do nothing on grounds to protect her so she should move to another school. The only option was Twilight Academy, an alternative school for students who had been in trouble, which was not the case with Doe. Nonetheless, seeing no other option she enrolled, only to find out that the "education" consisted of sitting silently at her desk completing worksheets. The court was also asked to consider that she was the third student to seek relief for a Title IX violation (National Women's Law Center, 2017). The case ended in a settlement in 2020. Similar lawsuits against universities for their inaction have been successful on the part of the plaintiffs.

A Title IX case involving a university student resulted in favor of the plaintiff's family, who filed it on behalf of Katie Hall. Hall had been murdered in her dorm room in 2015 by her boyfriend Gregorio Orrostieta during her first year as a student at Millersville University. The university was aware that while Orrostieta was not a student, he regularly stayed with Katie in her form room. Officials had received multiple reports of verbal and physical abuse but took no meaningful steps to address them. The district court initially dismissed the class, holding that the university was not responsible for the behavior of invited guests under Title IX. On appeal, the plaintiffs noted that the university had rules and procedures for checking in guests, indicating that it accepted responsibility for guest's behavior, and that it had taken action once to remove Orrostieta after a violent incident. The Third Circuit Court agreed and ruled against the university in 2022 (Public Justice, n.d.a).

Another Title IX case, *Roohbakhsh v. Board of Trustees of the Nebraska State Colleges*, asserted that Chadron State College had failed to adequately respond to reports of student-on-student dating violence. Fatima Larios, a student-athlete on the softball team, had told some teammates that her boyfriend had been physically abusing her. They reported it to one of their coaches. The college's Title IX Coordinator and other officials were also informed about the abuse, including subsequent reports detailing that it had escalated. Three months after the first incident was reported, Fatima was found hanging in the closet of her boyfriend's dorm room, having committed suicide. The case against the university was scheduled to go to trial in February 2020 but the parties reached a settlement (Public Justice, n.d.b).

In *Brown v. State of Arizona*, Mackenzie Brown, a student, filed suit alleging that the University of Arizona had violated Title IX in its failure to respond appropriately to physical abuse that she endured from her boyfriend, football player Orlando Bradford, a fellow student. The university had previously been made aware that Bradford had assaulted two other female students the year prior, one of them as many as 100 times. During April of that year, Bradford's freshman year, one of those female students obtained a no contact against him, which forbid him from making contact with her either on campus or off of it. Yet university officials did not the university's athletic director or his coaches about the order. Both Brown and Bradford lived in off-campus housing, Bradford in a house with other football players. The football players had received special permission to live off campus on the condition that they would be on good behavior (Brown v. Arizona, n.d.).

Bradford reportedly abused Brown over several months, between four and 10 times, with the abuse escalating to two especially violent attacks on successive nights in September 2016. On those nights, Bradford dragged Brown by her hair, locked her in his room, kicked her, scratched her, and choked her. He also sent her numerous threatening text messages.

Brown saw her family doctor on September 16, where she presented with the following:

> ...psychological trauma, burst blood vessels in the eye, bruising on the lower part of the neck, likely concussion, intractable acute posttraumatic headache, neck pain from direct trauma (kicking and hitting) as well as from strangulation, upper back pain, left rib pain with breathing and movement, left upper abdominal pain, abdominal contusions, . . . head tenderness from hitting a cabinet and being punched in the head during the attack, scratches on her forehead, upper arm contusions, circular contusions circling the base of her neck, and contusions with tenderness over her left rib area. (Brown v. Arizona, n.d., p. 20)

Had the athletic department and/or his coaches known not only this but about his previous assaults, he would have lost his football scholarship, been kicked off the team, and been expelled from the school. Bradford was finally arrested on September 14 and received an interim suspension notice. He was expelled a month later. Bradford pleaded guilty to two counts of felony aggravated assault and domestic violence. He received a sentence of two to five years in prison (Brown v. State of Arizona, n.d.).

The lawsuit was initially ruled in favor of Bradford, but the decision was overturned in Brown's favor. The federal appeals court found that the school had both "actual knowledge" of the incidents and the potential danger Bradford posed. As well, it found that the school exhibited "deliberate indifference," the two criteria outlined in precedent cases related to Title IX lawsuits (Brown v. State of Arizona, n.d.).

One concern about Title IX suits is that they require schools and universities to have actual knowledge of incidents that have occurred. Since many students do not report incidents to officials, this means the school or university would likely not be found liable. The actual knowledge requirement, many say, disincentivizes officials from finding better ways to encourage reporting (Curcio, 2017). As Curcio (2017) explained,

> To the extent schools comply with Clery Act reporting requirements, they create potential tort liability by establishing foreseeability of future acquaintance assaults. Thus schools have potential legal liability reporting disincentives both when it comes to reporting generally and when it comes to disclosing the fact that most of the on-campus assaults are occurring in their dorms. (p. 47)

Curcio (2017) expressed that universities have largely, and to their detriment, ignored the important factor of *where* incidents of sexual violence occur on campus. Most often sexual violence is perpetrated by an acquaintance or partner, so the same concern holds true more broadly of dating violence. She noted that most sexual assaults, and by extension, most sexual and physical incidents of dating violence, occur in dorm rooms/residence halls. Failing to adequately address this in prevention programs or in institutional policies and procedures can

> ...provide students with a false sense of security once they arrive at the dorm, therefore potentially contributing to dorm-based assault risks because potential victims, and bystanders who might intervene, are not aware of the risks in the dorm itself and thus may be unaware of the need to address those risks. (Curcio, 2017, p. 33)

While campuses receiving federal funding are required to provide prevention and awareness education, these more often focus on "stranger danger" and on safety on campus grounds but not in residence halls. Curcio (2017) explained,

> For example, students are told to watch their drinks, take buddies to parties, and leave people and places that might make them feel unsafe. Campus safety precautions also focus on preventing stranger attacks. For example, schools emphasize the presence of blue call boxes along campus paths, security escorts, and the swipe cards or other identification methods that limit entry into a dorm61 This focus on security measures external to the dorms may give students a false sense of security when they reach their dorms because no one talks to them about the fact that the majority of on-campus rapes occur in the dorms. (p. 41)

Additionally, Curcio (2017) asserted that tort lawsuits can help move institutions of higher education toward a more comprehensive approach to keeping students safe from sexual and dating violence. .

> Negligence claims may provide a basis for liability because, unlike the Title IX "actual knowledge" standard, negligence claims allow for liability if a school knew or should have known of a risk. Additionally, unlike the high bar of the Title IX "deliberate indifference" standard, negligence claims may succeed upon proof the defendant failed to act with reasonable care in light of the circumstances, a calculus that often involves calculating the risk of harm and the cost of preventing that harm. Thus, negligence claims may fill a regulatory and Title IX enforcement action gap when it comes to motivating schools to engage in meaningful awareness and risk reduction education. (Curcio, 2017, p. 54)

Colleges and universities that receive federal funding are already required to collect and report data about crime committed on campus. This is per the Clery Act of 1990. It is named after Jeanne Clery, who was 19-years old when she was raped and murdered in her residence hall at Lehigh University in 1985. In just three years there had been at least 38 violent crimes on Lehigh's campus, and Clery's parents argued that had they and she known that she would not have chosen to enroll at the university. The family sued and were awarded $2 million. The Clery Act requires that campuses report a host of crimes committed "on campus, in or on noncampus buildings or property, and on public property." Reports have to identify where the crimes occurred and, if it was on campus, whether the incident(s) occurred in campus residential housing. All reported incidents must be included in the report even if they did not result in an investigation or disciplinary action, nor if the victim reported to law enforcement. The Clery Act has been amended five times since 1990. The Clery Act includes Sex Offenses and that category includes domestic violence, dating violence, and stalking.

As noted above and in previous chapters, one challenge in addressing abuse is that many victims do not tell anyone about the abuse. Obviously school and campus officials cannot respond to things that they do not know about, nor can they be held legally liable. One study cited in *Business Wire* (2014) found that 40% of teens in abusive relationships had not told anyone about the abuse. There many reasons why victims do not disclose abuse, including but not limited to fear of retaliation from both the perpetrator and their peers, shame, concern it will affect their reputation in school, not knowing where to seek help, not understanding that what they are experiencing is abuse, concern about involvement with formal investigation and justice systems, and feeling that reporting abuse is a sign of weakness. These are addressed in greater detail in previous chapters.

College students do not report for the same reasons but also for some different ones. One is that victims sometimes are engaged in rule-breaking or illegal behavior themselves. They do not want to report because they are afraid that they will get into trouble. For example, if the victim is underage drinking or using some illicit substance in violation of school policy or the law, he or she may wish to avoid interaction with authorities even if abuse is happening as well. Research is clear that victims of dating violence most often confide in a peer, however, when they tell an adult, a trusted educator is at the top of the list. As such, it is essential that students and school/campus personnel be equipped to assist people who may be experiencing dating violence. This means, at minimum, people must receive training and education on the signs of abuse, the dynamics of it, and any reporting requirements or protocols. Beyond legal liability, the educational purpose of schools, colleges, and universities should include this information.

Another way to consider legal liability is in terms of duty to provide reasonable care to students. Although there is mixed precedent on this in the US, the California Supreme Court reversed some state court cases related to school violence, asserting that "colleges have a duty to use reasonable care to protect their students from foreseeable violence during curricular activities." This, the court held, is owing to the special relationship schools have with students, "arising from the mandatory character of school attendance and the comprehensive control over students exercised by school personnel, 'analogous in many ways to the relationship between parents and their children'." In essence, it is the idea of in loco parentis, a term that was common in the US until the 1970s and means "in the place of the parent." This "special relationship gives secondary school personnel 'the duty to use reasonable measures to protect students from foreseeable injury at the hands of third parties acting negligently or intentionally'" (Coleman, 2023, p. 92).

Domestic and dating violence are the number one cause of mass shootings. This includes those that occur on school grounds. Thus, any comprehensive plan to protect schools and campuses against mass shootings should also include addressing the role that abusive relationships plays, especially that of breakup violence (as was discussed in Chapters One and Four). Although there is not a common definition of what constitutes a mass shooting, some organizations define it as an incident in which four or more fatalities are the result, excluding that of the offender. A study using this definition to analyze mass shootings occurring between 2014 and 2019 found that in two-thirds the perpetrator either killed a family member or intimate partner or had a history of domestic or dating violence (Geller et al., 2021). We can look to specific examples to illustrate this issue.

On May 18, 2018, Dimitrios Pagourtiz killed 10 people and wounded 10 others at his at Santa Fe High School in Santa Fe, Texas. Not randomly, Pagourtiz targeted students who had bullied him as well as a girl who had rejected his sexual advances. On February 14, 2018, Nikolas Cruz killed 17 people at Marjorie Stoneman Douglas High School in Parkland, Florida had been abusive to his adoptive mother as well as to a former girlfriend. The police had been called more than 30 times to the home, where Cruz and his brother Zachary would assault Lynda Cruz, broke things in the home, and called her a "useless bitch" (Italiano, 2018).

There have also been a number of campus shootings that are connected to gender-based violence more broadly, if not specifically dating violence. Some of these have been perpetrated by men who identify as voluntarily celibate, or incels. While not necessarily abusive to dating partners, as their biggest concern is that they do not have romantic or sexual relationships with women, these men tend to target females more generally due to their disdain for women (Bates, 2021). One of the most notorious incel mass shooters was Elliott Rodger, who attacked 20 people near the University of California-Santa Barbara campus in 2014. Although Rodger killed men, he mostly target women using knives, guns, and his car, killing six and wounding 14 before killing himself. Rodger had been very active in online incel forums and had made a Youtube video and manifesto about his hatred toward women (BBC, 2018).

LAWS REGARDING SCHOOL EDUCATIONAL REQUIREMENTS FOR DATING VIOLENCE

In addition to laws relevant to protecting students and reporting crime, there are some state laws related to how schools must handle dating violence incidents, including educational initiatives. Texas was the first state to pass legislation requiring that schools enforce dating violence protection orders. The law also requires the school districts train and educate students and teachers about dating violence and provide resources to victims. Like so many laws in the United States, the Texas law came after a tragedy occurred in 2003. Ortralla Mosley was 15-years-old when she was murdered by her abusive exboyfriend, 16-year-old Marcus McTear, at Reagan High School in Austin, Texas. McTear stabbed Mosley six times in the back, neck, and head.

There were some classic warning signs that McTear was abusing Mosley. As well, he had been suspended for three days during the prior school year for hitting a different girlfriend in the head during a class. In the five years prior to murdering Mosley there were at least six reports of disturbing behavior. At the time, "school administrators in 2003 weren't versed in the concept of teen dating violence. They didn't recognize the warning signs. They didn't have procedures to defuse these volatile situations." In fact, on the day that she was murdered an assistant principal told Mosley just to "stay away from him." McTear admitted guilt in a juvenile court and was sentenced to 40 years in prison. In addition to the Texas law, the murder of Mosley helped prompt Congress to declare February to be National Teen Dating Violence Awareness and Prevention Month (Grumet, 2024).

As of June 2022, 37 states as well as Washington, DC had some type of law addressing dating violence in schools. In 28 states plus Washington, DC, dating violence education is required in schools while in nine others it is encouraged but not required. Only 14 states require school districts to enact district-wide policies to address dating violence. Ten states have laws dedicating funding for dating violence prevention programs and policies, and 12 states laws articulate specific consequences for school districts that are noncompliant. State laws vary as to who must be taught about dating violence, with some specifying only students and others adding staff, parents, or including all three (Peetz & Baker, 2023). Most often, dating violence education is integrated into health classes although it can be placed elsewhere in the curriculum. Some state laws specify that it must be included in health class (Adhia et al., 2022).

These laws also vary in regard to the content that must be included. Less than half of state laws specifically require teaching about warning signs of abuse, although this would likely be amongst the most helpful things for students, staff, and parents to know. When the details of the curricula are articulated in state law, the most common language is that schools should teach about "healthy relationships" or to provide the vaguely worded "awareness education." Unlike colleges and universities who have to follow Title IX's requirement that at least one person on campus be designated to address dating violence (discussed below), fewer than one third of states require that a specific school official do so (Adhia et al., 2022).

Approximately one-third of states require that dating violence prevention be evidence-based, meaning that the curricula has been evaluated. About one quarter of state laws require that dating violence education be done in consultation with a community organization like a domestic violence shelter. The other states require that prevention programs be reviewed, which is typically done by the school board. Although middle school is an ideal time to address these issues as it is before most students begin dating in earnest, most state laws require prevention education target high school students (Adhia et al., 2022).

Some states have expansive antibullying laws that could potentially cover dating violence (Cascardi & Avery-Leaf, 2014; Cornell & Limber, 2015). The limitation of this approach, however, is that previous Supreme Court decisions have said that schools have different responsibilities related to harassment and bullying than to abuse (Adhia et al., 2022).

As of January 2025, 11 states have mandated that schools have in-school threat assessment teams. These are multidisciplinary groups intended to identify students who are at risk of committing violence and getting them the mental health and other resources they need (Everytown Gun Law Rankings, 2025).

At the collegiate level, in addition to Title IX, the Violence Against Women Act (VAWA) first enacted in 1994, provides federal funds available to institutions of higher education for reducing domestic violence, dating violence, sexual assault, and stalking. In 2001, the Department of Education Office for Civil Rights stated that "[S]chools need to ensure that employees are trained so that those with authority to address harassment know how to respond appropriately, and other responsible employees know that they are obligated to report harassment to appropriate school officials." The OCR issued additional guidelines in 2011 via what is known as the "Dear Colleague Letter." It required that every campus receiving federal funding implement prevention programs in orientations for students, faculty, and staff. It specified that "These programs should include a discussion of what constitutes sexual harassment and sexual violence, the school's policies and disciplinary procedures, and the consequences of violating these policies." It also required that campuses designate a specific individual to be a Title IX Coordinator to ensure compliance (Marshall, 2014).

Another law that requires training and education on campuses receiving federal funding is the Campus Sexual Violence Elimination Act (SaVE Act), which was passed into law in 2013 as section 34 of the VAWA reauthorization. It requires that colleges and universities in the United States to provide training on sexual assault, stalking, sexual harassment, and domestic violence to all incoming students (NSVRC, n.d.). It also requires counseling, medical care, and legal assistance to sexual assault survivors.

AN INTERNATIONAL AND HUMAN RIGHTS VIEW OF SCHOOL AND STATE RESPONSIBILITY REGARDING DATING AND DOMESTIC VIOLENCE

Outside of the US, there is more precedent for school responsibility to protect students from violence. Looking at international human rights treaties like those included in the Introduction, it can be asserted that the US has a responsibility to protect schoolchildren as a fundamental human right (Finley, 2023). As criminologists Rothe and Mullins (2006) explained, States should look beyond their own laws to ensure that they are compliant with fundamental human rights.

Leila Sedat (2022) professor of international criminal law and advisor to the United Nation's prosecutor on crimes against humanity for the International Criminal Court, that the frequency and trauma of violence in schools, in particular gun violence, may be in violation of the U.N. Convention Against Torture and Other Cruel, Inhuman and Degrading Treatment (UNCAT). Sedat explained that the UNCAT requires preventative measures. Given the links explored in this book about dating violence and guns as well as abusers as school shooters, this interpretation suggest that states could be culpable for violating international human rights if they do not adequately respond to and try to prevent abuse from occurring on school grounds.

Although not a decision that is binding for the United States, there is precedent in the European Court of Human Rights (ECHRs) to hold states responsible for failing to protect students from school shootings, which would include those occurring as a result of abusive relationships. The ECHR determined in September 2020 that Finland had violated its duty to protect the lives of nine students and a teacher who were killed in a shooting at a vocational school. Sheppard (2020) wrote,

> The court ruled that by not confiscating the attacker's semi-automatic pistol after he made internet postings that cast doubts on his suitability to safely possess a weapon, Finnish police failed to observe a special duty of diligence incumbent on authorities. Such a duty existed, the court said, because of a particularly elevated risk to life inherent in any misconduct involving firearms.

Another time the ECHR ruled that a state was responsible for failing to protect students was after a terrorist group killed more than 180 schoolchildren in Beslan in 2004. According to the ECHR, school authorities had enough evidence that an attack was imminent and did not do enough to prevent it. As Sheppard (2020) wrote for *Human Rights Watch,*

> The European Court's decision delivers a powerful new perspective on government's human rights obligations to prevent gun violence, such as school shootings, when there are warning signs. The ruling sets a high standard for governments but does so to save lives. If other international and regional treaty bodies and domestic courts follow suit, they could too.

Some countries have more fully adopted school-based prevention and response policies as well. Portugal launched "Portugal + Equal" in 2018, which includes as one of its strategies to promote gender equality and reduce gender-based violence a provision to address dating violence specifically in school-based programs. It specifies that primary prevention be targeted at all levels of education (Neves & Correia, 2024).

Since 2019, England has required all primary school children to learn about healthy friendships, stereotypes, and other concepts that are often referred to in the United States as "social-emotional learning." In secondary schools, students in England are taught about safety in relationships, including with dating partners. They must also be taught to identify sexual harassment and sexual violence (Youth Endowment Fund, 2025).

Wales enacted the Relationship and Sexuality Education Code in 2022, which required that all students "develop an understanding of the social, emotional, physical and legal nature and impact of harmful behaviours, including all bullying, and LGBTQ+ based bullying, sexual violence and gender-based violence in a range of contexts, including online" (Youth Endowment Fund, 2025). Research by the Youth Endowment Fund (2025) found that such programs are effective at reducing dating violence, as much as 17%.

Australia mandates comprehensive education about gender-based violence in higher education but not in K-12 schools.

TRAINING AND EDUCATION IN OTHER INSTITUTIONS

Given the ubiquity of abuse, people involved in virtually any institution are likely to encounter victims. While those individuals mandated to report also vary by state, they generally include childcare providers, clergy, coaches, counselors, healthcare providers, law enforcement, principals, and teachers.

As was noted in Chapter Four, healthcare professionals can sometimes be the first to identify abuse or have it disclosed to them. Most states have such laws for child abuse and elder abuse, but some have added domestic violence. In 40 states, healthcare providers are required to report injuries that are likely to have been inflicted by guns, knives, or other deadly weapons. This is regardless of who the perpetrator is but would apply to domestic violence in cases in which the abuser used a deadly weapon. Eighteen states plus Washington, D.C. have legislation requiring the healthcare providers report injuries that were likely caused by criminal activity. These vary in terms of the seriousness of the injury and whether it was likely intentionally inflicted. Six states specify that healthcare providers are mandatory reporters of domestic violence. In California, for instance, healthcare practitioners must report to law enforcement if they reasonably believe that the injuries they treated were the result of domestic violence. Five states have no mandatory reporting laws at all, while some states make reporting voluntary (Mandated Reporter Training, 2022).

Although many people support the idea of mandatory reporting for certain offenses or injuries, including those resulting from domestic violence, others contend that these laws can put survivors and their children at greater risk. Since research shows that abuse tends to escalate when there is a sign that the victim is no longer going to accept the abuse, victims and advocates worry about retaliatory violence. Further, there are concerns about undermining survivor autonomy. The Family Violence Prevention Fund explained,

> In domestic violence cases, patients are competent adults who should be granted the ability to make critical life decisions; if they believe calling the police will jeopardize their safety, then that opinion should be respected. These types of cases can be distinguished from child abuse cases, where the victim is a minor. Mandatory reporting not only impinges on the patient's self-determination, but in the process perpetuates harmful stereotypes of battered women as passive and helpless. By taking away patient autonomy, mandatory reporting revictimizes battered patients: their relationships with the batterers were ones in which the batterers controlled the decisions in their lives. (Mandated Reporter Training, 2022)

Regardless of whether healthcare professionals are required to report domestic violence, most major medical bodies recommend screening of patients to assess for abuse. These include the American Medical Association, the American Academy of Pediatrics, the American Academy of Family Physicians, and the American College of Obstetrics and Gynecologists. Screening can help identify abuse or encourage victims to disclose it. Once identified or disclosed, healthcare providers can provide victims with various resources and support to improve their safety and health. There are numerous simple tools that have been developed to conduct screening. The most commonly used screening tools are the Hurts/Insults/Threatens/Screen (HITS) scale (and its extended version), Humiliation/Afraid/Rape/Kick, and Partner Violence Screen (Miller et al., 2021).

Several states require that healthcare providers take continuing medical education (CME) courses on domestic violence. These include Connecticut, Florida, Kentucky, and Texas, although the frequency of the training requirement and which type of professionals must specifically complete the requirement varies (Board Vitals, 2025). Since 2006, this author has been able to provide the domestic violence CME for healthcare providers in South Florida. It has been well-received, and my experience is that many doctors and healthcare professionals are screening for domestic violence even though Florida law does not require it nor are they mandatory reports of it. Yet in all, screening is still inconsistent across different areas of healthcare. Some of the lowest rates are in emergency rooms, but research is clear that victims of domestic violence use emergency services far more frequently than do those who are not victimized. This may be because of embarrassment in presenting signs of abuse to their primary care physician and/or the acute damage of the incident requiring emergency services (Miller et al., 2021).

Law Enforcement and First Responders

While police training academies generally include domestic violence, often it is only a small portion of the overall training. Twenty-six states require some type of continuing education for law enforcement officers related to domestic violence. Forty-three states have some type of law requiring training on interacting with specific populations, with some of them including domestic violence, sexual assault, human trafficking, elder abuse and other victims. Some states require continued training, such as Illinois, where officers must attend training on domestic violence every five years. Arkansas requires "16 hours of training related to behavioral health crisis intervention in a law enforcement context," which might include addressing both victims and offenders. No state that I could find requires that police have training about dating violence (Law Enforcement Training, 2024).

It is not clear how many states require domestic and/or dating violence for other first responders. A number of state and local governments offer such training, however, even if it is not required.

Some other countries have better institutionalized training for first responders. In 2012, the United Nations Office on Drugs and Crime created a curriculum for police officers in Vietnam that has been used in police academy (UNODC, 2012).

The Police Academy in Croatia also has a training program for police officers, which it has shared with other countries like Ukraine. The war in Ukraine has exacerbated rates of abuse, something Croatia had dealt with as well. Joerg Einemann, Head of IBM and Law Enforcement Component at European Union Advisory Mission explained,

> Croatia is the only EU country with direct experience in addressing domestic violence in a postwar setting. That's why its lessons are particularly relevant for Ukraine. At EUAM, we are glad to facilitate this exchange of knowledge to help ensure that Ukrainian police officers are better equipped to handle domestic violence cases, especially given how the war continues to heighten the risks and vulnerabilities. (European Union EAUM Ukraine, 2025)

Ukraine kicked off a training program for police officers in 2021 modeled on others like Croatia's (European Union EAUM Ukraine, 2021).

Legal Institutions

In the United States, there is no uniform requirement for lawyers regarding domestic violence training. Many states do mandate domestic violence training for judges, however. A 2019 survey found tremendous variation in states' training requirements for the judiciary. Thirty-one states plus Washington, DC have some legal provision for judges to be trained about domestic violence while 15 states require it. What specifically is included varies, as only 11 state laws specify what the training must cover. Those include how to promote victim safety; risk and lethality factors; the characteristics of domestic violence offenses; the dynamics of abuse; the effects of abuse on adults, children, and families; culturally responsive approaches to serving victims; and community resources and programs. Five states require that domestic violence be included in training for new judges (Kalsem, n.d.).

Other countries have mandated training for judges. The following are some examples, albeit not an exhaustive list. Serbia trains prosecutors, judges, and other professionals who are charged with enforcing its Law on the Prevention of Domestic Violence (United Nations, 2024).

Canada has also developed a national online training for judges. It covers myths and stereotypes about abuse, barriers victims face in leaving abusers and in reporting abuse, services available to victims, and more (Government of Canada, 2022).

CONCLUSION

This chapter has shown that schools and universities have a legal responsibility to protect students from dating violence, even though the legislative and case precedents are a bit hodge podge. From an international human rights perspective, states should also protect young people from violence in school and on campus, per many treaties and decisions. Further, in many states medical professionals, police officers, lawyers, and other professionals are legally mandated to be trained about abuse. The following chapters will share some curricula and teaching/training ideas to meet these legal requirements.

REFERENCES

Adhia, A., Kray, M., Bowen, D., Kernic, M., & Miller, E. (2022). Assessment in variation of US state laws addressing the prevention of and response to teen dating violence in secondary schools. *JAMA Pediatrics, 176*(8), 797–803.

Bates, L. (2021). *Men who hate women: From incels to pickup artists: The truth about extreme misogyny and how it affects us all.* Sourcebooks.

BBC. (2018, April 25). Elliott Rodger: How misogynistic killer became "incel hero". https://www.bbc.com/news/world-us-canada-43892189

Board Vitals. (2025, May 6). *Continuing medical education: CME state requirements.* https://www.boardvitals.com/blog/cme-requirements-by-state/

Brown, v., & State of Arizona. (N.D.). *United States Court of appeals for the ninth circuit.* https://cdn.ca9.uscourts.gov/datastore/opinions/2023/09/25/20-15568.pdf

Cascardi, M., & Avery-Leaf, S. (2014). Case study of a school-based universal dating violence prevention program. *Sage Open, 4*(3), 1–9.

Coleman, P. (2023). Targeting school shootings: Using three warning signs—Animal abuse, domestic violence, and conduct disorder—To help prevent massacres. *Widener Commonwealth Law Review, 32,* 65–142.

Cornell, D., & Limber, S. P. (2015). Law and policy on the concept of bullying at school. *American Psychologist, 70,* 333–343.

Curcio, A. (2017). Institutional failure, campus sexual assault and danger in the dorms: Regulatory limits and the promise of tort law. *Montana Law Review, 78,* 31–70.

European Union EAUM Ukraine. (2021, February 15). *EAUM and Patrol Police kick off training programme on combatting domestic violence.* https://www.euam-ukraine.eu/news/euam-and-patrol-police-kick-off-training-programme-on-combating-domestic-violence/

European Union EAUM Ukraine. (2025, May 21). *E-learning solution for police training on domestic violence: Croatia shares experience with Ukraine.* https://www.euam-ukraine.eu/news/e-learning-solution-for-police-training-on-domestic-violence-croatia-shares-experience-with-ukraine/

Everytown Gun Law Rankings. (2025, January 15). *Everytown for gun safety.* https://everytownresearch.org/rankings/law/school-threat-assessment-teams/

Finley, L. (2023). Examining U.S. school shootings as state crimes of ommission. *Contemporary Justice Review, 26*(3), 250–261.

Geller, L., Booty, M., & Crifasi, C. (2021). The role of domestic violence in fatal mass shootings in the United States, 2014–2019. *Injury Epidemiology, 8*(1), 1–8.

Government of Canada. (2022, December 6). *Improving access to justice for Canadians through judicial training on intimate partner and family violence in the family justice system.* https://www.canada.ca/en/department-justice/news/2022/12/improving-access-to-justice-for-canadians-through-judicial-training-on-intimate-partner-and-family-violence-in-the-family-justice-system.html

Grumet, B. (2024, November 11). Sharing Ortralla Mosley's story turned teacher's grief toward helping others. *Austin America-Stateman.* https://www.statesman.com/story/news/columns/2023/03/28/ortralla-mosley-murder-austin-school-teen-dating-violence-awareness/69954596007/

Italiano, L. (2018, February 17). School gunman has history of abusing his mother. *New York Post.* https://nypost.com/2018/02/17/school-gunman-has-history-of-abusing-his-mother/

Kalsem, K. (n.d.). *Judicial training on domestic violence: A 50-state survey.* https://ucracegendersocialjustice.com/wp-content/uploads/2019/12/judicialtrainingsurveyarticlefinal.pdf

Law Enforcement Training. (2024, June 18). *National conference of state legislatures.* https://www.ncsl.org/civil-and-criminal-justice/law-enforcement-training

Mandated Reporter Training. (2022, October 13). *Which states have mandatory domestic violence reporting?* https://mandatedreportertraining.com/resources/blog/which-states-have-mandatory-domestic-violence-reporting/

Marshall, R. (2014). *Will it really SaVE you? Analyzing the Campus Sexual Violence Elimination Act* (Vol. *6*(2), pp. 271–293). American University Legislation and Policy Brief.

Miller, C., Adjognon, O. L., Brady, J. E., Dichter, M. E., & Iverson, K. M. (2021). Screening for intimate partner violence in healthcare settings: An implementation-oriented systemic review. *Implementation Research and Practice,* 7(2), 1–47.

National Women's Law Center. (2017, August 9). *Jane Doe is standing up for herself and other teen dating violence survivors.* https://nwlc.org/jane-doe-is-standing-up-for-herself-and-other-teen-dating-violence-survivors/

Neves, S., & Correia, A. (2024). Dating violence in Portugal: How can it be handled in secondary schools and universities? *Frontiers in Global Women's Health, 5,* 1–3. https://pmc.ncbi.nlm.nih.gov/articles/PMC11446891/

NSVRC. (n.d.). What do you need to know about sexual assault on college campuses? https://www.nsvrc.org/what-do-you-need-know-about-sexual-assault-college-campuses/#:%7E:text=The%20Campus%20Sexual%20Violence%20Elimination,%2C%20dating%20violence%2C%20sexual%20assault%2C

Peetz, C., & Baker, L. (2023, May 11). Map: Does your state require education on teen dating violence? *Education Week.* https://www.edweek.org/leadership/does-your-state-require-education-on-teen-dating-violence/2023/05

Public Justice. (n.d.a). *Hall v. Millersville University.* https://www.publicjustice.net/case_brief/hall-v-millersville-university/

Public Justice. (n.d.b). *Sexual harassment.* https://www.publicjustice.net/student-civil-rights-project/sexual-harassment/

Rothe, D., & Mullins, C. (2006). *Symbolic gestures and the generation of global social control: The International Criminal Court.* Lexington.

Sedat, L. (2022). Torture in our schools? *Harvard Law Review Forum.* https://openscholarship.wustl.edu/law_scholarship/67/

Sheppard, B. (2020, October 1). *European court's school shooting ruling and its wider implications.* Human Rights Watch. https://www.hrw.org/news/2020/10/01/european-courts-school-shooting-ruling-and-its-wider-implications

United Nations. (2024, May 13). *A digital pioneer in the fight against domestic violence.* https://serbia.un.org/en/273069-digital-pioneer-fight-against-domestic-violence

UNODC. (2012, May 8). *UNODC develops domestic violence prevention training for Vietnamese police.* https://www.unodc.org/unodc/en/frontpage/2012/May/unodc-develops-domestic-violence-prevention-training-for-vietnamese-police.html

Youth Endowment Fund. (2025). *New research finds that schools delivering Relationship and Sex Education lessons can significantly reduce violence in partner relationships.* https://youthendowmentfund.org.uk/news/new-research-finds-that-schools-delivering-specialist-relationship-and-sex-education-lessons-can-significantly-reduce-violence-in-partner-relationships/

CHAPTER 6

PREVENTION CURRICULA AND PROGRAMS FOR SCHOOLS AND OTHER INSTITUTIONS

ABSTRACT

In Chapter 6 the emphasis is on reviewing prevention curricula and programs. This includes packaged programs like *Safe Dates* and various bystander intervention programs. Also included in the chapter are model programs that can be used in other institutions, for instance, by medical professionals and employers, as well as community-based educational programs.

Keywords: Prevention; curricula; bystander intervention; training; *Safe Dates*; DELTA

INTRODUCTION

Curricula related to dating violence are largely intended to be used in schools to teach youth about healthy and unhealthy relationships. They range from short in-class only programs to lengthier modules that include full school components and in some cases, training for parents as well. Among the most frequently used curricula are *Safe Dates, The Fourth R, Love is Not Abuse,* and *Shifting Boundaries.* Some of the curricula have been evaluated and found to be effective in some way. Programs that have been

Teaching and Making Peace in Every Relationship, pages 121–137

doi:10.1108/978-1-80686-961-920261007

rigorously evaluated and found to work are considered evidence-based programs (De La Rue et al., 2017). As noted in the previous chapter, some state laws require that schools use only evidence-based curricula. However, it is important to note that many of the evaluations of curricula, both those deemed evidence-based and those that are not, do not focus on actual reductions of dating violence or sexual assault (Stone, 2025). Laurie Graham et al. (2021) reviewed articles evaluating nine studies of seven distinct programs. Most measured changes in knowledge and attitudes, not in behaviors. Only one program reduced self-reported sexual violence among men.

Safe Dates is a primary and secondary prevention curriculum intended to challenge traditional gender norms, help teen recognize the signs of healthy and unhealthy relationships, improve conflict resolution skills, support help-seeking behavior, and encourage peer support. It is conducted in nine 50 minutes interactive sessions for middle and high school students. It can stand alone or be integrated into health or life skills class. It can be used in conjunction with substance abuse education as well as with other general violence prevention programs. The program is also designed to reach additional students through a poster contest and a 45-minute school play. Students and parents also receive booklets to have at home. The modules focus on the following: (1) Defining Caring Relationships. This introduces students to the program and emphasizes articulating how they want to be treated in dating relationships. (2) Defining Dating Abuse, which presents statistics and examples to identify unhealthy dating relationships. (3) Why Do People Abuse? This module uses discussions and scenarios to explore the causes and consequences of dating abuse. (4) How to Help Friends. Here students identify the challenges in leaving abusive relationships and, through exercises and a dramatic reading, consider how to help a friend in need. (5) Helping Friends further elaborates on helping those in need and in confronting abusers. It used stories and role-playing activities to do so. (6) Overcoming Gender Stereotypes, which emphasizes how "traditional" gender role norms may contribute to abusive relationships. In this module, students study scenarios, engage in small-group discussions, and complete a writing exercise. (7) Equal Power Through Communication, in which students learn eight skills for effective communication and participate in role-plays to practice them. (8) How We Feel, How We Deal. This module focuses on effective ways to recognize anger and to manage it in healthy ways. Students discussion managing "hot button" issues that can lead to abusive behavior and use a diary to consider their healthy anger management strategies. (9) Preventing Sexual Assault. The final module introduces helps students understand what constitutes sexual assault. They learn through a panel of peers, a caucus, and a quiz.

Safe Dates has been used in all 50 states. Australia, Canada, Chile, Greece, Iceland, Ireland, Japan, the Netherlands, Switzerland, Taiwan, Thailand, and the UK have also used it (National Institute of Justice, 2011).

Foshee et al. (1998) evaluated Safe Dates. Their study involved eight and ninth grade students at 14 public schools in eastern North Carolina. Some students were randomly assigned to receive the program and others were not. Treatment adolescents were exposed to school and community activities, whereas control adolescents were exposed to community activities only, not the school program. Sixteen teachers (10 men and 6 women) taught the program after having received 20 hours of training. Almost 91% of the curriculum activities were covered by the teacher and attendances ranged from 95 to 97% during the sessions, meaning that the treatment students received the bulk of the curriculum. A total of 1886 adolescents completed a baseline questionnaire before the program started and 90% of them completed a questionnaire again one month after it ended. The sample included 51.1% female, 19.1% African American, and 77.1% White students. Their ages ranged from 11 to 17 years, with a mean age of 13.8. Approximately 70% of the adolescents reported dating on both the baseline and postprogram questionnaire. Of those who reported that they were dating before the program, 34.9% of the girls and 38.0% of the boys reported being a victim of dating violence at least once.

The follow up showed positive effects of the program. There was 25% less psychological abuse perpetration, 60% less sexual violence perpetration, and 60% less violence perpetrated against the current dating partner reported on the follow up questionnaire among students in the treatment schools than in control schools. In particular, the study found that the program effectively challenged gender role stereotyping, dating violence norms, and awareness of services which were all connected to the reduction in perpetration.

Foshee et al. (2014) conducted a study of the original Safe Dates randomized control trial that addressed the effectiveness of the program in preventing victimization/perpetration and in weapon carrying at school one year afterward. It also analyzed the role of sex in gender in moderating the effectiveness of Safe Dates. Ninety percent of the eighth and ninth grade students who completed a baseline questionnaire at the start of the program completed the one-year follow up assessment. It found that there was 12% less victimization and 31% less weapons carrying among those that completed the program than from those in the control group. The program was significantly associated with perpetration for the minority group (23% less perpetration) but not for White adolescents who completed it.

Ending Violence is a school-based program delivered by attorneys to high school students. It teaches about healthy and unhealthy relationships as well as legal rights, focusing on criminal laws prohibiting dating and domestic violence and resources available to victims through the legal system. Ending Violence includes three classroom sessions delivered during health classes. Jaycox et al. (2006) published an evaluation of the impact of the curriculum on ninth grade students from Los Angeles Unified School District over a three year period (2001–2004). The focus was on large urban high schools with populations of at least 80% Latino students. Students were assigned to one of three randomized tracks. The first cohort of the study involved six schools, the second cohort included five schools, and the third included six schools—five of which participated in the first and one that participated in the second cohort. In all, 2,540 9th grade students from 10 highs schools were included. 1,384 students in health classes were randomly selected to receive the intervention and 1,156 were randomly selected to receive the standard health curriculum. A preassessment found that at baseline the control group reported less acceptance of female-on-male aggression and greater likelihood of help-seeking if they were victims. The researchers followed up with both groups six months after the intervention. The study measured self-reported knowledge of dating violence and laws, the degree to which students approved unprovoked male-on-female and female-on-male aggression, perpetration of dating violence, and dating violence victimization.

Students who received Ending Violence reported increased knowledge, less acceptance of female-on-male aggression, and an increased likelihood of help-seeking due to more knowledge about resources. However, no differences were found in regard to recent abusive or fearful dating experiences, violence victimization, or perpetration of violence (Jaycox et al., 2006).

The Fourth R is classroom-based as well and focuses on reducing violence of various sorts. It was first used in Canada and found to reduce physical dating violence amongst ninth grade students. Its comprehensive program includes material for students, teachers, parents, and the community. Activities include peer mentoring and role modeling. The community involvement component helps students and parents know about available resources (Fourth R Programs, n.d.). It has not, however, been found by the Office of Juvenile Justice and Delinquency Prevention (OJJDP) to be an evidence-based program.

Cissner and Ayoub (2014) evaluated The Fourth R program in a study that included seventh grade students in 10 middle schools in the Bronx. Incoming seventh-graders were randomly assigned to class sections and then those sections were randomly assigned to present either the Fourth *R* or a standard seventh-grade curriculum during the 2011–2012 academic year. The study, which involved 570 students initially, included preprogram surveys, postprogram surveys, and a follow-up survey administered at the conclusion of the following school year that included 517 students. At the beginning of the study, 57% of the student respondents reported that they were dating and eight percent reported that they were sexually active. On the baseline survey 20% of the students reported experiencing dating violence, including physical and sexual harassment or assault, and 21% reported perpetrating sexual harassment or assault against peers. Twice the number (41%) reported being a victim of any type of sexual harassment or assault. More than half of the sample (56%) reported perpetrating either physical, emotional or psychological abuse from a peer, and 68% reported being the victim of one or more of those forms of abuse. The study found that the program did not generally reduce dating violence or bullying but students who received some of the program were more likely to delay sexual activity, and those who received more of it delayed sexual activity event further. Those who received more of the curriculum were also less likely to perpetrate bullying and had greater changes in attitude than those who did not receive it or received less of it. The program did reduce dating violence amongst those student who were considered at high-risk because they reported experiencing or perpetrating abuse at the baseline (Cissner & Ayoub, 2014).

Another curriculum focuses at the middle school level is Shifting Boundaries. It focuses on dating violence as well as sexual harassment and includes both a classroom curriculum and a school-wide component. For sixth grade students there are four lessons, which cover boundaries, personal space, and identifying resources and safe spaces at school. The seventh grade curriculum includes six lessons that emphasize the same topics as well as helping students know how they can help those in need (Stein, 2010). The school-wide component includes how to utilize temporary school-based restraining orders, increasing staff presence and security presence in parts of the schools identified as "hot spots," and using posted to increase awareness and reporting of dating violence and harassment.

Taylor et al. (2011) evaluated Shifting Boundaries. The study involved 30 public middle schools in New York City that were randomly assigned to receive the program. 117 sixth- and seventh-grade classes (over 2,500 students) were included. Surveys were administered before the program, immediately after completion, and six months later. They measured knowledge, attitudes, behavioral intentions, intention to intervene as a bystander, perpetration and victimization of peer and dating partner physical and sexual violence, and perpetration and/or victimization of sexual harassment. The researchers also conducted qualitative focus groups with students and educators involved with the program. At the baseline, about half of the students reported having been in at least one dating relationship. Some 20% reported having been the victims of dating violence. The study found that the students who received the classroom and building interventions had increased knowledge about laws relevant to sexual harassment and dating violence as well as the consequences of engaging in those behaviors. Further, those receipt of both interventions was associated with a 26% reduction in sexual harassment victimization and a 34% reduction in perpetration of sexual harassment. Those who received the building intervention were less likely to perpetrate abuse immediately after the intervention and approximately 50% less likely to report perpetration or victimization of physical or sexual violence six months afterward. As well, students who received the building only intervention were more likely to report positive intentions as bystanders in the six months following the intervention.

Another study of middle schools in New York City that used Shifting Boundaries in 2009 and 2010 found that hot spot mapping and then placing adults in those places was really helpful. This involved asking students where incidents of sexual harassment and abuse most commonly occurred. It also found that institutionalizing Respecting Boundaries Agreements helped normalize a respectful environment (Stone, 2025).

The Centers for Disease Control and Prevention (CDC) also has a school-based program called *Dating Matters.* It is directed at middle school students and also contains a school-wide component. Further, Dating Matters includes material for parents and the community that address not only dating violence but also other risk-taking behaviors, including unprotected sex and substance abuse. It has been implemented and evaluated in several urban, high crime neighborhoods and found to be effective at reducing risky behaviors (Debnam & Temple, 2021). Dating Matters started as a pilot program in four cities: Baltimore, Chicago, Oakland, and Fort Lauderdale. At that time, the CDC was examining the feasibility of offering the program, including its cost and sustainability, as well as its effectiveness at preventing teen dating violence. Middle school students were recruited by local health departments from neighborhoods that had been identified as having above average rates of crime and poverty. This was a unique approach, as prior research had not assessed the effectiveness of prevention programs specifically targeted to youth in high-risk communities. A total of 46 middle schools were involved in the study and were randomly assigned to either implement Dating Matters or their standard curriculum related to health. Students were surveyed at the beginning of the program as well as annually until they began high school, allowing for a rigorous, randomized control (Public Health, 2024).

In the eighth grade program the CDC used Safe Dates, as it was considered the most widely used evidence-based program. The CDC also developed its own programs for sixth and seventh grade students. The curricula focused on the following: 1) Healthy and unhealthy behaviors in all relationships, including peers, family members, and dating partners; 2) The role of social media, cell phones, text messaging, and phone applications in relationships; 3) Other risk factors for dating violence, such as substance use, risky sexual behavior, and poor coping skills (Public Health, 2024).

The parenting program was adapted from an evidence-based program called Parents Matter! Its focus is on promoting positive parenting skills and open communication about dating relationships and sexual health.

For eighth-grade parents, the CDC used Families for Safe Dates, an evidence-based program for family conversations about healthy and unhealthy relationships (Public Health, 2024).

Communications program, i2i®: What *R* U Looking 4? was developed by the CDC based on communications best practices and using theoretical models of behavioral change. The CDC held workshops with youth to co-create the program so that the communications materials developed, especially social media messages, would be perceived as more credible and authentic to young teens (Public Health, 2024).

One study conducted by the CDC compared youth who participated in Dating Matters with those who received the previously mentioned Safe Dates program. Schools were randomly assigned to see which was more effective. Students in the study were surveyed multiple times, first in the start of the fall of sixth grade, before receiving any prevention program. They were surveyed again in spring and fall of eighth grade and once a year in high school to assess longitudinal effects. In addition to comparing the effects of the models, the study also examined differences between boys and girls (Public Health, 2024).

At the middle school level, the students who received Dating Matters reported less teen dating violence, both perpetration and victimization. They also reported less bullying perpetration, less physical violence perpetration, less weapon carrying, less alcohol and substance abuse, less delinquency, less sexual harassment (both inside and outside of dating relationships), and less use of negative conflict resolution strategies than students in comparison schools. Only females reported less cyberbullying perpetration and victimization and less sexual violence perpetration and victimization (Public Health, 2024).

Importantly, the CDC research found that many of those effected persisted into high school. Students in the 9th–11th grades who received Dating Matters reported less dating violence perpetration and victimization, less use of negative conflict styles, and more positive relationship skills (Public Health, 2024).

Liz Claiborne, Inc., Education Development Center, Inc., with the nonprofit organization Break the Cycle, developed a curriculum called Love is Not Abuse. It focuses on helping students understand dating violence as well as increasing help-seeking behavior. The group, known as the Love is Not Abuse Coalition also wanted to give adults resources to be allies for young people (Maina, 2025). Over time, Break the Cycle managed the program. In 2016, Break the Cycle created a movement where young people to share their relationship experiences called Let's Be Real. I was unable to find any evaluations of Love is Not Abuse but testimonials showed it to be well-received.

There are many programs or curricula focused specifically on sexual assault. As noted at the beginning of the chapter, many colleges use programs that do not seem to effect actual behavior. Some of these are discussion-based and focus on men. The Men's Program is a one-hour discussion for male undergraduates about consent, the impact of rape on survivors, and male-on-male rape. Evaluations of it found no significant difference in perpetration compared to those who did not attend the discussion. RealConsent includes six thirty-minute online sessions. An evaluation found decreases in reported sexual abuse, but 2/3 of the sample was not included in the follow up, making claims of effectiveness somewhat questionable. The Men's Project, another campus-based discussion group, found lower rates of reported sexual aggression four months after the program but not seven months later (Stone, 2025).

Flip the Script with EAAA® (pronounced E-triple A), which was developed by Charlene Senn for university women in Canada, has been found to be effective at not just changing attitudes and beliefs but in an actual reduction of sexual assaults and rapes. According to Sexual Assault Resistance Educate Center,

> ...the 12-hour small-group, evidence-based intervention designed specifically for 17–24-year-old university students of all sexual identities who identify as women. The program is based on theory, research evidence, and best practices for providing young women with the knowledge and tools to defend themselves against attempts to sexually coerce or assault them.

The program consists of mini-lectures, games, audio and video clips, individual, small, and large group application activities, and two hours of empowerment-based self-defense designed to teach women how to protect themselves but also to help challenge rape culture. Senn's study of 1,000 first-year students who completed it found they were 63% less likely than a control group to experience sexual assault and 46% less likely to experience rape (Stone, 2025).

As the above examples show, prevention efforts that involve school-wide programs have been shown to be the more effective because they are more comprehensive and holistic (Adhia et al., 2022). In addition to the curricula presented above, bystander interventions are popular ways to help change school cultures. Rather than focus on would-be victims or offenders, the goal of bystander intervention programs is to educate and empower youth who might witness or know about troublesome behavior. Bystanders can be either active or passive. Passive bystanders are those who witness or know about problems but do nothing to disrupt them. Active bystanders are those who take action. Not all action is good, though. Some active bystanders are negative bystanders. That is, they say or do something to egg on or encourage troublesome behavior. Think about the young people who circle around two classmates who are fighting, whooping and yelling out words of encouragement rather than telling their peers to stop. The same happens with dating violence, where some active bystanders say things that encourage the abuse, rather than try to stop it.

Bystander intervention programs try to give young people the skills to disrupt bullying, harassment, and abuse. Typically, bystander education involves instructing young people about five steps: Seeing a situation, recognizing it as problematic, feeling responsible to do something about it, knowing what to do, then taking action. Some states (less than one-quarter) require bystander education (Adhia et al., 2022). Gabriela Mujal et al. (2021) conducted a systematic review of 44 articles about bystander intervention between 2007 and 2017—most focused on changes in attitudes like rape myth acceptance but only one study measured actual behavior. Nadia Elias-Lambert and Beverly Black (2016) studied fraternity men who had received a 90 mins program called Bringing in the Bystander. In the short-term attendees reported less intention to commit sexual coercion or abuse but five weeks later that was not maintained (Stone, 2025). Between 2014 and 2022 the CDC funded 49 studies of programs to prevent sexual assault, child sexual abuse, dating violence, and domestic violence. Eight programs were specific to men and boys. None of those were found to be effective in preventing sexual assault, child abuse, dating violence, or domestic violence. Of eight programs focused on bystanders, two showed changes in actual sexual assault. Of the nine studies focused specifically on prevention of dating and domestic violence there were mixed results (Stone, 2025). One of the reasons some of these programs may not be effective at changing actual behavior is that many of them, like Bringing in the Bystander, are voluntary and lack institutionalization. Because many of the programs are voluntary, they may not reach all of the students, especially those that might need them the most.

One popular bystander education program for college students is Green Dot. Developed by Dr. Dorothy J. Edwards, former Director of the UK's Violence Intervention and Prevention Center, Green Dot was first implemented in 2007. It focuses on teaching potential bystanders how to safely and effectively interact with perpetrators and victims, including helping victims find needed resources. Green dots are small actions to counter unhealthy or abusive situations, called red dots. Coker et al. (2015) found significantly lower rates of sexual harassment and stalking among students who completed Green Dot at the University of Kentucky but no difference in intimate partner violence.

There are two components of Green Dot. One involves mini-motivational speeches that trained staff provide to students in introductory-level college courses. In the speech, staff explain what active bystanders are and why they are important as well as share information about available resources. The second components includes a comprehensive bystander training program. Green Dot has been evaluated and found to reduce dating violence, in particular amongst populations considered high risk, such as those who grew up in homes where there was abuse (Mennicke et al., 2022). As well, students in the UK who received the Green Dot bystander training program reported using more bystander behaviors than those that only heard the speech, while both those who heard the speech and completed the training reported using more bystander behaviors than students who received no training. Further, those who received the Green Dot program were significantly less likely than students in comparison campuses to report violent victimization, and male participants reported lower rates of perpetration (Coker et al., 2015).

Another popular bystander program is Mentors in Violence Prevention (MVP). Created by gender studies scholar and activist Jackson Katz, MVP was initially designed to train male collegiate student athletes to be active bystanders. It later expanded to include males and females as well as high school students. It uses a mentoring approach whereby older students are trained and then mentor younger ones about what bystander intervention entails and why it is important. Mentors use a variety of hypothetical situations involving abuse, harassment, and bullying to help their mentees consider various interventions and weigh the pros and cons of each (Katz, 1995).

MVP has also been used in the United Kingdom, with Scotland in 2012 and England in 2025. By 2019, more than 130 high schools in Scotland. By 2019, at least 51 schools in England had implemented MVP. MVP has been evaluated in the United States and in the United Kingdom. These have varied in terms of research design, with some focusing on just one college or high school, others focusing on a region, some including pre and postintervention evaluations while others are cross-sectional. The most useful studies, as noted in earlier parts of this chapter, are those that compare control and intervention group. In general, findings are mixed about the effectiveness of MVP (see for examples Fox et al., 2020; Hunter et al., 2021; MVP Progress Report, 2019).

Coaching Boys into Men is another prevention program that is designed to be delivered by athletic coaches to high school male athletes. It has been found to increase bystander efficacy and reduce abuse perpetration by male athletes in some studies but others have found mixed results (CBIM Works! n.d; Stone, 2025).

Teaching women self-defense has been a controversial approach. While it does not change the societal norms and beliefs that underly abuse, some like Stone (2025) recommend certain types of self-defense training because it can prepare someone for what to do in the moment when they are under threat. Backlash about self-defense putting ownership on women. She has faced backlash for promoting self-defense among some liberal feminists who see it as putting the ownership for change on would-be victims, not offenders. Stone (2025) recognizes that some programs like the police-led Rape-Aggression-Defense (RAD) do include elements that ask women to alter their behaviors so as "not to be assaulted," for instance, not wearing their hair in ponytails when walking alone. This, she asserts, is advice not based on any evidence. What Stone (2025) promotes is self-defense that comes from a feminist lens. She wrote,

> The self-defense with the strongest evidence are the ones that each women that we are not the problem, the ones that help us learn how easily gender inequities creep into our intimate relationships and what we can do to recognize and resist coercion. (Stone, 2025, p. 141)

Psychologists Crann et al. (2022) studied 445 college women who told about their experiences using what they learned in a self-defense course. Nearly half said they learned a skill from a feminist self-defense course and 78% found it to be helpful. Notably, it was around prioritizing their safety and comfort rather than feeling compelled to please and placate men. Jocelyn Hollander (2014) found that women who took self-defense reported being more assertive with friends and intimate partners, having more positive body image, being less worried about being perceived as rude, and taking up more space in public. There was a statistically significant decrease in fear of taking public transportation, going to bars, or doing laundry after dark. Many described feeling better about setting limits and boundaries with partners. Siller et al. (2021) found increased confidence, strength, and assertiveness among indigenous girls who took self-defense on a Midwest reservation.

PREVENTION EFFORTS FOR YOUNGER LEARNERS

With younger learners, one curriculum is the Nest Foundation's You Belong Here. Designed for ages 5–18, this a violence-prevention curriculum designed to transform schools. It is based on a social-ecological model and is evidence-based. Lessons focus on the root causes of violence. Specifically, lessons address what healthy relationships look like, including setting boundaries, self-regulation, nonviolent problem-solving, managing conflicts with respect, and more. The curriculum also emphasizes developing media literacy, help-seeking behavior, upstander behavior, critical thinking, and assertive communication. It encourages prosocial behaviors like collaboration and norms that encourage nonviolent conflict resolution. The Kindergarten curriculum emphasizes kindness, managing one's feelings, setting boundaries, bullying and upstander behavior, respecting others, and dealing with grief and loss. Students in grades one through five continue to study these issues in developmentally appropriate ways. Importantly, the curriculum is student-centered. As such, classrooms are conceived as mini-learning communities that adapt to students' different cultural and learning needs. Additional detail about You Belong Here can be found at this link: https://www.nestfoundation.org/curricula/you-belong-here.

Since dating and domestic violence are very similar to bullying in terms of the root cause—the need for power and control—bullying prevention curricula for can potentially prevent later abuse. This includes for older children as well as for younger ones. One longitudinal study of 14–20 year-olds who reported being bullied in the past year found that, seven years later, they were more than twice as likely to have experienced domestic or dating violence (Adhia et al., 2019).

One bullying prevention program is Stomp Out Bullying. It is focused broadly on addressing hate, discrimination, and violence and transforming schools into those that promote civility, diversity, inclusion, equity, and equality. Students are taught how to identify various forms of bullying and discriminatory behavior. Started in 2005, Stomp Out Bullying has reached more than 5.5 million students and has worked with more than 90,000 school partners. Additional information about the programs can be found at https://www.stompoutbullying.org/

Pioneering Norwegian antibullying scholar Dan Olweus, PhD (1931–2020) studied and promoted antibullying programs for more than 40 years. In 1983 he piloted his Olweus Bullying Prevention Program (OBPP), which was then evaluated in a longitudinal study that followed approximately 2,500 students. Results indicated significant reductions in self-reported bullying and victimization. OBPP is a school-wide program intended to reduce the prevalence of bullying, prevent future incidents, and build a sense of community (Olweus & Limber, 2010). OBPP was implemented in the United States in South Carolina in the mid-1990s, focused on students in grades 4–8. It has received recognition from numerous bodies for being an evidence-based practice that reduces bullying. A 2010 review in Norway found that OBPP reduced bullying by 30–50% eight months after implementation in an elementary school (Olweus & Limber, 2010). More information about OBPP can be found at https://clemsonolweus.org/history.php.

CURRICULA AND PROGRAMS FOR OUTSIDE OF EDUCATIONAL SETTINGS

As noted throughout this book, many domestic violence centers or shelters provide educational training and programs in their community upon request. Some are specifically targeted toward children who have been exposed to domestic violence, others to populations seeking to meet recommended or required training requirements (for instance, medical professionals or attorneys), and others more generally to school-aged youth. One example of a community-based program is Youth Relationships Project, which focuses on youth who are identified as being at high risk for experiencing abusive relationships. It was evaluated once in 2016 and has been rated "promising" by the OJJDP. In that study, youth who received the program were significantly less likely to perpetrate physical abuse, showed less trauma symptoms, and had a lower likelihood of emotional abuse and threatening behavior victimization when compared with youth in the control (Program Profile: Youth Relationships Project, n.d.).

Between 2002 and 2013, the CDC has funded the Domestic Violence Prevention Enhancement and Leadership Through Alliances (DELTAs) Program. It focuses on primary prevention, with funding provided to statewide coalition for training, technical assistance, and other support for community prevention efforts. From 2008 to 2011, the CDC, with collaboration from the Robert Wood Johnson Foundation, funded DELTA PREP (Preparing and Raising Expectations for Prevention) to an additional 19 state domestic violence coalitions. As well, from 2013 to 2018 the CDC funded 10 state domestic violence coalitions with the program DELTA FOCUSs (Focusing on Outcomes for Communities United with States). This program was intended to address the social and structural determinants of health in communities and at the societal level, using a social-ecological model. From 2018 to 2023 the CDC funded DELTA Impact to nine state domestic violence coalitions to focus on strategic, data-driven plans, evaluating success, and sustainability at the community and societal levels. The most recent program funded by the CDC is DELTA AHEADs (Achieving Health Equity through Addressing Disparities). Since 2023, funding has been provide to 13 state domestic violence coalitions to help address risk factors and strengthen protective factors regarding domestic and dating violence. Special focus is also placed on working with rural communities and indigenous populations. Further, DELTA AHEAD is a collaborative effort in which the CDC has partnered with the Family Violence Prevention and Services Office of the Administration for Children and Families, the National Resource Center on Domestic Violence, the Intimate Partner Violence Prevention Council, Prevent Connect, and the National Network to End Domestic Violence (CDC, 2024).

For healthcare providers needing or wanting training on domestic and dating violence, there are also many curricular resources. In 2019 the World Health Organization launched a training curriculum for healthcare providers, especially nurses, doctors, and midwives. The curriculum was developed by the WHO's Department of Sexual and Reproductive Health and Research (SRH), the WHO's Regional Office for the Americas/Pan-American Health Organization and was piloted in the Bahamas, Guyana, Myanmar, Namibia, Pakistan, Uganda, Zambia, East Timor and Geneva It released a revised version in 2021 that included five additional modules. In all, there are 17 sessions in the curriculum that focus on understanding violence against women as a public health issue, understanding the survivor's experiences, guiding principles for healthcare responses to abuse, communication skills for working with survivors, identifying referral networks and resources for support, using the LIVES strategy (Listen, Inquire, Validate, Enhance Safety, and Support), note-taking and documentation, forensic examination and clinical care, mental health and self-care for providers, ensuring privacy for survivors, creating prevention strategies, and more. The program is intended to reach healthcare providers specifically in low-and middle-income countries (WHO, 2021).

Futures Without Violence commemorates an annual Health Cares About Domestic Violence Day in October. In doing so, it provides several training videos, sample social media posts, and educational materials relevant for healthcare providers (Futures Without Violence, 2025).

I have been fortunate to be able to provide domestic violence Continuing Medical Education to thousands of healthcare providers in South Florida in the last 15 years, per a Florida state law requiring it. We cover the scope and extent of dating and domestic violence, victim and offender characteristics, risk factors for abuse, challenges in reporting abuse and leaving abusers, the physical, behavioral, and societal effects of abuse, the specific effects of abuse on children, screening for abuse, protocols once abuse has been disclosed or identified, Florida reporting requirements, and additional resources. My experience has been that this training is well-received and that many healthcare providers in the area are screening for abuse and are available to help victims find needed resources. There are also CME trainings on domestic violence available online.

For those working in the legal system, sometimes local experts will provide Continuing Legal Education (CLE) training. Attorney General's Offices in most states also provide such training. Another option is to take an online CLE course. There are many resources that offer these for free. Lawline (https://www.lawline.com/cle/topics/domestic-violence?topic=Domestic%20Violence) provides a variety of sessions, for example.

CONCLUSION

The good news is that there are many curricula and programs available for schools, colleges, and universities that can potentially help change knowledge, attitudes and beliefs. Some, however, sound good but have not been found to be effective, or the results of evaluations are mixed. Fewer still have been found to actually prevent bullying, abuse and assault, although many have never been evaluated specifically for behavioral change. More research is needed to see whether some of these widely-used programs are effective and, if not, why that might be. Interested persons can also use guides like the one created by the OJJDP to identify what are considered model programs (many of which were included herein). Model program can be found at the link here, which is a searchable database about various topics: https://ojjdp.ojp.gov/model-programs-guide/all-mpg-programs.

Research does show that more comprehensive and holistic programs are best. Comprehensive programs, as this chapter showed, tend to be lengthier and more involved and include elements to create school-wide change or even community change. Further, holistic programs reach attendees through multiple methods, addressing different learning styles and using emotional engagement to challenge beliefs, ideas, and norms. Stone (2025) refers to this as belief perseverance, or "the tendency to hold on to our existing beliefs even after we learn evidence that contradicts them" (p. 56). Further, creative, holistic programs can help reach more people, thereby potentially changing more than just beliefs but also actual behavior.

The following chapter describes a case study of a comprehensive and holistic program. While not yet evaluated for changing actual behavior due to financial and capacity constraints, it shows promise in changing campus norms around abuse and assault.

REFERENCES

Adhia, A., Gordon, A., Roberts, A., Fitzmaurice, G., Hemenway, D., & Austin, S. (2019). Longitudinal associations between bullying and intimate partner violence among adolescence and young adults. *Violence & Victims, 34*(6), 1011–1029.

Adhia, A., Kray, M., Bowen, D., Kernic, M., & Miller, E. (2022). Assessment in variation of US state laws addressing the prevention of and response to teen dating violence in secondary schools. *JAMA Pediatrics, 176*(8), 797–803.

CDC. (2024, February 8). *Domestic violence prevention and leadership through alliances: Achieving health equity through addressing disparities.* https://www.cdc.gov/intimate-partner-violence/programs/index.html

Cissner, A., & Ayoub, L. (2014). *Building healthy teen relationships: An evaluation of The Fourth R curriculum with middle school students in the Bronx.* Center for Court Innovation. https://www.ojp.gov/pdffiles1/nij/grants/248486.pdf

Coker, A., Fisher, B., Bush, H., Swan, S., Williams, C., Clear, E., & DeGue, S. (2015). Evaluation of the Green Dot Bystander Intervention to reduce interpersonal violence among college students across three campuses. *Violence Against Women, 21*(12), 1507–1527.

Crann, S., Senn, C., Radtke, H., & Hobden, K. (2022). "I felt powerful and confident": Women's use of what they learned in feminist sexual assault resistance education. *Psychological Women Quarterly, 46*(2), 147–161.

Debnam, K., & Temple, J. (2021). Dating Matters and the future of teen dating violence prevention. *Prevention Sciences, 22*(2), 187–192.

De La Rue, L., Polanin, J. R., Espelage, D. L., & Pigott, T. D. (2017). A meta-analysis of school-based interventions aimed to prevent or reduce violence in teen dating relationships. *Review of Educational Research, 87*(1), 7–34.

Elias-Lambert, N., & Black, B. (2016). Bystander sexual violence prevention program: Outcomes for high-and low-risk university men. *Journal of Interpersonal Violence, 31*(19), 3211–3235.

Foshee, V., Bauman, K., Arriaga, X., Helms, R., Koch, G., & Linder, G. (1998). An evaluation of Safe Dates, an adolescent dating violence prevention program. *American Journal of Public Health, 88*(1), 45–50.

Foshee, V., Reyes, L., Agnew-Brune, C., Simon, T., Vagi, K., Lee, R., & Suchindran, C. (2014). The effects of the evidence-based Safe Dates dating abuse prevention program on other youth violence outcomes. *Prevention Science, 15*(6), 907–916.

Fourth R Programs. (n.d.) *The fourth R.* https://youthrelationships.org/pages/fourth-r-programs

Fox, C., Ralph, N., Harrison, E., McElwee, J., Bagnall, C., & Garnett, N. (2020). *Evaluation of the Mentors in Violence Prevention (MVP) program in the West Midlands (final report).* Keele University.

Futures Without Violence. (2025). *Health cares about domestic violence day.* https://futureswithoutviolence.org/initiative/national-health-cares-about-domestic-violence-day/

Graham, L., Embry, V., Young, B., Macy, R., Moracco, K., Reyes, H., & Martin, S. (2021). Evaluations of prevention programs for sexual, dating, and intimate partner violence for boys and men: A systematic review. *Trauma, Violence, & Abuse, 22*(3), 439–465.

Hollander, J. (2014). Does self-defense training prevent sexual violence against women?. *Violence Against Women, 20*(3), 252–269.

Hunter, S. C., Russell, K., Pagani, S., Munro, L., Pimenta, S., Marín-López, I., Hong, J., & Knifton, L. (2021). A Social-Ecological approach to understanding adolescent sexting behavior. *Archives of Sexual Behavior, 50*(6), 2347–2357.

Jaycox, L., McCaffrey, D., Eiseman, B., Aronoff, J., Shelley, G., Collins, R., & Marshall, G. (2006). Impact of a school-based dating violence prevention program among Latino teens: Randomized controlled effectiveness trial. *Journal of Adolescent Health, 36*, 694–704.

Katz, J. (1995). Reconstructing masculinity in the locker room: The mentors in violence prevention project. *Harvard Educational Review, 65*(2), 163–175.

Maina, E. (2025, January 16). Teaching love, fighting abuse: A look back at the love is Not Abuse curriculum. *Break the Cycle.* https://www.breakthecycle.org/loveisnotabuse/

Mennicke, A., Bush, H., Brancato, C., & Coker, A. (2022). Bystander program to reduce sexual violence by witnessing parental intimate partner violence status. *American Journal of Preventive Medicine, 63*(2), 262–272.

Mujal, G., Adney, M., Fry, J., Gochez-Kerr, T., & Weaver, N. (2021). A systemic review of bystander interventions for the prevention of sexual violence. *Trauma, Violence, & Abuse, 22*(2), 381–396.

MVP Progress Report. (2019). *MVP progress report 2018–2019.* Education Scotland.

National Institute of Justice. (2011, June 4). *Program profile: Safe dates.* https://crimesolutions.ojp.gov/ratedprograms/safe-dates#2-0

Olweus, D., & Limber, S. (2010). The Olweus bullying prevention program: Implementation and evaluation over two decades. In S. Jimerson, S. Swearer, & D. Espelage (Eds.), *Handbook of bullying in schools: An international perspective* (pp. 377–401). Routledge.

Program Profile: Youth Relationships Project. (n.d.). https://crimesolutions.ojp.gov/ratedprograms/youth-relationships-project

Public Health. (2024, May 16). The science behind Dating Matters. *CDC*. https://www.cdc.gov/intimate-partner-violence/php/datingmatters/the-science-behind-dating-matters.html

Siller, L., Edwards, K., Leader Charge, L., Bordeaux, S., Leader Charge, D., & Herrington, R. (2021). "I learned that I am worth defending": A process evaluation of a sexual assault prevention program implemented on an Indian reservation. *Journal of Community Psychology, 49*(7), 2221–2237.

Stein, N. (2010). *Shifting Boundaries: Lessons on relationships for middle-school students.* https://www.wcwonline.org/images/stories/projects/datingviolence/ShiftingBoundaries.pdf

Stone, M. (2025). *The cost of fear: Why most safety advice is sexist and how we can stop gender-based violence.* Beacon Press.

Taylor, B., Mumford, E., & Stein, M. (2011). *Shifting Boundaries: Final report on an experimental evaluation of a youth dating violence prevention program in New York City middle schools.* Office of Justice Programs. https://www.ojp.gov/ncjrs/virtual-library/abstracts/shifting-boundaries-final-report-experimental-evaluation-youth

WHO. (2021). *Caring for women subjected to violence: A WHO training for healthcare providers.* Revised edition, 2021. https://iris.who.int/server/api/core/bitstreams/8b6d4b89-007c-45df-9483-32f44affbd92/content

CHAPTER 7

USING POPULAR CULTURE TO ADDRESS DATING AND DOMESTIC VIOLENCE

ABSTRACT

Chapter 7 presents examples of popular fiction books, films, TV shows, and music that address dating and domestic violence. It also includes examples that can be used with younger children to teach acceptance, kindness, and prevent bullying. While not an exhaustive list, the examples included herein have been used by educators in many disciplinary areas to teach about the scope and extent of abuse, the forms of abuse, the dynamics of abusive relationships, barriers to leaving, and the inadequacy of available resources.

Keywords: Popular culture; movies; TV shows: music; bullying; books

INTRODUCTION

Media and popular culture are powerful ways to reach young people, given our media saturated world. Berns (2004) explained that all media helps influence public perceptions about social problems, be they positive or negative perceptions. It is not just factual media but also fiction movies, TV, novels, and music that "teach" about social issues like domestic and dating violence. In fact, many assert that fiction is better suited to help us tap into emotions (Finley, 2016). As Banks (2008) explained, fiction is not entirely

Teaching and Making Peace in Every Relationship, pages 139–161

doi:10.1108/978-1-80686-961-920261008

"fictional," given that it is written by real people, sometimes who have experienced what they are writing about or conducted extensive research about it. For example, author Joyce Carol Oates, whose novels address many social issues including domestic violence and sexual assault, once told an interviewer that she sees herself as not just a writer "but as a witness to history" (Germaine, 1989, p. 137). Critically assessing what is depicted in various forms of media and popular culture can help students understand the dynamics of abuse, the difficulties victims have in leaving abusers, and needs in terms of resources and help. As well, examining media and popular culture can help identify unhealthy relationships and differentiate them from healthy ones. McDaniel (2013) asserted that

> ...fiction is a rich resource for examining beliefs about partner violence...the popularity of some fiction extends its reach considerably farther than that of policy, advocacy or even the law in its likelihood to influence social expectations, norms and values, and beliefs about what is or is not acceptable behavior. (p. 18)

Many of the curricula discussed in the previous chapter include reading requirements of recommendations for students. This section discusses some additional books that can be used at specific levels to help facilitate conversations about violence, especially abuse in relationships.

USING BOOKS TO ADDRESS ABUSE

Even students who are not yet elementary school age can be taught about accepting difference, treating people kindly, and taking action to make the world a better place. There are many board books that emphasize these concepts. I am a fan of Todd Parr's books, which also include colorful illustrations. *It's Ok to Be Different, Be Who You Are, The Kindness Book, The Peace Book,* and many others are cute but can also help stimulate conversation with little ones.

Since the connection between bullying and abuse is clear, books for elementary school students focus on that issue and can thus be useful in teaching about healthy relationships of all sorts. Here I include just a few examples. Ana Galan's *Billy Bully* shows how bullying ruins friendships but also how to mend them. *The Recess Queen* by Alexis O'Neill tells the story of Mean Jean, the schoolyard bully and the new girl, Katie Sue, who isn't scared of her like the other kids are. Katie Sue is nice to Jean which then helps her be nice to others. Another book that emphasizes the importance of treating everyone kindly is Jacqueline Woodson's *Each Kindness.* It focuses on how ever act of kindness makes the world a better place. Maya is the new girl and Chloe does not show her kindness. But when Maya is gone, Chloe realizes her mistake. It is unclear where Maya goes, which leaves readers wondering and can prompt pondering about what might have been different if Chloe would have welcomed her.

For middle school students, Sarah Dessen's *Dreamland* emphasizes how seemingly "perfect" partners can be not-so-perfect. Caitlin is rebelling against her parents when she starts dating Rogerson. He becomes abusive, just as is Caitlin's dad. Eventually she admits she needs help. Similarly, S.M Parker's *The Girl Who Fell* describes how young people who are enamored with their partners often miss warning signs that they are manipulative and controlling. Zephyr, like Caitlin, realizes she needs to end the relationship with Alec before it is too late, which helps young people understand the way that abusive relationships may start with subtle controlling behaviors but can escalate dramatically.

One of the most widely used book to address dating violence is Alex Flinn's *Breathing Underwater.* Nick is abused by his father and then becomes abusive with his girlfriend, Caitlin. Unlike many other books, this one is written through the abuser's—Nick's—perspective, which can be helpful in talking to students about why someone abuses others. It also emphasizes the connection between child abuse and dating violence. Flinn was inspired to write it after having volunteered at a domestic violence shelter and realizing how little there was written about teen dating violence. Lily and Taylor starts with the worst case scenario—Taylor's older sister is murdered by her abusive partner. She moves to a new town and makes a new friend, Lily, but soon her own boyfriend Devon becomes abusive and with a friend, Connor, takes both Taylor and Lily hostage in a remote cabin. The book shows how Taylor has internalized abuse, believing that she deserves it. In Jennifer Brown's *Bitter End,* we again have a popular guy—Cole—who everyone, including his girlfriend Alex, thinks is amazing. She dismisses the early signs of his controlling behavior and jealousy of her friendship with Zack, but over time he becomes increasingly verbally and physically abusive. Some assert that it is too predictable and formulaic, but for readers who don't know much about the dynamics of abusive relationships, this book can help point out the warning signs and escalation.

In *Breaking Beautiful* by Jennifer Shaw Wolf, Allie survives a car accident that kills her abusive boyfriend, Trip. She does not remember the details of the accident but is in many ways happy to be free from the abuse. Meanwhile, few know about the abuse so the town memorializes Trip and starts to ostracize Allie because she wants to move on with her life. *The Burning* by Laura Bates explores a unique type of abuse—cyber abuse. Anna is the victim of cyber abuse and stalking. The book addresses the ways that technology can be used as a tool of control, as well as how adults are often unprepared to help teens in need. In *Falling for You,* Rae, who is dealing with many tough things in life like a lazy and mean stepfather, falls in love with new guy Nathan. Before long she realizes that what she thought was honest affection had become dangerous obsession.

Although it is about sexual violence, Laurie Halse Anderson's *Speak* illustrates the stigma and shame that many survivors feel. The rape occurred at a party and Melinda called the police, who break up the party. Her peers are upset about that. Melinda never expressed why she called the police, so they had no idea. She becomes increasingly isolated and virtually stops speaking before expressing herself and starting to heal through art. Rape is the subject of Courtney Summers' *All the Rage* as well. Romy is mistreated by her peers after she tells that her crush—Kellen, the popular son of the local sheriff—rapes her at a party. Because she was intoxicated and because Kellen is so well-liked, almost no one believes Romy. As well, Romy left the party with him when she was junk and never contacted authorities, making others doubt that she is really a victim. The book offers a powerful indictment of rape culture and the unfair expectations many people have in regard to how victims are "supposed" to behave. Also about rape, Christa Desir's *Fault Line* is also told from a male's perspective but in this case, it is Ben who is not the perpetrator but rather the boyfriend of Ani, who is raped by multiple guys at a party she attends without him. She does not remember the details and when Ben tries to console her, she pushes him away. This emphasis illustrates how important but difficult it is to support victims.

Alyssa Sheinmel's *What Kind of Girl* follows Maya, whose boyfriend Mike Parker hit her. She tells the school principal and then word gets around, with many people taking sides—more often, Mike's. They do not understand why she went to the principal not the police or why she stayed with him if he was abusive. Things are really intense when Mike is expelled, and Maya and others are dealing with mental health issues. The book is a thought-provoking examination of victim-blaming.

In Deb Caletti's *Stay,* Clara flees her city with her father to a small town in order to get away from her boyfriend Christian, who at first seemed intense but loving. Yet even far away she remains fearful that he will find her, as he promised not to let her go. The book is written from Clara's point of view and offers an interesting view into how victims may grapple with love for someone who is also hurting them.

Other young adult novels show deeply problematic views on relationship violence. Bannar (2010) analyzed the four books in Stephenie Meyer's *Twilight* series and found 172 examples of unhealthy relationship behavior exhibited by Edward against Bella. These range from controlling who she sees to stalking and more. One concern is that some young adult novels like these feature abusive protagonists who are sexy and dangerous and make the relationships look interesting rather than healthy and mundane. Such depictions may make abusive behavior seem normal, even exciting, and like

Bella, young people can mistake abuse for love (Bannar, 2010). This is especially true given that the target audience of the books and films was teenage girls (Collins & Carmody, 2011).

Novels directed at older readers can also be useful tools for addressing dating and domestic violence. Below are just a sample of examples. Suzanne Redferns's *Hush Little Baby* tells the story of Jillian and Gordon. With their two children, Jillian and Gordon appear to have the perfect family. The truth is far from it-for nine years Gordon abused Jillian. She went to great lengths to hide the injuries she sustained, knowing that her police officer husband would never let her leave him alive. As noted in previous chapters, approximately 40% of police officer families experience domestic violence, which is much higher than the 10% of the general population (Police Family Violence Fact Sheet, 2013). It is obvious the danger that this poses, given that police officers have ready access to firearms and are trained to use them. They also typically know the location of domestic violence shelters, which is not made public for the safety of victims. Gordon gets away with the abuse for a very long time, which is unfortunately common when police officers perpetrate abuse (Police Family Violence Fact Sheet, 2013).

Gordon uses many forms of power and control against Jillian. He verbally disparages her and physically assaults her. Like many victims, Jillian changes her behavior to try to please Gordon and prevent another incident. She explains in the book how she dote on Gordon in weeks after an attack. While it is not every time, Gordon is often drunk when he physically assaults Jillian. Like many victims, Jillian blames the abuse on alcohol. As was noted in an earlier chapter, there is a high correlation between substance abuse and domestic violence, although advocates caution against the conclusion that drug or alcohol use causes domestic violence. Another form of abuse Gordon uses is financial. Jillian learns that he has bankrupted the family. The book also shows how abuse affects children. As the story unfolds, readers learn that their son Drew has begun getting into some minor trouble and his grades at school are not very good. Jillian tries to deal with it because she knows Gordon is already too pushy with their son. After another attack Jillian realizes she has to leave Gordon and take the kids. She starts planning how to do so. In reflecting on why she endured abuse for nine years, Jillian lists "Pride, obstinacy, vanity, arrogance" (p. 68). Gordon responds as many abusers do when she says she wants a divorce–he cuts off her access to bank funds. He also locks her out of the house, even inviting her to stay with him and the woman with whom he has been having an affair. Jillian finally tells a colleague everything. It has become increasingly clear that it will be difficult for her to prove that the abuse happened, given that she has no hospital records, and no one saw the bruises. She is concerned that her inability to prove the abuse will result in Gordon having custody of the children. This is not far-fetched, because as soon as she files the paperwork, Gordon levies bogus allegations about her in an attempt to get full custody. After Gordon kills Jeffrey, a man with whom she has had an affair and loves deeply, Jillian knows that she absolutely has to take the kids and flee town. Gordon eventually finds them, and Jillian is arrested for taking the kids against court order. At this point, she knows that the only thing that is keeping her from being killed is the fact that she is pregnant. She is unsure whether the baby is Gordon's or Jeffrey's but lets Gordon think it is definitely his. Eventually, Gordon's actions catch up with him. He beats the woman he is living with and is suspended from work. At the custody hearing Jillian is given custody of the kids and obtains a restraining order to prohibit Gordon from seeing them. He does not take this well, as he grabs the kids and hides. Jillian knows, however, that he will eventually come back when the baby is born. He does and when he attacks her Jillian kills him.

Another novel that shows the way that abuse can have long-term effects is Elizabeth Haynes' *Into the Darkest Corner*. Cathy/Catherine was verbally, physically, and sexually abused by her boyfriend, Lee, until he was convicted and sentenced to prison for attacking her. Like Gordon in Hush Little Baby, Lee is a police officer. When Cathy/Catherine tried to leave hum he formed her to perform oral ex, beat her, cut her with a knife, then urinated onn her before locking her out of the home. Catherine/Cathy suffers from panic attacks and Obsessive-Compulsive Disorder. She used to be the life of the party and now is largely isolated because most of her friends did not believe that Lee was abusing her. The novel later reveals that her fiend Sylvia had lied at Lee's trial, claiming that Cathy/Catherine-had harmed herself. This was a significant reason for Lee's short sentence. The book later reveals that Sylvia was in a relationship with Lee. Cathy/Catherine was briefly institutionalized, making others believe that she was the problem, not Lee. A compelling part of the story is when Cathy/Catherine describes how difficult the trial was. Thus is one reason that victims do not report abuse to police—not only do they fear not being believed and that the abuser will retaliate, they do not want to relive the trauma in court. Cathy/Catherine is constantly concerned that Lee will be released and will kill her, which is not hard to believe given that he has killed a woman before. He does indeed track her down after his release. Cathy/Catherine eventually opens up to her neighbor Stuart, gets some counseling, and the two begin a relationship. Lee tries to attack the two but because Cathy/Catherine is so observant of details she realizes that someone has been in her apartment and is messing with her mind. The book ends with a letter Lee wrote to Cathy/Catherine from prison, claiming that he loves her and won't rest until they can be together. The book also nicely shows the importance of victim advocates, as the one assigned to Cathy/Catherine, Sam Hollands, is tremendously helpful.

TELEVISION SHOWS AND MOVIES TO ADDRESS DATING AND DOMESTIC VIOLENCE

TV shows and movies are also a great way to teach people about dating and domestic violence. Some shows offer examples that are unrealistic or problematic but can still be used to highlight misconceptions and to correct them. One of my favorites because I believe it is one of the most accurate depictions is the Netflix series "Maid." Adopted from Stephanie Land's (2019) book *Maid: Hard Work, Low Pay, and a Mother's Will to Survive,* the series debuted in 2021 and stars Margaret Qualley as a Alex, survivor who has left her abuser and is trying to make her way as a poor, single mother. According to domestic violence advocates, the show gets a lot right about abuse. One thing that is accurately depicted is that abuse is often not physical but that victims sometimes deny those forms of abuse as being what they are. For instance, "Alex tells a social worker in Episode 1, 'Maddy's dad drinks and he blacks out and punches stuff.' *Punches you or Maddy*? the social worker asks. Alex responds, 'No,' and goes on to say, 'I'm not abused'." "Maid" also emphasizes that financial control is common, is one of the man reasons that victims stay with abusers, and is tremendously difficult to overcome. As well, the abuse escalates when Alex tells her husband that she is pregnant, which is also common. Alex also has flashbacks to her own childhood, when she hid while her father abused her mother, which highlights the cycle of violence. Finally, the show illustrates that survivors are not always treated nicely, by family, friends, or even the services that are there to supposedly help them (Kippert, 2021). Alex is judged for leaving her sick daughter at daycare so she can work, but she absolutely has to work because she does not get paid if she takes a day off. Further, the show also has Alex straying in a shelter for a short time, which is not often included in popular culture depictions of abuse. One thing that experts say the show got wrong is in a scene in which a social worker tells Alex that she needs to have reported the abuse to police in order to get help, which is not the case (Kippert, 2021).

"Big Little Lies," the 2017 series based on Liane Moriarty's book, also accurately depicts the dynamics of abusive relationships. Everyone thinks that Celeste's (Nicole Kidman's) relationship with her husband Perry (Alexander Skarsgård) is great, the truth is much different. Behind closed doors he is verbally and physically abusive. As is usually the case, the abuse escalates until Perry physically attacks Celeste in public. The show illustrates the harsh reality that many people who know and love someone have no idea of their suffering. Bernstein (2019) explains," In many of the series' most potent scenes we see the quickness with which Perry transforms from doting to monstrous, and also see the ways that Celeste is increasingly frightened by her husband's behavior, even as she struggles to keep from admitting that she (and her children) might well be in real danger." In the book, like so many victims, Celeste naively believes that her twin sons have no idea about the abuse and honestly believes that while Perry is bad to her, he is a good dad. That falsehood is shattered when she learns that one of the twins, Max, has been bullying girls at his school and that the new woman in town's (Jane) son Ziggy has been taking the blame for it. She realizes that the boys are manifesting the abuse they have witnessed. Celeste does try to seek help, but as a woman of means she chooses a counselor rather than a shelter and finds one some distance away. But when Perry finds out she might be considering leaving him, the abuse escalates and he beats her worse than he ever has (Finley, 2017).

Episode two focuses on the lingering effects of the abuse, even after Perry is no longer around. Unfortunately, since Celeste seems to "have it all" and Perry is good-looking, wealthy, and seemingly put together, some viewers have a hard time empathizing with her or criticizing him. This, however, can offer a good entry point to a conversation about "ideal" victims and offenders. Further,

> In the second, Big Little Lies considers how the effects of abuse linger even after the abuser is out of the picture. Celeste mourns Perry's death, even though she knows intellectually that she deserved a life free from his violence and rage. Her therapist wisely counsels her to understand her longing for her husband as a kind of PTSD, not dissimilar to how some soldiers find it hard to adapt to civilian life because they don't find it stimulating enough. "You miss the war," she tells Celeste, who doesn't quite believe her. She's safe but hungry for the kind of intimacy that Perry offered. (Bernstein, 2019)

A show that was very popular with teen viewers when it debuted in June is "Euphoria." Maddy (Alexa Demie) and Nate (Jacob Elordi) have what many call a "dramatic" relationship, but in reality, Nate is very controlling. Later in the show, we see his father Cal (Deric Dane) abusing him so it clearly shows the cycle of violence. The abuse escalates to Nate strangling Maddy when she tries to leave him. Of concern is that Nate is attractive and popular, with some critics contending that he is the ideal model of masculinity. Like many victims, Maddy tries to hide her bruises with makeup. School officials do notice though and take it seriously. Nate is arrested but Maddy then denies he did anything. She does not want him to go to jail, which is sometimes the case in real life as well. As is often the case, Maddy gets back with Nate. Demie explained that her character grew up in a dysfunctional home and therefore found a dysfunctional teen relationship to be "normal" (Chuba, 2019).

Alice, Darling (2022) stars Anna Kendrick as Alice, who is in a psychologically abusive relationship with Simon (Charlie Carrick). It depicts the ways that abusers can make victims feel as though they have lost their minds—"crazy making"—and the dangers of psychological abuse in general. It also shows the lengths that abusers will go to in order to isolate their victims from loved ones. After Alice loses a gift from Simon—an earring—she repeatedly mutters "I can't do another thing wrong." This is how many victims feel, as their abusers usually tell them that the abuse is their fault. Thankfully, Alice's friends are understanding and supportive when she tells them, and they even intervene when Simon tries to make Alice go away with him. While the film is not a true story, Kendrick says that she drew on her own experience with emotional abuse to portray Alice. Kendrick said that she remembers writing in her journal "I'm just going to try a little harder. If I could just get it right, if I could make it perfect, if I could just say it in the perfect way, I'll be OK." Her castmate Kaniehtiio Horn, who plays Alice's friend Tess, related. "Unfortunately, I've been in a lot of emotionally and other types of abusive relationships. It's pretty safe to say 85% of my relationships were pretty abusive" (O'Neal, 2022).

The film 2007 *Waitress,* which has a Broadway show of the same name, also accurately shows how abusers often rely on gender stereotypes for their expectations of their partners as well as how the typically minimize, dismiss, and gaslight their victims. It stars Keri Russell as Jenna, a waitress who is in an abusive relationship with her husband Earl (Jeremy Sisto). Earl is controlling, demanding, verbally abusive, and physically assaults Jenna. Jenna's dreams of leaving Earl seem to be squashed when she finds out that she is pregnant. The musical, while it won many awards, was criticized for minimizing the abuse portion of the storyline.

Girl on a Train, the 2016 film adaptation of Paula Hawkin's 2015 Hawkin's 2015 book of the same title, stars Emily Blunt as Rachel, an alcoholic who aimlessly rides the train every day because she is depressed about the loss of her job and her marriage and her infertility. She seems to be fixated on her exhusband Tom (Justin Theroux), who is remarried to Anna (Rebecca Ferguson). Rachel also follows the lives of Tom and Anna's neighbors, Scott and Megan Hipwell. Megan had worked for a while as Anna and Tom's nanny. As the story unfolds it is revealed just how horrible Tom was to Rachel and that he murdered Megan because she was pregnant with his child, a fact he did not want revealed. Tom is also the one who fueled Rachel's alcoholism and "implanted" memories about how certain things in their relationship happened that were completely false, causing her to blame herself. "As we can see, Tom is a typical gaslighter who rejects women's intelligence and tries to make his partners 'crazy' by undermining their self-confidence and self-belief" (Zani, 2022).

A film that is based on a true story is The Burning Bed (1984). Farrah Fawcett stars as Francine Hughes, a Michigan woman who had grown up in an abusive home and was enduring severe verbal and physical abuse from her estranged husband Mickey. He routinely threatens her and their children, sexually assaults her, and sabotages her efforts to study for a secretarial course. Having had enough, fearing for her life after Mickey's latest threat and enduring a brutal rape, Francine sets his bed afire and leaves the drunken man to die. She was tried but found not guilty by reason of insanity. Her case helped bring about the concept of Battered Woman Syndrome and defense, as was discussed in Chapters Two and Four. The film also nicely shows the cycle of violence and the way abuse tends to escalate. Shelter staff said that after the release of The Burning Bed they were flooded with calls. While this might appear to be a bad thing, in reality, the film increased awareness and encouraged help-seeking.

A Cry for Help: The Tracey Thurman Story (1989), a made-for-TV movie, tells the true story of Tracey Thurman. Nancy McKeon stars as Tracey, who is estranged from her husband Buck (Dale Midkiff). It opens with Nancy being rushed to the hospital after Buck attacked and nearly killed her. It then follows a flashback to show how the two met, how the abuse began, and how it escalated. Buck is at first charming when Tracy, who is working at a hotel in Florida, meets him and his construction worker colleagues. As the relationship progresses so too does Buck's verbal and eventually physical abuse. He also tells Tracey that he was abused by his mother when he was a child. Feeling bad for Buck, she agrees not to leave him. Tracey thinks that Buck will be pleased when she tells him that she is pregnant, but as in many cases, Buck reacts violently, punching her in the face and kicking her in the stomach. Tracey decides to leave and stay with some friends in Torrington, Connecticut. But Buck finds her there and apologizes. He promises that he has changed and asks Nancy to marry him, offering to stay and settle down in Connecticut. She is hesitant but agrees. Soon after they wed, their son C.J. is born. But Buck has not changed, and his failure to find work exacerbates the situation. They move back to Florida, where Buck gambles away all of their money. Tracey again leaves him for Torrington and once again, Buck chases her there. He claims that he has a job but this time Tracey tells him to leave. He does, but with C.J. in tow. Tracey contacts the police and they find Buck at the diner he is working at, feeding their son. The police actually tell Tracey that she can have her son back if she agrees to reconcile with Buck. Instead, Tracey decides to divorce him and is awarded full custody of C.J. On June 10, 1983, Buck attacks Tracey in broad daylight outside of her home, stabbing her multiple times and stomping on her head. The police had been called yet stood by doing nothing as Buck assaulted Tracey. She was left partially paralyzed and with permanent scars, both emotional and physical. The film also covers Tracey's legal battle, as she filed a federal lawsuit against the Torrington Police Department alleging that they violated her constitutional right to equal protection under the law. She is awarded $2.3 million in damages, setting a precedent that domestic violence is a violation of civil rights. The case, and the movie about it, helped usher in many reforms. This included new protocols requiring police to arrest domestic abusers, thereby removing officer discretion and inertia to do nothing (Brasson, 2025).

While some criticize Lifetime channel movies as "cheesy" and only for women (Finley, 2024), the channel takes on many serious issues, including domestic violence. A Lifetime movie about another true domestic violence story, *Cries Unheard: The Donna Yaklich Story* (1994). There are some similarities to Tracey's story, in particular the fact that the abuse escalates after Donna (played in the film by Jaclyn Smith) tells her husband Dennis that she is pregnant. Also like the Tracey Thurman story the film uses flashbacks to show the abuse that escalated, although in this case to the point that Donna felt she had no choice but to have her husband killed. Dennis, a Pueblo, Colorado Narcotics Detective, is handsome and charismatic, so no one wants to believe bad about him. The two met when she was 22 and he was 30, and Donna moved in with Dennis, his three-year-old daughter, and his three stepchildren ages 9, 11, and 12. She claims that Dennis became abusive only one month after she moved in, which was also fueled by his steroid use. Despite her fears, Donna marries Dennis, who has an outburst during the wedding leaving her to spend her wedding night in fear. When she tells Dennis she is pregnant she begs Dennis to stop using steroids. He does not, instead escalating the abuse to greater violence and even rapes her. She tries to leave with their son but Dennis stops her. When Donna contacts a friend, Jerry, asking for his help in getting Dennis to stop using the steroids Jerry tells Dennis about the conversation. He responds by threatening to kill her and he rapes her again. Five years later Donna tries to leave again, this time to a local shelter. But Dennis uses his contacts to find her, and again threatens to kill her. Seeing no other option, Donna contacts Eddie Greenwell and pays him to murder Dennis. He and his brother shoot Dennis in their driveway. But, Charlie's girlfriend tells the police and the brothers inform them that Donna paid for the murder. Donna is found guilty of conspiracy to commit murder and is sentenced to 40 years in prison. In 2005, Donna was released to a halfway house. Dennis's partner Pueblo police Sgt. Jim Ruggieri called the decision a travesty and maintained that the entire story of abuse was a fraud (Malone, 2005). The film is important in many ways, including that it shows police-perpetrated domestic violence. Research has shown that there is 40% more abuse in police families than in those in which the spouse is not an officers.

The 1991 film *Not Without My Daughter* tells the supposedly true story of Betty Mahmoody (played by Sally Field), a Michigan mother who agreed to visit Tehran in 1984 with her Iranian husband Dr Bozorg "Moody" Sayyed (Alfred Molina) only to find that he does not let her and their daughter Mahtob return to the United States. Betty claimed that the two agreed to a two-week visit while Moody has always insisted she knew the plan was not to leave Iran. The story was originally detailed in a 1987 book. According to Betty, she and Mahtob were trapped in postrevolution Iran where women had few rights and were subject at that time to strict Islamic law. Moody became increasingly violent toward both of them. Betty and Mahtob do eventually escape through a complicated plan involving many others helping them navigate the international landscape from Iran and into Turkey. Some have expressed concern about the film, however. On the surface, this is one woman's inspiring story of having survived domestic violence against all odds. But the book and its movie adaptation (1991) also fed American biases against Muslims and Islam: portraying her husband, his family, Iranians, and all Muslims as dirty, dangerous, violent, and especially abusive of "their" women (Goodwin, 2019).

What's Love Got to Do with It (1993), the biopic about musician Tina Turner and her abusive husband Ike was important because it showed how abuse can and does happen even to famous people. Angela Bassett received Oscar nomination for her depiction of Tina and Lawrence Fishburn received one for playing Ike. Some expressed concern, however, that in a society where there remain too many negative depictions of people of color, the graphic showing of Ike shoving cake down Tina's throat while a White woman watched on in horror might further negative stereotypes (Shoos, 2003). Tina first broke the silence about Ike's abuse in 1981, telling People magazine that she was "insanely afraid of that man." She reported that Ike made her watch a live sex show at a brothel on their wedding night, beat her while she was pregnant, hit her with a coat hanger, and threw scalding coffee at her. Tina said that in 1968 she tried to take her own life. Ike always denied that he was abusive and claimed that Tina and the media had demonized him. He died in 2007. Lenore Walker, director of the US Domestic Violence Institute, explained,

> In 1981 we were just learning about the extent of domestic violence in homes. It was often thought to be only poor women without resources who were abused. When Tina Turner spoke out about her life, it brought awareness to the fact that domestic violence was everywhere.

She asserted that Tina's courage to share her story helped many others.

> Women were not believed when they spoke out about domestic violence, so when Tina Turner, a well-respected and famous singer, spoke out, it gave other women the courage to do so, also. We needed 'influencers' such as Tina Turner to speak out about domestic violence, so that my work on battered woman syndrome was introduced in the courts, and juries began to believe women acted to protect themselves and their children. (Bushby, 2023)

Another movie that depicts a real-life situation is I, *Tonya*, about figure skater Tonya Harding (played by Margot Robbie) While the focus on

Harding has for long been about the attack she coordinated on Olympic competitor Nancy Kerrigan, Harding was a victim of abuse. Harding was first abused by her mother LaVona Golden (played by Allison Janney, then her exhusband, Jeff Gillooly. Harding claims that not a week went by without her getting beat when she was a child. There's a scene in the film showing LaVona throwing a steak knife at young Tonya, although LaVona claims that never happened (ABC News, 2018). The film also highlights the point that not all victims are "likeable." Harding behaves horribly, but that does not dismiss the fact that she was a victim and never really received help for it. She claims that police generally did not believe her because of who she was (University of Oregon School of Law, n.d.).

Some books for adults, as well as their film adaptations, depict troubling images of abusers and victims. For example, Bonomi et al. (2013) conducted a content analysis of the *50 Shades of Gray* trilogy. Their findings were concerning, as it is clear that the main male character Christian (played by Jamie Dornan in the film) was emotionally abusive to Anastasia (Dakota Johnson in the film). Christian also stalked, isolated, intimidated, and humiliated Anastasia. What was presented as sexy often met the legal definition of sexual violence (Finley, 2017). Advocates were deeply troubled by the series and used the hashtag #50dollarsnot50shades to try to garner support for domestic violence resources rather than for a movie that glorifies abuse (Child, 2015).

Many people love the 2002 film *Enough* starring Jennifer Lopez as abused victim Slim. It does nicely show how sometimes victims tell loved ones about abuse only to be dismissed. Slim tells her mother-in-law about it, and she asked what Slim did to "set him off." As is often the case, the abuse escalates after Mitch (Billy Campbell) finds out she told. However, there are many problems with this film. While it accurately depicts the fact that abusers can be relentless in their pursuit to control their victims, the "answer," according to the film, is for Slim to train in martial arts, lie in wait, and physically confront her husband then kill him. While victims might need to sometimes fight back, this show disingenuously makes it look like women who simply train enough are able to "fix" their abusers. As Shoos (cited in Metz, 2018) explained, "as any kind of real-life solution, this is totally fantastical and in fact dangerous; women who confront their abusers typically are attacked and killed themselves."

The 1991 film *Sleeping with the Enemy*, which starred Julia Roberts as Laura Burney, is another film that some have taken issue with. The film is based on Nancy Price's 1987 novel, also called Sleeping with the Enemy. Her husband Martin (Patrick Bergin) is a successful businessman who is also emotionally, physically, and sexually abusive. While it shows the cycle of violence and the escalation of abuse, Laura's decision to fake her own death is unlikely and extreme. Both of these films do, though emphasize the lack of resources available to victims. Diane Shoos, author of *Domestic Violence in Hollywood Film: Gaslighting*, asserted

> Most of these films acknowledge that there are shelters, hotlines and personal protection orders, but then make a point of showing that these resources are not only inadequate, they are total failures. This throws everything back onto the woman's shoulders. She is completely isolated, and then the narrative drives toward a confrontation between her and her abuser.

Although there definitely are many middle- and upper-class victims, Shoos (in Sidortzova, 2018) asserts that Hollywood tends to overrepresent them. This can be dangerous in that they often have more resources to escape, which can reinforce the belief that easy escape from abusers is a reality for all victims.

> One of the big absences is the lack of any attention to abuse suffered by poor women and women of color. We don't take into account enough how race, class, education and other factors intersect when it comes to domestic violence. For example, the way in which an abuser might act out—his strategies—are very different depending on his social identity and situation.

Even though it is the oldest film on her list as it came out in 1944, Shoos (in Sidortzova, 2018) says *Gaslight* does the best job of portraying psychological abuse. This film is where the term derives from. It tells the story of Paula (Ingrid Bergman), who is newly married to Gregory (Charles Boyer). He makes her repeatedly question her sanity doing such things as dimming the gaslights in their home and making her question whether it is real. "We should absolutely be concerned about physical violence, but that isn't the primary form of abuse. Often, long after physical abuse may have stopped, the control that abusers exert over women may still be present."

The horror genre is replete with examples of domestic abuse. Johnson (2025) refers to some of these films as a subgenre, domestic horror. Films in this subgenre take place largely in a confined space like a home, with a female protagonist whose freedom has been restricted. They involve at least one male antagonist in the same dwelling who cannot be easily removed. Further, domestic horror films feature the infliction of violence against female protagonists that centers on sex, reproduction, and/or children. Finally, movies in this subgenre are either implicitly or explicitly connected to legal conflicts related to women's rights. She has asserted that there are several horror films that helped raise awareness about domestic violence, which in turn helped promote legislative changes and increase services for victims. Johnson argues that as a genre, horror is

> …one of the most acutely participatory art forms out there: By design, horror triggers a physiological response in a reader or viewer. Even though we know

> we are merely witnessing events on the screen or page, we *feel* endangered, we *feel* like we're right there with the horror protagonists. (p. 3)

Further, Johnson (2025) maintained that violence against women is typical of horror in general, citing the famous quote by Director Alfred Hitchcock that the crucial thing in making horror movies was to "torture the women!" (p. 4). Yet she also notes that

> ...horror also has a deep and enduring relationship with American feminism. In fact, American feminism and American horror have been—for more than half a century—allies on issues of domestic abuse, reproductive control, and women's restricted rights relative to men. (p. 5)

Instead of fetishizing abuse and suffering, these films

> *humanize* it, make it palpable, exportable to the viewers' own minds and bodies. They invite viewers into the lived, embodied experiences of abuse women; women barred from power, barred from speaking for themselves, barred from defending themselves; women who aren't taken seriously by the people from whom they sought aid—doctors, police, lawyers, psychiatrists, husbands, coworkers. (Johnson, 2025, p. 9)

One classic horror film that depicts domestic violence as well as child abuse is *The Shining*. Even the movie posters show a terrified Shelley Duval, who plays Wendy Torrance, her mouth open in a scream behind a bathroom door while her husband Jack (Jack Nicholson) crazily tries to smash through it with an ax. The couple and their son Danny (Danny Lloyd) have moved into the isolated Overlook Hotel, where Jack will be the winter caretaker and will have time to focus on his passion–writing. Wendy is dubious because they will be alone in the hotel, which turns out to have a very dark past. A snowstorm makes the isolation even worse and presents a major barrier for Wendy and Danny to flee Jack as he descends into madness and becomes increasingly abusive.

At one point Wendy takes Danny to a doctor because he has had some type of seizure and she reveals that previously drunk Jack had dislocated Danny's shoulder. Jack first becomes verbally abusive to Wendy, shouting at her and mocking her. He gaslights her when she tells him she thinks there is something wrong with the place, even though it is him that is losing his mind. As Jack's mental state worsens, he begins conversing with Delbert Grady, who was a previous caretaker at Overlook who murdered his wife and children there. Grady tells Jack that Danny is "very naughty" and needs "correction." By this, he is referring to physical abuse if not murder, like he did. When Wendy finally confronts Jack, he refers to her as "Wendy, darling, light of my life!" before saying he won't hurt her then declaring "I'm just going to bash your brains in." Wendy hits Jack with a bat and while he is unconscious tries to flee but finds out that Jack has sabotaged their snowcat, the only vehicle available to get them down the mountain in the blizzard conditions. This type of sabotage of a vehicle is a common tactic abusers use so that their victims cannot escape. When Jack comes to, Grady tells him he needs to "deal with this matter in the harshest possible way," to which he responds, "There's nothing I look forward to with greater pleasure." This obviously means he intends to kill Wendy and Danny, which precipitates the scene with the ax. Miraculously the two escape and Jack freezes to death.

The Color Purple's description of the abuse faced by Celie, first by her dad and then her husband Albert "Mister" Johnson, was deeply disturbing to readers when Alice Walker's 1982 book was released. Celie is poor and has no financial means of her own to leave the verbally, physically, and sexually abusive Mister. She faces the double discrimination of race and gender (Lewis, 2017). Further, Mister has isolated Celie to the point that she sees almost no one, especially her sister Nettie, who is in Africa. Celie does not know that Nettie is even alive, since Mister keeps all the letter Nettie sent her. Other female characters in the book (and later film) face violence and discrimination due to their race and gender, including Sophia and Squeak. Lewis (2017, p. 9) explained,

> Celie's status as an African American woman determines her willingness to come forward about her abuse. Early 20th century society has deemed her less than human because of her combined gender and race. Societal constructs create Celie's low self-confidence and tendency to direct her blame inward, which is shown through her decision to confess her abuse only through letters to God.

The first film adaptation of it in 1985 starring Whoopi Goldberg as Celie and Danny Glover as Mister was equally disturbing. Some Black advocacy organizations called for a boycott of it, asserting that it fueled negative perceptions of Black men (Evans, 2023). The 2023 film starred Fantasia Barrino as Celie and Colman Domingo as Mister. Evans (2023) asserted that both films are important vehicles to talk about the overrepresentation of Black women as victims of domestic violence.

Another film that some see as problematic is *It Ends with Us*, the screen adaptation released in 2024 of Colleen Hoover's book with the same title. As of June 2025, the book had sold 20 million copies and it had more than one billion tags on TikTok. The film was also a box office success (Rufo, 2025).

Critics have contended that trailers for the film, which features Blake Lively as Lily Bloom, a victim of horrible abuse from her husband Ryle Kincaid (Justin Baldoni, who also directed the film), make it seem lighthearted and romantic. On the press tour, Lively showed up in floral outfits, and the press was told to keep questions "fun and light-hearted." A domestic violence survivor explained, that they were promoting the film like it was "the sequel to Barbie" (Rufo, 2025). One domestic violence advocate explained, "When we use trauma as entertainment, it can feel really exploitative, and just irresponsible, and, in many ways, tone-deaf to the actual issue" (Wise, 2024). Others have criticized that the book and film have been categorized as "romances," which might normalize the abuse that is portrayed. Fans were really upset when the book's publisher, Atria, announced its intent to release a coloring book to go with the novel. They immediately pulled it (McNeal, 2024).

There was also significant controversy about the climate on the film set. Lively accused Baldoni of sexual harassment and starting a smear campaign against her. She filed a legal suit, which Baldoni countered. His was dismissed in June 2025. Lively's suit also named Baldoni's production company, Wayfarer Studios, and alleged that he and Wayfarer CEO Jamie Heath engaged in repeated sexual harassment and other disturbing behavior. According to the filing, other female castmates and crew members had similar experiences. Further, it says that Lively, Baldoni, and other involved with the production of the film held a meeting, which her husband Ryan Reynolds attended, to address the hostile work environment. Allegedly Baldoni and Heath agreed to several terms, including to refrain from "descriptions of their own genitalia," to hire an intimacy coordinator to be used at all times when Lively was on set, and not to allow any visitors or friends of either of the men to be on set during scenes in which Lively was in a state of nudity. Many female celebrities stood with Lively, and the organization Vital Voices rescinded a women's solidarity award that Baldoni was scheduled to receive. On December 31, 2024, Baldoni sued the New York Times for libel, which was dismissed in June 2025 (Rufo, 2025).

Yet, the film, and even more, the book, highlight some important concepts. One is that Lily grew up with an abusive father and then finds herself in an abusive relationship. As has been noted throughout this book, this cycle of violence is all too common. Further, Ryle's abusive behavior is a slow escalation, and is often justified through Lily's eyes as a child survivor. He gradually becomes more controlling, and as he does, she reconnects with Atlas (Brandon Sklenar), a young man she befriended and fell in love with when she was young who is also a survivor of deep family trauma. Ryle becomes increasingly jealous and violent the more Lily reaches out to Atlas, eventually attempting to rape her. Lily gets pregnant but, despite Ryle's promises to improve, divorces him so that the cycle of violence ends with her and her child. Hoover has said she wrote the book based on her own experience growing up with a father who was abusive to her mother. Baldoni has been outspoken about wanting the film to change how people see domestic violence, while Lively has said "This is a story that covers domestic violence but isn't about domestic violence" (McNeal, 2024).

A Vigilante stars Olivia Wilde as Sadie, who tries to help victims of domestic violence escape their abusers. Sadie fled her own abusive husband and now hunts down other abusers to exact revenge. Wilde said about the film,

"I think this film can be seen as an allegory for fighting the patriarchy. It's about the abuse of power. And what we're sensing right now is we've had enough of that" (Waxman, 2018). Wilde has been applauded for her raw and nuanced approach to her character. While she is avenging, she is also still struggling from enduring her own abuse and in specific moments, barely holds it together. Director Sarah Daggar-Nickson has also been praised for the script, which tackles women's anger, of course, but it's most concerned with their pain, and how that affects their healing process. And most significantly, it explores that trauma in a way that feels mostly divorced from the men who inflict it" (Cohen, 2019).

Fewer films focus on dating violence. One that does is the 1996 thriller *Fear*, which starred Reese Witherspoon as Nicole Walker and Mark Wahlberg as David McCall. It is not long into their relationship that David shows his true colors, prompting Nicole to break up with him. While David's actions are really extreme, the film highlights the escalation that often occurs after victims say they are leaving the relationship. As well, David attacks the family pet, which not uncommon.

Another older movie that focuses on dating violence is *No One Would Tell* (1996). Made for the Hallmark Channel, this film stars Candace Cameron Bure as Stacy Collins, who begins dating Bobby Tennison (Fred Savage), an attractive and popular boy at her school. Like most abusive relationships, things begin with Bobby's controlling behaviors and escalate to verbal and physical abuse. Given its platform, the film does not show any graphic violence but it is definitely implicit. No One Would Tell also nicely shows the emotional rollercoaster Stacy is on, as Bobby is sometimes sweet and repentant and other times vicious. Another important thing that the film underscores is that people who were in a position to help Stacy did not do so. This includes people who strongly suspect what is going on as well as those who are certain that abuse is happening.

USING MUSIC TO TEACH ABOUT DATING AND DOMESTIC VIOLENCE

Music is another genre of popular culture that can help prompt discuss about dating and domestic violence. The Dixie Chicks' "Goodbye Earl" accurately describes how many victims try to hide the abuse by covering bruises with clothing or makeup. Yet it was controversial for emphasizing that Wanda's only alternative was to kill Earl. This is similar to Martina McBride's "Independence Day," which also makes it seem like killing the abuser (in this case, burning down the house) is the only option. Christina Aguilera's "Fighter" describes how she was lied to and abused but came out with the strength to leave the abusive relationship. Kelly Clarkson's "Since U Been Gone" tells how she can breathe for the first time after she left her abuser.

Lauryn Hill's "I Get Out" offers a similar refrain, calling out her abuser for using her, victimizing her, then guilt tripping her as if it was her fault.

Hozier's "Cherry Wine" offers an important glimpse into a case in which the abuser is a woman. The music video that accompanies it, with Saoirse Ronan playing the woman, concludes with the hashtag #FaceUpToDomesticViolence.

Some songs are from the perspective of child witnesses to abuse. For example, Christina Aguilera's "Oh Mother" is written from the perspective of a daughter who eventually thanks her mother for leaving their abusive father. She chose to do that when her husband began also abusing the kids. As was discussed in Chapter Two, the correlation between child abuse and domestic violence is about 50%. Pink's "Family Portrait," also written from the child's view, describes the home as a war zone. Tracy Chapman's haunting acapella "Behind the Wall" focuses on how children see and hear more than we know, enduring sleepless nights and fear. The song also gets at the fact that oftentimes neighbors or others who suspect something is happening refuse to intervene. As well, it emphasizes that sometimes police dismiss domestic violence as an issue between "a man and a wife." The powerful refrain "the police always come late, if they come at all" is a testament to how many victims and their children feel. Suzanne Vega's "Luka" emphasizes that children often blame themselves for the abuse. Luka tries not to "talk too loud" for fear of exacerbating the abuse. He knows that the neighbors have seen and heard things but think it is none of their business so do nothing to help the victim or her hurting child. "Face Down" by Red Jumpsuit Apparatus focuses on the abuse that lead singer Ronnie Winter and his brother witnessed as children. Lyrics discuss watching mom cover up with makeup, hearing her tell herself it will never happen again, and swearing through tears that he loves you. The chorus interrogates how the abusive dad must feel, asking whether pushing around his partner makes him feel manly.

Even songs that are problematic can and should be addressed by educators. For example, Eminem and Rhianna's "Love the Way You Lie" describes abusive relationships as "stormy" and includes the refrain "I like the way it hurts." This implies something positive about these relationships and can reinforce the inaccurate notion that some people "like" abuse.

CONCLUSION: TEACHING IDEAS

Educators at many levels and in different disciplinary areas can use popular culture to teach about dating and domestic violence. As noted in the introduction to the chapter, seeing or reading about characters in fictional works can help students to develop empathy for victims in a way that presenting statistical information cannot. Reviewing the examples included herein and countless more can also enhance students' critical media literacy skills. The following is just a sample of teaching ideas for different age levels as well as disciplinary areas.

Lesson ideas can include reading/viewing/listening with book reports, reflective essays, presentations, visuals, and more. Simply reading out loud to elementary school students and discussing the key themes is an easy recommendation. Students can also be asked to write and illustrate their own book about kindness or write simple songs or poems about treating others with respect and disrupting bullying. Middle grade and more advanced students can study statistics and the characteristics of abuse and then "fact check" a particular example or set of examples for accuracy. Older students can also read the recommended novels and discuss them in a book club style. They can also be asked to research additional examples of domestic or dating violence in popular culture and write or present about what they "learned," both what is accurate and what is not.

For Peace and Conflict Studies folks, students at a young age can be introduced to restorative practices. Rooted in restorative justice, these are communication processes that are used to build strong relationships and communities, especially in cases in which there is some disruption or conflict. There are five core components of restorative practices, referred to as the "5 Rs': Relationship, respect, Responsibility, Repair, and Reintegration." While most often used as an alternative to exclusionary and negative disciplinary practices, educators can integrate the ideas of restorative justice by meeting with students in circles to discuss difficult topics in a safe and meaningful way. In such a way, restorative practices help to teach pro-social skills (Ferlazzo, 2024).

Students can be asked to consider the conflicts in the relationships they read about, viewed, or listened to and to think about how restorative practices might have resulted in different outcomes. They can re-write scenes or stories to reflect their understanding of the key components of restorative practices.

College students in Peace and Conflict studies would likely learn about restorative justice and restorative practices early in their careers. They could also apply their knowledge to consider the benefits and the challenges of using restorative practice in domestic and dating violence cases. A creative activity could be to ask students to write a short story or song in which the parties use nonviolent language, conflict resolution, and/or restorative practices in a relationship.

In Criminology classes like those that I teach, I often assign students to watch one of these films on their own and then apply criminological theories we have been studying. After studying domestic and dating violence, I would facilitate dialog about what the films get right and what they do not (much like what was presented in this chapter). We also discuss what is missing from these depictions based on what we know. As was mentioned in this chapter and others, women of color are overrepresented as abusers but underrepresented in Hollywood depictions. As well, there are very few depictions of males as victims or of LGBTQ victims.

In Social Work, students can consider how help-seeking is presented. Further, students can make recommendations about services that need to be enhanced or provided for different populations, based on what they reviewed in popular culture examples. Further, Social Work, Sociology, Criminology, and Political Science students can compare what is depicted in popular culture to the various human rights treaties described in the Introduction to assess to what degree the phenomenon of abuse is presented as a fundamental human right. They can also take what they read, view, and/or hear and use it to make policy recommendations.

Students in health and wellness classes can compare what they consume from popular culture to what they are taught about establishing healthy boundaries. They can also do research to assess the short and long-term effects of the abuse they see depicted.

Another idea is for students to explore cases in which celebrities have been abusers or victims. Many high profile actors, directors, and musicians have histories of domestic violence that has influenced their work. For example, Rihanna was a victim of abuse by former boyfriend Chris Brown. Johnson (2025) wrote about horror directors who abused women, including sometimes the actors in their films.

REFERENCES

ABC News. (2018, January 11). *Tonya Harding's mother says steak knife incident never happened, denies former Olympic skater's abuse allegations.* https://abcnews.go.com/US/tonya-hardings-mother-steak-knife-incident-happened-denies/story?id=52261073

Banks, S. (2008). Writing as theory: In defense of fiction. In J. Knowles & A. Cole (Eds.), *Handbook of the arts in qualitative research* (pp. 155–164). Sage.

Bannar, K. (2010). *The romanticism of teen dating violence: The Twilight series as a case study.* Honors thesis. American University. https://aura.american.edu/articles/educational_resource/The_Romanticism_of_Teen_Dating_Violence_The_Twilight_Series_as_a_Case_Study/23830134?file=41814114

Berns, N. (2004). *Framing the victim: Domestic violence, media and social problems.* Aldine de Gruyter.

Bernstein, A. (2019, June 17). War at home: How Big Little Lies deftly dissects domestic violence. *The Guardian.* https://www.theguardian.com/tv-and-radio/2019/jun/17/big-little-lies-domestic-violence

Bonomi, A., Altenburger, L., & Walton, N. (2013). Double crap! Abuse and harmed identity in *Fifty Shades of Grey. Journal of Women's Health, 22*(9), 733–744.

Brasson, B. (2025, July 10). Tracey Thurman vs. The System: The domestic violence case that shook the nation. *The Medium.* https://medium.com/@brandontbrasson/tracey-thurman-vs-the-system-the-domestic-violence-case-that-shook-the-nation-5a261d576c91

Bushby, H. (2023, May 25). How Tina Turner "broke the silence" on domestic abuse. *BBC.* https://www.bbc.com/news/entertainment-arts-65673196

Child, B. (2015, February 5). Domestic violence campaigners call for boycott of Fifty Shades of Grey film. *The Guardian.* https://www.theguardian.com/film/2015/feb/05/domestic-violence-campaigners-boycott-fifty-shades-of-grey-film

Chuba, K. (2019, July 16). "Euphoria" star on portraying abusive teen relationships, shooting that choking scene. *Hollywood Reporter.* https://www.hollywoodreporter.com/tv/tv-news/euphoria-star-portraying-abusive-teen-relationships-choking-scene-1224454/

Cohen, A. (2019, March 28). Olivia Wilde gives a brutally raw performance in A Vigilante. *Refinery.* https://www.refinery29.com/en-us/2019/03/228156/a-vigilante-movie-review-olivia-wilde-domestic-abuse

Collins, V., & Carmody, D. (2011). Deadly love: Images of dating violence in the "Twilight Saga". *Feminist Inquiry in Social Work, 26*(4), 382–394.

Evans, M. (2023, December 26). For all of its joy, "The Color Purple" is also a chance to talk about Black women and intimate partner violence. *Los Angeles Times.* https://www.latimes.com/entertainment-arts/story/2023-12-26/for-all-of-its-joy-the-color-purple-is-a-chance-to-also-talk-about-black-women-and-intimate-partner-violence

Ferlazzo, L. (2024, February 27). What do restorative practices look like in schools? *Education Week.* https://www.edweek.org/leadership/opinion-what-do-restorative-practices-look-like-in-schools/2024/02

Finley, L. (2016). *Domestic abuse and sexual assault in popular culture.* Praeger.

Finley, L. (2017). Examining the depiction of domestic violence in popular adult fiction: A review of six novels. *Factis Pax, 11*(1), 1–27.

Finley, L. (2024). Using popular culture to teach about domestic abuse and healthy relationships. In L. Finley (Ed.), *Teaching peace through popular culture* (2nd ed., pp. 85–102). Information Age.

Germaine, D. (1989). Author Oates tells where she's been, where she's going. In L. Milazzo (Ed.), *Conversations with Joyce Carol Oates.* University of Mississippi Press.

Goodwin, M. (2019, May 29). Abusing religion: Race, Islam, and not without my daughter. *The Revealer.* https://therevealer.org/abusing-religion-race-islam-and-not-without-my-daughter/

Hawkins, P. (2016). *The girl on the train.* Thorndike Press.

Johnson, E. (2025). *Scream with me: Horror films and the rise of American feminism (1968–1980).* Atria Books.

Kippert, A. (2021, December 15). Netflix's "Maid" highlights truth about domestic violence. *Domestic Shelters.* https://www.domesticshelters.org/articles/identifying-abuse/netflix-s-maid-highlights-truth-about-domestic-violence

Land, S. (2019). *Maid: Hard work, low pay, and a mother's will to survive.* Hachette Books.

Lewis, J. (2017). Gender, race, and violence: A critical examination of trauma in The Color Purple. *Sacred Heart University Scholar, 1*(1), 1–38.

Malone, P. (2005, October 21). *Yaklich released to halfway house.* The Pueblo Chieftan. https://www.chieftain.com/story/news/2005/10/21/yaklich-released-to-halfway-house/8649668007/

McDaniel, D. (2013). *Representations of partner violence in young adult literature: Dating violence in Stephenie Meyer's Twilight saga* (Doctoral dissertation). University of Texas, Austin, Texas.

McNeal, S. (2024, August 9). What is going on with the It Ends With Us Controversy?. *Glamour.* https://www.glamour.com/story/how-do-you-solve-a-problem-like-it-ends-with-us

O'Neal, L. (2022, December 29). "I'm the evidence": Anna Kendrick opens up about the abuse that shaped her new film. *Los Angeles Times.* https://www.latimes.com/entertainment-arts/movies/story/2022-12-29/anna-kendrick-alice-darling-emotional-abuse

Police Family Violence Fact Sheet. (2013). National Center for Women & Policing. http://womenandpolicing.com/violencefs.asp

Rufo, Y. (2025, June 10). Blake Lively and Justin Baldoni: What you need to know. *BBC.* https://www.bbc.com/news/articles/cewxj0qw2p9o

Shoos, D. (2003). Representing domestic violence: Ambivalence and difference in What's Love Got to Do With It? *NWSA Journal, 15*(2), 57–77.

Sidortzova, S. (2018, March 3). *Big little representations: How Hollywood shapes our views of domestic violence.* Michigan Tech University. https://www.mtu.edu/news/2018/03/big-little-representations-how-hollywood-shapes-our-views-of-domestic-violence.html

University of Oregon School of Law. (n.d.). *An interview with Tonya Harding.* https://law.uoregon.edu/news/tonya-harding-interview

Waxman, S. (2018, March 10). Olivia Wilde on "fighting the patriarchy" and directing her first movie. *The Wrap.* https://www.thewrap.com/olivia-wilde-on-fighting-patriarchy-and-directing-her-first-movie-video/

Wise, A. (2024, August 28). The movie "It Ends With Us" faces criticism for glamorizing domestic violence. *NPR.* https://www.npr.org/2024/08/28/nx-s1-5088075/movie-it-ends-with-us-faces-criticism-glamorizing-abuse

Zani, T. (2022, August 1). Psychological aspects in the novel: "The girl on the train" and gaslighting as a form of abuse. *The Medium.* https://medium.com/@tatsherm/psychological-aspects-in-the-film-the-girl-on-the-train-and-gaslighting-as-a-form-of-abuse-fbbe9be61c3b

CHAPTER 8

SCHOOL-CAMPUS PARTNERSHIPS

ABSTRACT

In Chapter 8 the focus is on how to build school/campus-community partnerships to address abuse and to educate students and the broader public. In doing so I provide a case study of the College Brides Walk, an initiative that has been held in South Florida since 2011. The emphasis is on holistic campaigns that integrate community partners, allow students opportunities for service-learning, and engage not just women and girls but men and boys as well.

Keywords: Experiential learning; service-learning; engaging men; multimedia; brides March; clothesline project

INTRODUCTION

Research shows that students need safe and inclusive spaces on school and campus grounds, especially those who have been victims of abuse. Trauma-informed policies, practices, and training are essential to meeting the needs of survivors but also to creating spaces in which abuse is not tolerated. Considering not just risk factors but also individual and systemic strengths—including community partnerships—can help ensure that schools and campuses meet the safety needs of students, faculty, and staff (Gezinski et al., 2025). Often, students are not aware of local resources for many reasons, including being new to the area or not feeling as though they need to

Teaching and Making Peace in Every Relationship, pages 163–175

doi:10.1108/978-1-80686-961-920261009

access them. Bringing community partners to school and campus educational efforts not only allows students to know about resources for support but also can invite them to engage in advocacy and activism.

BIRTH OF THE COLLEGE BRIDES WALK (CBW)

In an earlier chapter, I discussed the tragic murder of Gladys Ricart by her abusive exboyfriend. While the case is horrific, one good thing that came out of it was the first Brides March and subsequently, the college brides walk (CBW).

Myhosi "Josie" Ashton is a survivor of dating violence who, at the time she heard about the murder, had worked in domestic violence advocacy and was completing a criminal justice degree at Florida International University. Ashton did not know Ricart but was outraged not only at what happened, but that media coverage often seemed to blame the victim and justify the behavior of the abuser.

Ashton pondered what she could do to help. As a person of deep faith, she has said that she had a vision of herself walking in public, wearing a wedding gown in honor of Gladys. This, she thought, would prompt people to ask her questions and thus allow her the opportunity to break the silence about domestic violence. She contacted the Ricart family and they gave her their blessing. On September 26, 2001, the anniversary of Ricart's death, Ashton walked 1,600 miles from Ridgefield, New Jersey (where the murder happened) to Miami, earning internship credit from Florida International University (FIU). Ashton collaborated with several New York City organizations, including the Dominican Women's Development Center, the Violence Intervention Program, the Northern Manhattan Improvement Corporation, the Dominican Women's Caucus and the National Latino Alliance for the Elimination of Domestic Violence, helped Josie organize the first March, which served as a sendoff for her 1,600-mile journey. The family and friends of Gladys also joined her on the first leg of her walk from Gladys's home in New Jersey to the Church in Queens were Gladys was to marry that September 26, 1999. She stayed in 14 domestic violence shelters and visited 22 cities, facilitating dialog about abuse as she went along. September 2025 saw the 25th Annual Gladys Ricart and Victims of Domestic Violence Memorial Walk, also known as the Brides March, in New York City. Marches have also taken place in Miami, FL., Lawrence, MA, Newburgh, NY, and Milwaukee, WI. In 2003 actress, Salma Hayek, in collaboration with Marie Claire Magazine, held a March in Washington, DC. In 2005 actor, author and child survivor of domestic violence, Victor Rivers participated in the New York City March (History, n.d.).

I met Josie at an event at Florida Atlantic University's (FAU) Davie campus in 2010. We were both there to share our work on domestic and dating violence. I was working with a nonprofit organization that helps victims called No More Tears and had previously worked with another Broward County, Florida agency, Women In Distress. My primary work with both was to educate. After listening to each other's presentations, Josie and I became friends and started to brainstorm how we could bring the idea of the Brides March to college students, given that I worked on a campus and she had a daughter at the time who was a high school junior. We are both well aware of the unique risk that college students face regarding dating violence, as was discussed in Chapter Two.

Further, we were concerned that college students were not getting much, if any, information about dating and domestic violence. While some colleges offer courses on gender-based violence, this varies tremendously depending on the school and what a student may major in or elect to take. Often, the only university-wide educational efforts occur during first-year orientation or as one-off lectures or events. While orientation might reach most students, coverage of these issues is still minimal and often delivered via passive, noninteractive lectures. Oftentimes, these events are required for student-athletes or fraternity or sorority members but not for other students (Finley, 2013). As Finley (2013) expressed,

> ...one-time events are far from adequate to change perceptions and beliefs, let alone to challenge the social norms that underlie abuse. Domestic violence is a complex issue that involves patriarchal social norms, gender expectations, intersecting inequalities, and legal, policy, and advocacy implications. One-off events or event short academic units simply cannot address the issue thoroughly. And, importantly, such cursory attempts fail to inspire students to take action to help end abuse. (pp. 110–111)

Finley (2013) explained that campuses need to draw on literature on peace education and human rights education to create transformative, holistic domestic violence awareness that tap into multiple ways of learning and are cross-disciplinary. Disciplines that are or can be involved include but are not limited to communications, public relations, marketing and business students, along with medical, nursing, psychology, sociology, social work, political science, education and other disciplines can and should be involved. "Further, such a program should integrate opportunities for students to design projects, to take action to serve their communities, and to share what they have learned through peer education initiatives" (Finley, 2013, p. 73).

Year One

When we began planning the CBW, we knew that we could do something at my campus but wanted to retain the visible component of the Brides March rather than simply have an event on campus. As well, we wanted to include other South Florida campuses, if possible. We began by asking the friends who had invited us to speak at FAU to help us plan. We also added a counselor at Barry and some colleagues at Nova Southeastern University. The initial idea was to walk from Barry University's campus in Miami Shores, Florida all the way to FAU's Davie campus. We soon abandoned that lengthy walk, given how long it would take, how unlikely college students would want to participate, and the difficulty of getting permits across county lines. We figured it would be best to stay in Miami Dade County and have our Broward County friends bring students to the event. We then found a contact at FIU's Biscayne Campus, which is, roundtrip of about 7.5 miles. We thought that might be doable, so set about getting permits to walk there, including accompaniment by police for safety purposes. The plan was to stop at FIU for a short break and program, and then walk back to Barry.

We also knew that we wanted to do more than just walk, we wanted the opportunity to share information about dating and domestic violence. We arranged to have an opening session in a large conference room at Barry in which we each spoke, our university president (at the time, Sister Linda Bevilaqua) spoke, and a survivor shared her story. After the walk, we fed everyone dinner. In all, the event lasted several hours.

We learned many things from that first effort, which was held in February 2011! First, the event was better attended than we had hoped. Some 300 people participated in the Opening, overflowing the room that we had reserved. One reason that attendance was good was that I teach two sections of a course that requires students to complete service-learning hours Society and Social Justice (SOC 200). I offered this as an option and it appealed to many of the students, as they could earn almost all of their hours on that day.

According to the National Service-learning Clearinghouse (2013), "Service-learning is a teaching and learning strategy that integrates meaningful community service with instruction and reflection to enrich the learning experience, teach civic responsibility, and strengthen communities." The goal is to bring together academic expertise with experiential learning, helping to enhance learning, create new ways of viewing the world, and help communities. Service learning allows students to make connections to one another, to develop a sense of empathy and pride, to enhance their critical thinking and writing skills, enhance their leadership skills, to make better connections between theory and practice, improve their interest in their coursework, develop stronger connections to faculty, and to see themselves as part of both the campus and community (Alberle-Grasse, 2000; Koliba 2000; Kuh, 1995; Parker-Gwinn, 1996; Roschelle et al., 2000). Additionally, research supports that students who participate in service learning related to domestic violence or other social issues may be more likely to enter careers in the nonprofit sector and advocacy organizations

(Alberle-Grasse, 2000). Religious-based institutions that include social justice in their missions, as is the case of Barry University, are particularly well-suited for this type of service learning (Roschelle et al., 2000).

The coupling of this initiative with the service-learning requirement for SOC 200 and other courses was and continues to bee helpful in increasing attendance but also in allowing attendees to see the real connections to their coursework and community. Part of the appeal is that it is on campus and the hours can occur over one or two weeks, making it easier for students without transportation or with challenging schedules to satisfy their service-learning requirement.

Approximately 100 people completed the actual walk in year one. Another thing we learned was that the walk was still way too long! Several students could not make the entire walk. We were grateful for the police, who served as a "sag wagon" to pick up those who were unable to finish and transport them back to campus. We had encouraged students to wear bridal gowns or formal attire, if they had it, or white if not. Unfortunately, we had not emphasized wearing tennis shoes so several students attempted the walk in heels!

We also found that we wanted to do even more with the education piece. Even though the 0pening was well-received, we wanted to incorporate other ways to teach attendees about dating and domestic violence. We began to brainstorm how else we could do that.

Year Three and Beyond

The next year, we decided to offer educational workshops during the walk, for those who either could not or did not want to participate in that component. We also decided to walk into the main part of town and have the midway point be outside of City Hall. The Mayor spoke and offered refreshments before the walkers headed back. In addition, we created some passive educational exhibits in the form of yard signs that contained photos of victims who had lost their lives to domestic violence along with a one sentence description of what happened. We placed these all along the walkways on campus so that even those not involved in the event could read and learn from them. Further, we began hosting a "clothesline project." This project was started in Cape Cod, Massachusetts in 1990 as a way for survivors to show one another support. People would decorate t-shirts with messages of tribute, hope, and solidarity and hang them from a clothesline. The choice of the clothesline is that historically it might be while hanging out the laundry that women met and got to talk with one another. Clothesline Projects have spread worldwide and have been supported by research on its ability to reach students emotionally. Cheek et al. (2007) found the Clothesline Project to be a positive learning experience for social work students (Finley, 2013).

We had students paint t-shirts and hung them on clothesline around campus as another passive visual display. Building on the previous year, we held an Opening Session with speakers and featured a Powerpoint presentation and moment of silence for the victims we had researched for the signs. Since the walk was shorter the event was shorter and we decided to start in the morning, so instead of dinner we fed everyone lunch. Year two was even more well-attended than year one! Despite heavy rain, close to 400 people attended the event in year two (2012).

One of our speakers was really impactful. She is the mother of a young man who was murdered with his female friend by her exboyfriend while they attended a Florida university. The pair had contacted police many times to report that the exboyfriend was stalking them but the police took no action. She spearheaded the effort to pass dating violence legislation in Florida. Another speaker focused on the connection between animal abuse and domestic violence and shared her advocacy to get the local shelter to coordinate help for the pets of abuse victims. One of the students who had attended in year one decided to coordinate a mid-walk tribute to persons who had been lost to violence. He grew up in an abusive home and had recently lost a close friend to violence, so he held a ballon release where attendees could write something to the person that they had lost before releasing the balloons (We have since learned that this is terrible for the environment so never did it again, but were impressed with the young man's desire to pay tribute to victims).

In year three we were able to get Grammy-nominated Latin artist Elain, an ambassador for the United Nation's UNiTE program, to performed at the opening event in front of powerpoint slideshow featuring pictures of those who had lost their lives to domestic violence in the last year. This was very emotional and shows the importance, as Lin (2006), Noddings (n.d.) and others have explained, of stimulating emotional responses and develop attendees' sense of caring, love and justice. Once again, our attendance grew, with year three (2013) host to more than 450 people and some 200 walkers, again despite rainy weather.

Over the years we have kept essentially the same model and added elements. For some years we were able to get some high school mentoring groups to attend, so by year eight had more than 1,200 attendees. We also integrated music, vocal performances, and dance performances in the opening so as to reach people in different ways. We've added other visual displays around campus and in some years included smaller events leading up to the CBW. In addition to the high school connections, we also continued to develop connections to other area colleges and universities, community organization, and clubs and organizations on campus (Finley, 2018). We partner with at least 10 different campus units or groups annually as well as, depending on the year, five or more community partners.

Another way that we tried to reach people was to ensure that there were "fun" elements. In 2012 and again in 2013, the university hosted a Zumba event to raise awareness. Zumba, a dance-based exercise class, originated in South Florida and is widely popular. Some 100 people attended the Zumba classes each year. While everyone had a good time and a good work out, we also placed information about abuse around the room and during breaks, and organizers shared more information about the issue and about local services as the event opened, midway through, and in closing.

The visuals we use have been a really important part of "passive" programming. Each year, organizers and/or students research domestic or dating violence homicides. We find an image of the victim(s) and then write a one-sentence summary of what happened. These we compile into a PowerPoint that runs as attendees arrive to the opening, allowing people the emotional experience of processing the worst case scenario—a fatality. We make note of important things for them to observe, such as the fact that women are more often killed by abusers, that sometimes there are multiple victims (for instance, an abuser kills his entire family), that abuse happens in same-sex relationships, that murder-suicides occur frequently, and that police officers responding to abuse can be killed in the line of duty). We also had some funding in the first few years to make yard signs out of these, which we display across campus in visible spaces. This allows people who are not participating to still learn about the abuse, and every year many people stop to read the signs. Although we no longer have funding to produce them in that form, we still print the new signs we add every year and hang them in visible areas.

Another thing we did via the CBW was to initiate a domestic violence peer education program titled peace in every relationship. With funding from an Avon Foundation grant, we started in 2011–2012, training graduate counseling students to present to college and high school youth about dating and domestic violence. We utilized a bystander intervention approach (as was described in the previous chapter) to empower attendees to see themselves as capable and to be willing to intervene to stop abuse. In 2012–2013, we received a grant from the City of North Miami to further support PIER although since then have been unable to fund the program.

In addition to reaching students, faculty, and staff, the CBW helps reach the community in various ways. One is that community members are invited. Since we hold it on a Friday in order to accommodate our students, we know that many cannot miss work to attend. But every year we do get some community members there, many who are survivors. We also reach the community through the visibility of the walk. Most people read the signs we carry as we walk and honk or yell out messages of support.

Another advancement is collaborating with campus-community efforts to address sexual violence. As previous chapters have explained, sexual violence often occurs within dating relationships. For several years, Barry University's campus has held a "Take Back the Night (TBTN)" event for Sexual Assault Awareness Month in April. This is coordinated by the office of Campus Recreation, Health, and Wellness. Coupling these events allows us to have a coordinated campaign about gender-based violence and both are great inspiration for continued activism. TBTN is the oldest worldwide movement against sexual assault, including when it occurs within intimate relationships. It began in Belgium in the 1970s and today reaches millions.

As the previous chapter explained, I have been dubious about self-defense training as a way to address abuse. However, having been inspired by Strong's (2025) book discussed in Chapter Seven, in 2026 we will be offering a feminist-based self-defense training for attendees. This is part of our collaboration with Campus Recreation, Health, and Wellness.

As noted, CBW always includes speakers during the opening and we typically change them each year. At least one speaker is a survivor who tells his or her story. If possible, we try to get a student, faculty or staff member, or alumni from the university or one of the partner universities to make it even more relevant to attendees. Some years we are unable to, as some people we find are not yet comfortable publicly sharing their stories. Last year, a student who had transferred to the university the previous term heard about the event from friends and contacted me to see how she could get involved. She had recently left an abusive relationship with a female and was still waiting for a court hearing after a violent physical attack. She was tremendously moving and we applaud her courage in sharing something so difficult that was still really raw.

Once we added the workshops, which we have also moved to after the walk so that walkers can also participate, we have tried to offer them on an array of topics. I personally have led some sessions, for instance one of race, ethnicity, religion and abuse and another specifically on guns and domestic violence. We have had two different community partners (Essential Haus and Pridelines) focus on domestic violence and LGBTQIA+ individuals. We have had other community partners focus on services they provide, such as those provided by domestic violence shelter Women in Distress and Miami's Coordinated Victim's Assistance Center. We are planning for the upcoming year a collaboration with another community partner that works on addressing abuse involving migrant workers. The coalition of immokalee workers works on fair wages and treatment of agricultural workers, many of whom are migrants. Sexual harassment, sexual assault, domestic violence, and trafficking are all too common for workers in the fields. This will also help serve as a vehicle to discuss domestic violence and immigrants more broadly.

Because we know that attendees are reached in many different ways, we always make sure to include music in the opening session. Sometimes we have live performers, like Elain in year three. For several years we have had the local folk duo Piper and Nightingale perform live. Their performances include singing, ukelele, and flute. The duo selects songs that are relevant to gender inequality, abuse, and female empowerment, and in some years has performed songs that Laura Sue Wilansky (Nightingale in the duo) wrote. Some examples of songs that Piper and Nightingale have performed are Lady Gaga's "Until it Happens to You" and a reworking of Stone Temple Pilots' "Sour Girl." We also typically include a live dance performance to a relevant song, performed by Barry's Repertoire Dance Troupe.

In other years, we have utilized music videos of songs that connect to the issue. One video we showed was in 2017, not long after the Women's Marches that were held all around the world in protest of the election of Donald Trump as President. We showed the spoken word poem that Halsey performed at the New York Women's March. It is a powerful testament about the frequency of abuse women endure, the fact that many do not believe women when they tell others about the abuse, and a shout out to activists and celebrities who have tried to shift the conversation and holds abusers accountable. It is linked here but readers should note that it begins with a caution that it might be distressing. https://www.youtube.com/watch?v=kU6mNXAFj6Y.

With help from Barry University's marketing and public relations teams, we typically get some type of media coverage of the event. It is promoted on social media and a press release is sent to local media stations so that they can cover it, if possible. In some years we have been able to have more detailed packages, depending on what else is going on at the time. For instance, in 2025 I was interviewed as was our survivor speaker, the Barry female student I described earlier in the chapter who had approached me to share her story. As well, another survivor who heard about the event from a social media post and wanted to attend spoke fluent Spanish, so a Spanish-language channel from South Florida interviewed her about the importance of the event.

Media coverage is really essential, as it not only helps promote the event but it also helps inform the public about the reality of domestic and dating violence. In all of my years working in the antidomestic violence movement, I have encountered hundreds of survivors who have said that some type of media or popular culture coverage was what made the "bell go off" that triggered their decision to leave their abuser.

We also want to ensure that attendees have ample time to process their experience. We usually hold "debriefing" sessions with students who have engaged in service-learning with the CBW, which not only helps them connect what they learned to course concepts but also allows for them to share any emotions they felt. This year (2026) we will be adding restorative justice circles as the way to debrief, which is something the university is prioritizing for helping students manage conflict and build community.

One of our goals was to spread the movement to other campuses. Although there is way more that can be done, in 2019 I was invited by a colleague who began teaching at Rochester Institute of Technology to speak about the CBW and to lead one on their campus. Josie has also consulted on other campuses.

CHALLENGES AND RECOMMENDATIONS

One challenge with efforts to address gender-based violence is getting men and boys involved. For one, men and boys are victims as well. Yet still many men believe abuse is a problem for only women and do not recognize that they too can be victimized. As well, many men see abuse as a "woman's problem," one that women need to handle. Further, while some men may be sympathetic, they often do not get involved, because they do not see it as important to them or they do not feel invited or welcomed. Research has shown that men often do feel interested in being involved in this kind of activism against gender-based violence but that they felt marginalized. As well, they want to be personally invited, not just recruited by generic flyers or marketing campaigns. Additionally, efforts to recruit men and boys that are overtly feminist or that seem to blame all men for victimization are often off-putting (Casey, Casey & Smith). With our campaign in particular, we are aware that the title and bridal imagery may reinforce the image that it is for women. We do not want to lose that, however, in order to stay true to the origin of the campaign and its tribute to Gladys Ricart.

We have found that how we approach men and boys makes a huge difference. We invite them to join us and to learn more about how they can be agents for change. As well, we have found that inviting men and boys to participate in service-learning with our CBW. While initially they may participate as a means of "earning their hours," we have found that once they get engaged they are moved to continue learning, staying involved, and even advocating afterward. For instance, one young man who participated as a way to finish his service-learning hours reached out to me one year later to thank me for the opportunity. While he acknowledged at the time it was interesting and impactful to some degree, he has since had (unfortunately) some experiences that made him see the issue in another light. Many other service-learners have returned for numerous years, including Kevin (a student whose name is changed to protect his identity), who started in year 1 as a service learner. The event hit close to home for him, as his mother was nearly killed by an abuser. Not only did Kevin participate in year two but in the following two years after that he helped his mother fly to South Florida from Chicago so she, too, could participate.

Another strategy we have employed to engage men and boys it so actively reach out to campus and community men's groups as well as to male faculty and staff members. For some time until it was not longer active, we worked with a club men achieving leadership excellence and success. We presented to them about the importance of male allyship and activism, often utilizing Jackson Katz's powerful Technology, Entertainment, and Design talk "Violence against women—it's a men's issue." We also emphasize more broadly, per work by gender studies scholar Michael Kimmel, that gender equality benefits everyone—not just women. We've tried also, with limited success, to reach out to student athletes. As well, we have found several male alumni who have enthusiastically embraced participating. One of them, after being in an abusive same-sex relationship, started a nonprofit for LGBTQ victims and has spoken, lead workshops, and walked in the event several years in a row.

For the last several years we have been hosting orientation sessions in the classes in which students will be participating for service-learning credit. This is for several reasons. One, it helps attendees know a little about abuse before the day of the event, which can help reduce the possibility that someone would unwittingly make an inappropriate or triggering remark. Second, it helps people understand the origin of the movement and what the day will look like, which makes things go more smoothly. Third, it is another strategy that has helped us reach males on campus.

The COVID-19 pandemic was a tremendous challenge! In 2021, the university was still completely remote so we either had to cancel or adapt the event. We chose to adapt. In many ways, that allowed us to expand the programming in ways that would not be as well-received as in-person events. We held several virtual events in the month of February, leading up to the actual CBW. Since we could not meet and do the walk in person, we held a virtual opening session then asked people to arrange their own walks and share them on the app Strava, which many athletes use to track their workouts. That way people could walk with their family or neighbors in ways that ensured no spread of the pandemic. We also asked for people to share photos of their walks.

The virtual prewalk events were well attended and include workshops and panels on a variety of topics, including creating healthy boundaries, legal issues related to abuse, and more.

Another challenge we faced was the logistical hoops required to get a permit to do the walk on public streets. While we managed to navigate it, the bureaucracy was not the easiest and it was stressful. Since the pandemic we have moved the walk to be around the outskirts of campus, rather than through town. This has meant that we can avoid the permit but because our campus is in the middle of the city, the outskirts still allow traffic and homeowners to see us, hence the goal of visibility is still achieved.

One of the biggest challenges has been institutionalizing the campaign. While we have had tremendous support from the university, it is not really "housed" in any particular division or department. Because no specific entity is responsible for coordinating the campaign, it is a scramble every year to pull the pieces together with no additional assistance or compensation. Further, greater institutionalization would likely increase attendance, as it would be someone's job responsibility for the event, not just mine. Over the years, many of the organizers have moved on to other positions and still help as they can, but I am the primary organizer at this point. It is a labor of love, but definitely a labor! While I indeed enjoy it and believe it to be an important part of our campus, it likely would end if I was not able to coordinate it for some reason. Indeed, one spring when I was on sabbatical there was no CBW because no one was interested or able to take it on. Some of that may be on me, as I tend to be good at getting things done but not necessarily asking for help or delegating.

CONCLUSION

As was previously mentioned, there has not yet been a rigorous evaluation of the CBW. Many years (but not all), we have done some type of pre and posttest to assess changes in knowledge and attitude. These have shown that the campaign does improve people's understanding of what constitutes abuse, the barriers to leaving, and the availability of local resources. We have also conducted satisfaction surveys to gauge how attendees feel about the event, which is overwhelmingly positive. The most frequent comments are related to the emotional impact of the day and the chance to reflect on the frequency of abuse, as well as the desire to do more to help address it.

As noted earlier in the chapter, this year (2026) we are partnering with Campus Health and Wellness, which hopefully can address the institutionalization component and, perhaps, provide some funding and support for greater evaluation of the campaign.

REFERENCES

Alberle-Grasse, M. (2000). The Washington study-service year of Eastern Mennonite University: Reflections on 23 years of service learning. *American Behavioral Scientist, 43*, 848–857.

Cheek, T., Rector, C., & Davis, C. (2007). The Clothesline Project: An experiential project with MSW students. *Journal of Teaching Social Work, 27*(1/2), 141–154.

Finley, L. (2013). Peace in every relationship: Building an interdisciplinary, holistic domestic violence program on college campuses. *In Factis Pax, 7*(2), 66–85.

Finley, L. (2018). *Engaging men in conversations and activities related to dating and domestic violence.* Intech Open. https://www.intechopen.com/chapters/64853

Gezinski, L., O'Connor, J., Voth Schrag, R., & Wood, L. (2025). Intimate partner violence and academic challenges among college students: The role of campus belonging and campus community safety. *Psychology of Violence, 15*(2), 154–163.

History. (n.d.). *Brides March.* https://bridesmarch.com/history/

Koliba, C. (2000). Moral language and networks of engagement: Service learning and civic engagement. *American Behavioral Scientist, 43,* 825–838.

Kuh, G. (1995). The other curriculum: Out-of-class experiences associated with student learning and personal development. *Journal of Higher Education, 66*(2), 123–155.

Lin, J. (2006). *Love, Peace and wisdom in education: Vision for education in the 21st century.* Rowman & Littlefield Education..

Noddings, N. (n.d.). *Caring in education.* Infed. https://www.uvm.edu/%7Ergriffin/NoddingsCaring.pdf

Parker-Gwinn, R. (1996). Connecting service to learning: How students and communities matter. *Teaching Sociology, 24,* 97–101.

Roschelle, A., Turpin, J., & elias, R. (2000). Who learns from service learning? *American Behavioral Scientist, 43,* 839–847.

CONCLUSION

ABSTRACT

This brief conclusion emphasizes that there is much more to done in order to create truly effective prevention strategies related to dating and domestic violence, but that education is the key. Many people hold misconceptions about abuse that shape their support (or lack thereof) for essential policies and resources. When we educate people—not just in a school setting but in others as well—we can correct those misconceptions and help move toward more just and humane approaches that honor the human rights of all.

Keywords: Prevention; evaluation; legislation; gender-based violence; survivor's voices; training

It is my hope that this book serves to not only help readers understand abuse and its effects but also how we can develop and implement effective prevention strategies. As an educator, I feel that it is my duty—not just because some state laws require it, as was discussed in this book—but because I care deeply, to ensure that I use my knowledge, skills, and passion to ensure that I am part of making my campus a safer space for all.

As with any book, the moment you stop writing is the moment the data is dated. I did my best to include updated statistics and examples, but of course (and sadly) more will come. I hope that what I presented here is enough to highlight the problem, however, and to inform educators and policymakers about the many ways that we can use that data to create innovative, holistic, prevention programs in schools, on campuses, in other institutions, and in our communities.

I know that there are so many other great resources about domestic and dating violence, so I hope that this book does justice to expanding knowledge

Teaching and Making Peace in Every Relationship, pages 177–178

doi:10.1108/978-1-80686-961-920261010

and informing education about abuse. I also want to continue to prioritize and lift up survivors' voices, as we have done with the College Brides Walk.

Moving forward, I would like to see a much greater focus on evaluating dating and domestic violence prevention programs (including my own College Brides Walk). Additionally, uniform federal legislation related to school and campus prevention would help ensure that every student, faculty, and staff member was aware of the scope and extent of abuse but also on how to assist victims and offenders. Moreover, legislation requiring prevention programming is an important first step in ensuring that schools and campuses ensure the human right to safety from gender-based violence,

I would also like to see greater emphasis on understanding abuse in many institutions. While I am grateful that I have been able to train healthcare professionals in Florida, that is not a requirement in every state. I believe it should be. Police officers, who interact with victims and perpetrators regularly, often have very little training on understanding abuse. That is unacceptable. As an educator, I am grateful that I am knowledgeable about these issues, but most teachers and professors are not, Again, that is unacceptable. Because abuse often follows victims to the workplace, human resource professionals should adopt policies and require training relevant to the issue.

Media and popular culture also can and should play an important role in educating about dating and domestic violence. As this book has shown, there are many misconceptions about abuse, most of which are fostered from popular culture. Realistic depictions that inform and inspire empathy, like some of those included in Chapter Seven, can change hearts and minds.

Mostly, it is my hope that the readers of this book are inspired to care more deeply. As I shared, I have not been a victim of domestic or dating violence. But that should not and does not stop me from doing what I can to help address it. I hope that others reading this feel similarly called to action and better informed on what to do.

www.ingramcontent.com/pod-product-compliance
Lightning Source LLC
LaVergne TN
LVHW021959100926
847717LV00023B/252
9781806869640